THE BIG BOOK OF JAPANESE GIANT MONSTER MOVIES

HEISEI COMPLETION

1989-2019

By John LeMay
Edited by Ted Johnson
Foreword by David McRobie

BICEP BOOKS

Roswell, New Mexico, U.S.A.

BICEP BOOKS

Roswell, New Mexico, U.S.A.

For my parents, who introduced me to these films, and for Scott, who discovered them alongside me.

TABLE OF CONTENTS

Acknowledgments

For this edition I'd first like to say thank you to Ted Johnson for editing it and putting your special touch on it. Second, thank you David McRobie for writing the foreword to this book a few years back, and also accepting my articles in a great little fanzine we all know as *Xenorama*. Thank you Kyle Byrd, Kevin Derendorf, and Matt Parmely for helping me find some of the rarer films in this book. And, an especially big thank you to Shinpei Hayashiya for allowing me use of his monsters Reigo and Raiga on the cover!

FOREWORD

John LeMay has written a pretty thorough set of books about Japanese monster cinema. He is fortunate as he got to witness the first (Showa) and second (Heisei) wave of kaiju eiga at a young age. I'm a little jealous as the age you see a movie at can really affect how much you love it. I love most of the "golden age" Japanese monster movies, but since the second wave didn't start until I was 20, my sense of wonder had changed. The newer movies just didn't have the awe and mystery the older ones did for me. John got to see all these movies as a young person and that can really influence how much affection you have for any given movie. His love of the entire genre really shines through in both books, which makes the set entertaining and informative to read.

John has even taken movies that have been written about frequently in the last fifteen years and wrote about them in a way that is fresh and fun. Most of these movies in Volume 2 have a lot more information available about them now, which makes his accomplishment even greater as he doesn't just retread previously published words.

This second book covers the Japanese monster movie experience clear up to the 2014 American *Godzilla*—which he has nicer things to say about than I do. He is always able to find something good to say about even the worst movies (hello "*Godzilla*" 1998) or will point out a plot hole in a fan favorite (see 2001's *Godzilla, Mothra, and King Ghidorah: Giant Monsters All-Out Attack*) so his even-handedness is quite refreshing.

Both books are fun to have available when watching any of the movies reviewed within, as his reviews are better than some of the movies presented within these pages. I'll let you figure out which ones they are as there are a few sprinkled throughout both tomes. I would like to read more of John's work and not just about giant monster movies. *That's* how good his writing is—that it makes me a fan of his style, not just the things he writes about. The humor is there but it never seems forced and you never get the feeling he is laughing at the movies either.

To wrap this up, John has done a remarkable job in writing about movies that in the last two decades, have been covered far more extensively than the movies in his first book. I applaud his work and am thankful he writes as well as he does. So with that, John, get to cracking on that next book!

David McRobie
December 2016

David McRobie, writer, publisher and custodian of the long running fanzine Xenorama, The Journal of Heroes and Monsters, *lives and works in Colorado. He has written for a wide variety of magazines, including* Famous Monsters of Filmland, Oriental Cinema, Prehistoric Times *and* G-Fan. *In his spare time he referees roller derby. His life is run by two cats who approve of his hobbies provided they get fed on a regular basis.*

THE HEISEI ERA

Though many consider the start of the Heisei era tokusatsu-wise to be 1984, the year that *The Return of Godzilla* was released, it technically didn't begin until 1989. By that time Teruyoshi Nakano had retired from Toho, and Koichi Kawakita had taken over the special effects department. Notably, his work on *Godzilla vs. Biollante* kicked off the Heisei era for Godzilla.

But, to explain *Biollante*, we still need to backtrack to 1985. That year producer Tomoyuki Tanaka was sifting through scripts solicited in an open story contest. Two winners were picked, and one went on to become *Godzilla vs. Biollante*. The other, in which Godzilla battles a super-computer, was reworked to exclude the kaiju king altogether and became a film called *Gunhed*. Unfortunately, both films were disappointments at the box office. *Biollante's* poor performance, in turn, cancelled an in progress Mothra movie entitled *Mothra vs. Bagan*, also written by Omori. Despite these setbacks, Omori was eventually called back in to direct "Godzilla 3". 1991's *Godzilla vs. King Ghidorah*, which reveals the origins of Godzilla, got lots of publicity on both sides of the Pacific and was a hit in Japan. The film's effects director Koichi Kawakita even won a special Japanese Academy Award for his work on the film (though some feel that in reality this award was for not recognizing his much better work in *Biollante*.

Toho hit pay dirt with 1992's *Godzilla vs. Mothra,* which became the highest-grossing entry of the new series of G-films (called the Heisei series in Japan)—though *King Kong vs. Godzilla* still wins when adjusted for inflation. It was also the highest-grossing domestic film released in Japan in 1992 at ¥2.22 billion. On a roll, Toho produced sequels for the next three consecutive years. In 1994, they released a big-budget non-Godzilla film, *Yamato Takeru*, based upon Japanese legends and a semi-remake of their 1959 hit *The Three Treasures*. The film was a massive flop, scrapping any further plans for kaiju films outside the Godzilla stable (as well as impacting the budget of the Godzilla movie following later). This same year, Sony's TriStar Pictures planned to release an American Godzilla film made by *Speed* director Jan de Bont. When the film's release was pushed back to 1997 over arguments about the budget, Toho decided to kill Godzilla in 1995's *Godzilla vs. Destroyah* to make way for the American version.

Even with Godzilla off the scene, Japanese movie screens were still filled with kaiju. In 1995, the recently-revived Daiei Motion Picture Company also revived its Gamera series to surprise critical and financial success. A sequel was produced in 1996, the same year that Toho tried their hand at a solo Mothra film, retitled *Rebirth of Mothra* internationally, though simply called *Mothra* when released in Japan as the "New Year's Blockbuster" leading into 1997. Though not the success Toho had hoped for, they still produced sequels in 1997 and 1998 rounding out a trilogy with Tomoyuki Tanaka sadly passing away during the making of the second film. Even Shochiku pondered resurrecting their old monster Guilala from *The X from Outer Space* (1967), though this didn't pan out. On top of this, Korea's *Yongary, Monster from the Deep* (1967) saw a CGI resurrection in the 1999 film reimagining, *Yongarry*. The film attempted to ride the hype surrounding the American *Godzilla,* which was released in 1998 to big box office but resoundingly awful critical reviews (notably from Godzilla fans who hated the beast's new design). Jan de Bont had dropped out of production long ago and was replaced by *Independence Day* helmers Dean Devlin and Roland Emmerich, who drastically changed Godzilla's appearance. Though there was talk of a sequel for several years, it never materialized. Instead, Godzilla would return to Toho Studios, who produced *Godzilla 2000* in time for December of 1999. The film rebooted itself from the Heisei continuity and was ultimately only mildly successful despite packed houses opening weekend. Ironically, it became the first Japanese Godzilla film released in the U.S. since *Godzilla 1985.* Unfortunately, it barely held its place in the top ten on opening weekend, cancelling any plans for the releases of sequels.

Ultimately, the 2000s ended up not unlike the 1970s in terms of financial success. None of the 2000-era G-films (known in Japan as the Millennium Series) garnered the attendance numbers of the Heisei films. Toho tried an experimental approach to the new series, with each film taking place in their own unique universe. These were best exemplified by Masaaki Tezuka's fan-pleasing, financial flop *Godzilla vs. Megaguirus* (2000) and Shusuke Kaneko's successful but polarizing *Godzilla, Mothra, and King Ghidorah: Giant Monsters All-Out Attack* (2001). Surprisingly, Toho chose Tezuka to helm further sequels, and as a result, he became the definitive director of the Millennium series helming three of its six entries. With the ticket sales again dwindling, Toho decided to retire Godzilla once again with the much-ballyhooed *Godzilla: Final Wars* (2004) which ended up being the biggest bomb of the series, only bringing in 13 million U.S. dollars on an unprecedented 18 million dollar budget (the highest of the entire series at that point). Kadokawa, who had since bought the again bankrupt Daiei, tried their hand at reviving Gamera in 2006's *Gamera the Brave*. Despite a packed opening night, it failed to find an audience afterward. Guilala finally saw his much-belated revival with the comedic *Monster X Strikes Back: Attack the G8 Summit* (2008), which did dismally at the box office. Even a few new kaiju such as the independently-made *Reigo the Deep Sea Monster vs. the Battleship Yamato* (2008) and *Death Kappa* (2010) were unleashed onto the public.

Back in 2004, Godzilla series producer Shogo Tomiyama had stated Toho wouldn't let Godzilla sit for longer than 2014, and followed through when Legendary Pictures announced a new Godzilla film for release in America in 2012, though it didn't come out until May 2014. The serious reboot helmed by Gareth Edwards, director of 2010's *Monsters*, owes its birth to an unlikely source: a quasi-sequel to *Godzilla vs. Hedorah* (1971). Announced in 2004 as *Godzilla 3-D to the MAX* (an IMAX 3-D short film to feature Godzilla battling a Hedorah-like foe called Deathla), the film lingered in development hell for several years before ultimately being snatched up by Legendary Pictures. It was then retooled into another big-budget American—but more faithful rendering of—*Godzilla*. The film, though still somewhat polarizing, was not the debacle that the 1998 *Godzilla* was, and ended up being a critical and financial success. Godzilla had once again reestablished himself for a new generation.

In a truly surprising move, Toho rebooted the Godzilla series in 2016. *Shin Godzilla* would not only go on to become the second-highest grossing Japanese Godzilla film, but in a first, also won Japanese Academy Awards for best picture and best director! Though Toho is not allowed to make any more live-action Godzilla films until the completion of 2020's *Godzilla vs. Kong*, the new film certainly revived Godzilla for a new generation in Japan!

THE FILMS
1989-2019

GUNHED

(TOHO/SUNRISE/KADOKAWA/BANDAI)

Release Date: July 22, 1989

Directed by: Masato Harada **Special Effects by:** Koichi Kawakita **Screenplay by:** Masato Harada and James Bannon **Music by:** Toshiyuki Honda **Cast:** Masahiro Takashima (Brooklyn), Brenda Bakke (Sergeant Nim), Aya Enjoji (Bebe), Kaori Mizushima (Eleven), Yujin Harada (Seven), James Brewster Thompson (Barabass), Randy Reyes (voice of Gunhed)

Widescreen, Color, 100 Minutes

In the year 2030, a new super-element capable of controlling computers called Texmexium [sic] is discovered. It is stored away on an island known as 8JO until the island's artificial intelligence Kyron-5 declares war on humanity. Eight years later, a group of scavengers and a party of Texas Army Rangers invade the island for different reasons. Of both parties, only Brooklyn and Sergeant Nim survive and band together with two children, Seven and Eleven, to survive on the island. To steal the Texmexium, Brooklyn repairs the sentient Gunhed, a transforming machine designed to battle Kyron-5, and storms the island. Nim, Brooklyn, and the children escape the island with the Texmexium before it self-destructs, while the Gunhed sacrifices itself so they may live.

Background & Commentary Though at first glance, this film may appear to be a rip-off of *The Terminator* (1984)—and to a degree it is— rumor has it that this film actually began life as the runner-up in a script contest for "Godzilla 2" in 1986. Tatsuo Kobayashi's story entry "Godzilla vs. the Robot Corps" would have pitted Godzilla against a sentient super-computer. Toho was so impressed with the "Godzilla vs. the Robot Corps" treatment that the studio had director Masato Harada and Jim Bannon rework the script to excise Godzilla and make an all-new original film. That said, the film ironically makes for an interesting companion piece to *Godzilla vs. Biollante*, as it shares that film's computer-animated simulations, the younger brother of *Biollante* actor Masanobu Takashima, and even that film's English dub cast.

Though produced by Tomoyuki Tanaka, *Gunhed* wasn't exclusively a Toho-made film, but a co-production with Sunrise (a Japanese animation company), Kadokawa Pictures, and Bandai. The expensive production was hyped as the first ever "live-action giant robot movie" and special effects director Koichi Kawakita's love of robotics shows through. Though shots of the miniature Gunhed are fairly obvious, the effects are still well done for the era. In addition to the miniature Gunhed, a full-sized six-meter version was also made (which was a highly-touted aspect of the film's publicity campaign). The film also represents classic 1980s bravado to a tee, right down to cheesy one-liners spouted off during gritty, often gruesome, action.

One of the film's biggest highlights is its synthesized score by Toshiyuki Honda, which is somewhat evocative of Mark Isham's score for *The Beast* (1988). *Gunhed*'s weak link is the Bio-Droid, sort of the film's Terminator, which suffers from a creepy but poor design. It also somehow becomes possessed by a dead member of the crew, Bebe, and the film would have been better off without this confusing twist.

Ultimately, *Gunhed* was a notorious flop at the Japanese box office. And yet, ironically enough, *Terminator* director James Cameron claims *Gunhed* is one of his favorite films.

Final Word Though its merits weren't recognized at the time, *Gunhed* should be quintessential viewing for fans of post-apocalyptic 1980s cinema.

GODZILLA VS. BIOLLANTE

(TOHO)
Release Date: December 16, 1989
Alternate Titles: *Godzilla: The Giant* (Germany) *Godzilla 1990* (Thailand/South Korea)

Directed by: Kazuki Omori **Special Effects by:** Koichi Kawakita **Screenplay by:** Kazuki Omori **Music by:** Koichi Sugiyama **Cast:** Kunihiko Mitamura (Kazuto Kirishima), Yoshiko Tanaka (Asuka Okochi), Megumi Odaka (Miki Saegusa), Toru Minegishi (Colonel Goro Gondo), Masanobu Takashima (Major Sho Kuroki), Koji Takahashi (Dr. Shiragami) **Suit Performers:** Kenpachiro Satsuma (Godzilla), Masao Takegami (Biollante Rose Form), Shigeru Shibasaki/Yoshitaka Kimura (Biollante Final Form)

Widescreen, Color, 105 Minutes

Geneticist Dr. Shirigami has been tasked with developing a new weapon called Anti-Nuclear Energy Bacteria (ANEB) using Godzilla cells found in the wreckage of a decimated Tokyo in 1984. Shirigami also experiments with the G-Cells by combining them with that of a plant infused with the DNA of his dead daughter, Erica. Rather than a new breed of super plant as Shirigami had hoped, a giant plant monster he dubs Biollante is born. At the same time, Godzilla is released by terrorists from his volcanic prison and makes a bee-line for his clone which he battles and destroys in Lake Ashino. Biollante's spores disappear into the sky as something even more horrible within them roars at Godzilla. As Godzilla treks across Japan, the military successfully fires the ANEB into his body but it doesn't take effect. Realizing that, as a reptile, his body temperature is too cold for the ANEB to work, the military devises a huge electrical attack on Godzilla in hopes of upping his body temperature. The attack is successful, but Biollante re-spawns herself in the process and attacks Godzilla in a second, more aggressive form (seen briefly as she disappeared the first time). Biollante isn't much of a match for Godzilla's rays but the ANEB takes effect and he collapses into the ocean while Dr. Shirigami is assassinated. After Biollante returns once again to the sky, the cold seawater drops Godzilla's temperature back to normal, and the monster revives and swims out to sea.

Background & Commentary Although the Godzilla series had effectively been rebooted with modern (for Japan) special effects and a more serious tone in 1984's *The Return of Godzilla*, it was this sequel that began the Heisei era of Godzilla films and set the template for the monster's adventures to come. Tomoyuki Tanaka solicited a story contest in which the winning entry would be adapted into the next film, something that had also resulted in 1975's *Terror of Mechagodzilla*. Like that film, the results breathed new creative life into the series thanks to the winning script penned by Shinichiro Kobayashi, a dentist who had also written episodes of *Return of Ultraman* in 1971. In the vein of the original series' way of preaching against nuclear testing, *Godzilla vs. Biollante* warned against the dangers of the new science of bio-engineering. Most of Kobayashi's elements survived the rewrite by director Kazuki Omori, the biggest casualty being a second monster, a giant rat/fish hybrid named Deutalious, who was excised entirely.

The title creation, Biollante, is a wonderfully designed monster that has two distinct forms starting a tradition, brought on by Koichi Kawakita, of transforming kaiju throughout the Heisei era. Biollante's first form reflects how the monster likely would have been designed in the Showa era: simplistic, beautiful, and elegant. Its second form reflects the post-*Aliens* cinema of the 1980s when the kaiju becomes a multi-tendrilled, giant-mouthed, acid-spewing monstrosity. The new special effects director Koichi Kawakita puts his best foot forward with Biollante, at the time the largest monster prop Toho had ever created. It was so heavy that to give it the illusion of movement onscreen it was placed on top of a dolly track and hauled across the set by a group of the crew!

Kawakita certainly wasn't afraid to try new things. There is a famous deleted scene wherein Biollante's tendrils and Godzilla are brought to life via stop motion animation. While impressive, it didn't mesh well enough with the standard suitmation footage to warrant inclusion. Godzilla himself gets a makeover in the film with a double row of shiny teeth (ironically the dentist/scriptwriter's idea) and a more feral appearance. Unlike the wildly changing designs of the Showa period, Godzilla's look would stay more or less the same throughout the rest of the series (though each new costume is distinct from the other Heisei suits). An animatronic Godzilla was built from the chest up for close-ups of the monster's facial movements. Unlike Tsuburaya's puppets that often didn't resemble the suits they were supposed to correlate to, Kawakita's animatronic was made from the same molds as the main suit.

When Akira Ifukube again declined to return, Koichi Sugiyama—composer of the popular video game *Dragonquest*—was chosen. Most fans have a lukewarm reception to the score, which features a rock version of Ifukube's classic Godzilla theme. The theme for the Super X2 is certainly a product of the 1980s and is vaguely reminiscent of John William's *Superman* theme, though Sugiyama's themes for Biollante have a certain poetic quality to them.

As to the cast, there are so many human characters in the film that they are sometimes hard to keep track of. In fact, it's such a problem to the story that it ends up having no true main character! The standouts, though, are Toru Minegishi as Goro Gondo, a lively fire-and-ice character that is killed by Godzilla at the end of the second act. The other is eighteen-year-old Megumi Odaka making her debut as psychic Miki Saegusa, a character that would serve as a continuity thread in all subsequent sequels.

With an attendance of only 2 million people, this film wasn't the big success Toho hoped for and it only grossed $2 million more than what it had cost to make. This poor performance axed a Mothra solo film planned to follow in 1990 and sent Toho back to the drawing board, still not content to give up on the Big G.

With New World Pictures' motion picture division bankrupt and gone, Toho had to turn elsewhere to release *Godzilla vs. Biollante* in the United States. Enter the Weinstein Brothers' Miramax, who allegedly made a deal to release *Biollante* theatrically in the U.S. in December of 1990. However, suddenly talks broke off, and in August 1990, Toho filed a lawsuit in Los Angeles against Miramax. Their suit claimed that Miramax had entered into an oral agreement with them in June to pay $500,000 for the North American, British, and Irish distribution rights for *Biollante* and then backed out of the deal. An out-of-court settlement was eventually reached, and Miramax purchased the rights for an undisclosed amount. *Biollante* was unceremoniously dumped onto VHS in October of 1992, licensed to HBO Video. It was the first American VHS release of a Godzilla film that was in its original widescreen format. It would be the last new Godzilla film to secure a home video release in America until 1998.

Final Word Even though it's the least successful film in the Heisei series from a financial perspective, fans in both the east and the west have voted *Godzilla vs. Biollante* as their favorite Godzilla film on two different occasions.

ULTRA Q
THE MOVIE

(TOHOKUSHINSHA/SEGA ENTERPRISES/SHOCHIKU)
Release Date: April 14, 1990
Japanese Title: *Ultra Q The Movie: Legend of the Stars*

Directed by: Akio Jissoji **Special Effects by:** Jun Oki **Screenplay by:** Mamoru Sasaki **Music by:** Maki Ishii **Cast:** Toshio Shiba (Jun Manjome), Keiko Oginome (Yuriko Edogawa), Mio Takaki (Mayumi Hoshino), Shingo Kazami (Ippei Togawa) **Suit Performers:** Masao Fukazawa (Wadatuzin Statue), Miho Nikaido (Wadatuzin), Ryoshi Matsuoka (Nagira)

Widescreen, Color, 112 Minutes

A bizarre set of murders and earthquakes plagues the excavation site of newly-discovered ancient ruins. A television crew there to report on the ruins instead begins an investigation into the killings. They are lead to a mysterious woman named Mayumi Hoshino. As it turns out, Mayumi is an alien called Wadatuzin that came to earth in ancient times to investigate the earth's environment. Displeased with what she is finding in the new world, Mayumi unleashes her monster Nagira on a small, coastal town as a testament of her wrath. Before she departs earth with a group of new followers, she warns that what Nagira did was only a small fraction of what she will do if the earth does not stop polluting the environment.

Background & Commentary Due to the cancellation of *Mothra vs. Bagan*, 1990 was the lone year that Toho didn't put out a giant monster film in the 1990s. Luckily for fans though, Tsuburaya put out their first giant monster movie since 1984's *Ultraman Story*. The film was co-produced with Tohokushinsha Co., Ltd., Sega Enterprises, and Shochiku, who also distributed.

The movie was written by one of the main writers of *Ultraman* and *Ultra Seven*. Apparently, this film has its origins in an unmade script from 1983 called *Ultraman: Monster Bible*. Like many kaiju films, this film's storyline was affected greatly due to issues regarding toy sales. In this case, as Sega Enterprises (also a toy producer) was a co-producer on the film, they mandated that a new monster be created because if classic monsters were used, then Bandai would be the only company allowed to make figures to tie in with the movie.

Had this not happened, the movie was to have been an anthology film à la *Twilight Zone: The Movie* (1983) and would have had three stories focusing around the monsters Kanegon, Garamon, and another mystery monster. This version was to have been directed by Shusuke Kaneko and written by Kazunori Ito but when the dispute arose over Bandai having sole marketing rights to the desired monsters, they left and Mamoru Sasaki, who had previously concocted the aborted *Ultraman: Monster Bible* scenario, was brought in.

The finished film has a creepy air to it through and through thanks to the atmospheric locations, direction by Jissoji, and the music by Maki Ishii. For those who might think that this film was influenced by the dark tone of *The X-Files*, that show would not premiere for another three years. The new monster Nagira is well-designed and fires a blue and orange atomic ray like Godzilla's. The monster is hinted at early in the film when its tail causes a well-done earthquake and briefly flays up from the ground like a giant whip. At the hour mark, the monster emerges from the ground to attack a group of policemen. Nagira appears once more during the climax and engages in some well-done city destruction. The film ends similarly to *The Day the Earth Stood Still* with alien Wadatuzin warning that this is only a taste of what's to come should earth not change its ways.

Final Word Though it has yet to be dubbed or subtitled into English, *Ultra Q: The Movie* is worth a watch for its creepy atmosphere and the monster Nagira alone.

GODZILLA VS. KING GHIDORAH

(TOHO)

Release Date: December 14, 1991

Alternate Titles: *Godzilla vs. King Ghidora* (original international title) *Godzilla: Duel of the Mega-Dinosaurs* (Germany) *Godzilla vs. the Evil Monster* (Brazil)

Directed by: Kazuki Omori **Special Effects by:** Koichi Kawakita **Screenplay by:** Kazuki Omori **Music by:** Akira Ifukube **Cast:** Anna Nakagawa (Emmy Kano), Kosuke Toyohara (Terasawa), Katsuhiko Sasaki (Professor Masaki), Megumi Odaka (Miki Saegusa), Robert Scott Field (M-11), Chuck Wilson (Wilson), Richard Burger (Glenchiko), Yoshio Tsuchiya (Yasuaki Shindo), Tokuma Nishioka (Takehito Fujio), Akiji Kobayashi (Dobashi), Kenji Sahara (Defense Minister Segawa) **Suit Performers:** Kenpachiro Satsuma (Godzilla), Ryu Hariken (King Ghidorah), Wataru Fukuda (Godzillasaurus)

Widescreen, Color, 103 Minutes

In early 1992, humans from the 23rd century arrive in Japan and tell of a devastating future wherein Godzilla reawakens and destroys the country. To prevent this, a special team led by Emmy Kano, a Futurian, her android M-11, and several observers from modern day Japan travel back to the 1940s to prevent Godzilla's irradiated birth. Then merely a remnant dinosaur, the time travelers displace Godzilla in the Bering Sea so he will not be mutated by radiation from a later atomic bomb test and turn into a monster. Upon returning to the present, new monster King Ghidorah has mysteriously taken his place. The time travelers have deceived the Japanese; Godzilla never did destroy the country in the future but now their controlled monster will. The Japanese decide their only option is to create a new Godzilla out of the dinosaur in the Bering Sea. However, not only does everyone remember Godzilla, but Miki can sense him. The Futurians didn't change anything; they only created the second Godzilla that appeared in 1984! A nuclear submarine encounters Godzilla and is destroyed by the monster. The nuclear energy cures Godzilla of the ANEB and increases his size from 80 meters to 100 meters. Godzilla resurfaces in Hokkaido and, with the help of the Japanese and a sympathetic Emmy raiding the Futurians' ship, succeeds in defeating King Ghidorah. Without anything to stop him,

17

Godzilla proceeds to ravage Japan but Emmy returns to the future promising to bring help. In the 23rd century, she revives Ghidorah in a mechanized form and returns to 1992 where she saves Japan from Godzilla. But after Emmy has returned to the future, Godzilla revives again...

Background & Commentary In the opening weeks of *Godzilla vs. Biollante*'s release, producer Tomoyuki Tanaka and director Kazuki Omori noticed theater houses were packed for the time travel extravaganza *Back to the Future Part II*, while *Biollante* was dwindling badly after the opening night. This laid the groundwork for the time travel elements of *Godzilla vs. King Ghidorah*. In addition to this, Toho also felt it would be safer to go with an established foe like King Ghidorah rather than try another new monster like Biollante. Or, at least, that's the story according to Omori. In fact, Toho tried and failed to remake *King Kong vs. Godzilla* first. Even after that, Omori wasn't the first-round pick for "Godzilla 3", but rather Koji Hashimoto, who had helmed the 1984 *Godzilla*. Some Toho executives eventually stepped in and suggested that Omori return, feeling that he had a better handle on younger audiences.

While Omori's love for western cinema, particularly the James Bond series, showed strongly in *Godzilla vs. Biollante*, it would be brought further to the forefront in *Godzilla vs. King Ghidorah*. In addition to time-traveling Futurians, there are also *Terminator*-inspired androids, notably M-11 played by Robert Scott Field. On the other hand, the film's bio-engineered Dorats and Godzillasaurus were innovations rather than copycats, as 1993's *Jurassic Park* was still two years away (though someone at Toho likely had read the book, released in 1990).

On a technical level, the new King Ghidorah is marvelous, but many fans were somewhat disappointed in the monster's new origin as a bio-engineered creature from the future. Originally, when the film was to be directed by Hashimoto, Tanaka wanted the monster's body to be discovered by the Futurians in the 23rd century on Venus, which they then cloned to make their own controllable Ghidorah. Omori disliked the idea and said he didn't want to make a film about "silly space monsters" and changed the space dragon's origins to something surprisingly sillier. Tanaka insisted there be a monster battle every thirty minutes, and he more or less gets his wish as the first act features the Godzillasaurus battling American troops, the second act has Godzilla battling King Ghidorah, and the third, Godzilla battling Mecha-King Ghidorah. Of the three battles, the middle one is the best as it intercuts spectacularly with the human heroes storming MOTHER, the time travelers' ship.

As for the Godzillasaurus, it was created as a way for Godzilla to show up early in the film. Otherwise, he doesn't make his true entrance until nearly 50 minutes in, accompanied by a wonderful harp orchestration by maestro Akira Ifukube, returning to the series after a 16 year absence. When the Big G emerges, he is now also 20 meters taller (in the script, due to his encounter with the nuclear submarine, but behind the scenes, this was to enable Koichi Kawakita to build smaller miniatures). Plus, most of Tokyo's buildings would now dwarf the 80 meter tall Godzilla from the previous two films. After 17 entries, this is also the first film in which Godzilla's origin is fully explained as a remnant dinosaur exposed to radiation in 1944.

That said, the origins of the original 1954 Godzilla remain a mystery. Many fans forget that the dinosaur irradiated on Lagos Island is the Godzilla that first appeared in 1984, not the one from 1954. In fact, the Futurians never erased the 1954 attack, nor did they seem to erase any of Godzilla's past attacks despite that being the goal! Actually, what many English-only speaking fans interpret as a plot hole (nothing changing in 1991 despite moving the Godzillasaurus in 1944) is just a misinterpretation. This is partly because the international dub doesn't address several important plot points in the movie. You see, the Futurians believed that the 1954 Godzilla and the 1984 Godzilla were the same monster. In fact, their actions are what caused the creation of the second Godzilla, who appeared in *The Return of Godzilla.* If one pays close attention, they will notice that Terasawa finds a newspaper article that details a nuclear sub running aground in the Bering Sea in 1977. This accident is, of course, what irradiated the Godzillasaurus into the second Godzilla. The only thing this film doesn't address is how the 1954 Godzilla came to be and how the Heisei Godzilla became buried under Daikoku Island between 1977 and 1984. Wilson is too egotistical to think they had done anything but succeed in their mission, despite the fact he and everyone else still knows who Godzilla is in the "altered" version of 1991. Even when Godzilla returns, he assumes that the monster was created recently.

Continuity issues now being cleared, let us continue on discussing the movie's other merits. Many familiar faces from past films such as Kenji Sahara show up in small roles and cameos. "I've been waiting for this role my whole life," Yoshio Tsuchiya said when offered the part of Yasuaki Shindo, one of the film's many memorable characters. He goes on to share a unique scene with a teary-eyed Godzilla, who recognizes him from the island forty years previous. Godzilla then promptly blasts him with his ray, as he also memorably does to human villains Wilson and Glenchiko.

The film was made at the height of Japan's "bubble economy" when Japanese stocks were soaring, and the tiny nation seemed poised to take over the world, something that actually happens in the film's fictional future. As Toho hoped, the return of King Ghidorah and the light adventurous tone lured in the coveted "family audience" Toho was targeting. As such, the film was considered a big hit in Japan, though it was only the 8th highest-grossing film that year (it earned the Silver Excellence Award at the Japanese Golden Gross Awards). Godzilla's battle in dinosaur form with American troops along with the Caucasian villains gave the film what U.S. media considered an anti-American slant, though director Omori—a great lover of American cinema—denies that was his intent. The film wouldn't be released in America on home video until 1998 in the wake of TriStar's *Godzilla* film.

Final Word One of the most energetic and best paced Godzilla films in the entire series. Though many U.S. fans criticize what they think to be time travel-induced plot-holes, these "plot-holes" are just a misinterpretation of a much richer backstory as to the creation of the 1984 Godzilla.

GODZILLA VS. MOTHRA

(TOHO)
Release Date: December 12, 1992
Alternate Titles: *Godzilla and Mothra: The Battle for Earth* (U.S. home video title) *Godzilla: Battle of the Dinosaur Mutants* (Germany) *Godzilla: The Dinosaur Mutant* (Argentina) *Godzilla and Mothra* (France/Portugal)

Directed by: Takao Okawara **Special Effects by:** Koichi Kawakita **Screenplay by:** Kazuki Omori **Music by:** Akira Ifukube **Cast:** Tetsuya Bessho (Takuya Fujito), Satomi Kobayashi (Masako Tezuka) Takehiro Murata (Ando), Shiori Yonezawa (Midori Tezuka), Makoto Otake (Tomokane), Megumi Odaka (Miki Saegusa), Akira Takarada (Joji Minamino), Saburo Shinoda (Professor Fukazawa), Akiji Kobayashi (Dobashi), Keiko Imamura & Sayaka Osawa (The Cosmos) **Suit Performers:** Kenpachiro Satsuma (Godzilla), Ryu Hariken (Battra Larva)

Widescreen, Color, 102 Minutes

In late 1992, a meteor that crashes into the ocean awakens both Godzilla and an ancient monster called Battra, whilst a typhoon unearths Mothra's egg on Infant Island. In December of 1992, an archeologist and his ex-wife are sent to investigate Infant Island along with a representative from the Marutomo Company, who owns the island. There, they find a set of six-inch tall twins, the Cosmos, who agree to accompany them to Japan along with Mothra's egg. Meanwhile, Battra appears in Japan wreaking havoc in Nagoya before suddenly disappearing. In the South Seas, Godzilla intercepts the egg being towed to Japan via ocean liner. It hatches a Mothra larva who begins a battle with Godzilla until Battra suddenly arrives and joins the fray. Mothra and the ship escape while the other monsters, fighting on the ocean's floor, are consumed by an underwater volcano. In Japan, the Cosmos are kidnaped and Mothra comes to the rescue in Tokyo. After the Cosmos are recovered, she builds a giant cocoon at the Diet Building. Godzilla causes Mt. Fuji to erupt and emerges from the volcano while both Mothra and Battra, also reborn, morph into their adult forms. The two leopedeprians battle in the air but then decide to join forces against Godzilla, whom they drop into the ocean. When Battra is killed by the conflict, Mothra agrees to complete his mission to destroy an asteroid headed for earth in 1999.

Background & Commentary Even before *Godzilla vs. King Ghidorah* had been released and proved to be a success, Toho had already announced the sequel as an updated version of *Mothra vs. Godzilla* (1964). Mothra had nearly returned before that in a 1990 solo vehicle entitled *Mothra vs. Bagan,* which was axed after the disappointing box-office take of *Godzilla vs. Biollante*. In later 1991, a treatment entitled *Godzilla vs. Gigamoth* was written where the monster king would battle a normal Mothra and its mutated counterpart, Gigamoth (an "evil Mothra" and proto version of Battra). In the end, the two insects fuse together into the "true" Mothra to battle Godzilla. This script by Koichi Kawakita, which featured a lone Shobijin named Mana, was eventually reworked to become something more traditional by Kazuki Omori—who combined the *Gigamoth* story with ideas and characters he created for *Mothra vs. Bagan*. As a result, it took Omori only three months to complete the shooting script.

Omori's love for American cinema, which had a strong presence in his previous two outings, is apparent here as well. An opening sequence set in Thailand pays homage to Indiana Jones. When it came time to shoot the picture, after two consecutive entries Omori stepped down as director to make way for Takao Okawara, who had previously been an assistant director on *The Return of Godzilla* and just completed his first picture as director, *Reiko* (1991).

Godzilla vs. Mothra continues the epic spectacle established by the previous film with battles taking place not only on land, but in the water, under the sea, and high in the air. The highlight is undoubtedly the aerial battle between Mothra and her dark twin, Battra (derived from "Batoru Mosura/Battle Mothra"). That said, the two marionettes for Mothra and Battra are unfortunately stiff and lack the grace of Tsuburaya's Mothra despite that monster's antiquated roots in the 1960s. Oddly enough, Battra's larva form is a more impressive creation than its adult stage and is brought to life by suitmation rather than a marionette. In fact, it's the true star of the film in certain respects and gets not only an excellent city destruction scene, but also a fantastic underwater battle with Godzilla. As for the Mothra larva, it too is inferior to the Tsuburaya version which had a weathered reality to it compared to Kawakita's polished artificial feel. Despite its title, the film pays homage to the original *Mothra* more so than 1964's *Mothra vs. Godzilla* with numerous scenes from the aforementioned film recreated here, most notably the ending wherein Mothra lands at a huge airfield to depart with the Cosmos.

Despite being what American fans consider to be a lukewarm entry in the Heisei series, the Japanese loved it and it became the second highest-grossing Godzilla film, at ¥2.22 billion ($19,900,080), a record that wouldn't be broken until 2016's *Shin Godzilla*. At the time, the gross also broke a 19-year record held by 1973's mega-successful *Submersion of Japan*. In addition to sweeping the box office, the film received numerous awards. Among them were Best Newcomer Awards for Keiko Imamura and Sayaka Osawa (the Cosmos), a Best Supporting Actor Award for Takehiro Murata, and a Lifetime Achievement in Music Award for Akira Ifukube at the Japanese Academy Awards for 1993. The film, not surprisingly, took the top prize at the Japan Golden Grosses Awards.

When it was finally released in the United States, to differentiate itself from the 1964 movie—which was more commonly known as *Godzilla vs. Mothra* on VHS—the new film was re-christened *Godzilla and Mothra: The Battle for Earth* on home video for its belated summer 1998 release.

Final Word A runaway success that officially cemented the fact that Godzilla was here to stay in the 1990s. And, as of 2017, *Godzilla vs. Mothra* was still one of the top five most popular Godzilla movies with Japanese fans.

GODZILLA vs. MECHAGODZILLA

(TOHO)

Release Date: December 11, 1993

Alternate Titles: *Godzilla vs. Mechagodzilla* (Japan) *Godzilla vs. Super-Mechagodzilla* (English copyrighted title) *Jurassic City: Godzilla vs. Mechagodzilla* (India) *Godzilla vs. Engineered Godzilla* (Greece) *Legend of Dinosaurs 2* (Russia)

Directed by: Takao Okawara **Special Effects by:** Koichi Kawakita **Screenplay by:** Wataru Mimura **Music by:** Akira Ifukube **Cast:** Masahiro Takashima (Kazama Aoki), Ryoko Sano (Dr. Azusa Gojo), Megumi Odaka (Miki Saegusa), Akira Nakao (Commander Takaki Aso), Yosuke Kawazu (Professor Omae), Kenji Sahara (Minister Segawa), Koichi Ueda (Commander Hyodo) **Suit Performers:** Kenpachiro Satsuma (Godzilla), Wataru Fukuda (Mechagodzilla), Ryu Hariken (Baby Godzilla)

Widescreen, Color, 107 Minutes

In 1994, using the remains of Mecha-King Ghidorah, the United Nations Godzilla Countermeasures Center (UNGCC) and its Japanese branch, known as G-Force, constructs the robot Mechagodzilla and the flying machine Garuda. Aoki, Garuda's designer, is begrudgingly assigned to Mechagodzilla's cockpit crew with G-Force. On Adonoa Island near the Bering Sea, a prehistoric egg is found by scientists. Before they can transport it to Japan via helicopter, the flying monster Rodan intervenes. Godzilla arrives moments later, and the two monsters battle as the helicopter escapes. Godzilla soundly thrashes Rodan. Back in Japan, Aoki sneaks into a lab to see the egg and begins a flirty relationship with the egg's adoptive human mother, Dr. Azusa Gojo. Godzilla shows up in Japan as the egg hatches to reveal a baby Godzillasaurus rather than a baby pteranodon as expected. Mechagodzilla is sent out to intercept him but is defeated by Godzilla, who unsuccessfully attempts to reunite with his young before returning to the sea. After having discovered that the baby has a secondary spinal brain, G-Force hatches a plan to lure Godzilla to Ogasawara Island with the baby as bait and kill him with the upgraded Mechagodzilla's new "G-Crusher" weapons. En route to the island, the baby and Gojo are intercepted by Rodan, who *has revived and been slightly mutated by Godzilla's ray. Aoki hijacks Garuda to save them and joins with Mechagodzilla in Chiba where Rodan is defeated. Drawn back in by the plaintive cries of the baby, Godzilla arrives and the rematch begins. Even though Godzilla is far more adept at physical fighting, the robot has more powerful laser weaponry and Mechagodzilla is victorious in killing Godzilla by destroying his spinal brain. Baby Godzilla calls out to Rodan, who awakens and uses his life force to regenerate the fallen monster king's secondary brain. Godzilla revives and, having gained an upgraded ray attack from Rodan, blasts Mechagodzilla to smithereens, then reunites with the infant, and the two peacefully swim out to sea together to live in peace.*

Background and Commentary Having successfully resurrected King Ghidorah and Mothra, Toho decided to next revamp the alien foe of 1974's *Godzilla vs. Mechagodzilla,* who next to King Ghidorah, ranked as Godzilla's most popular enemy. To pen the script, Shogo Tomiyama brought in Wataru Mimura, who gave Toho three different drafts over a six month period. Mimura's first draft was slightly more ambitious, as Mechagodzilla would have the ability to separate into two separate forms: one a tank and the other a flying machine. In one of these forms, it was to battle two white pteranodons on Adonoa Island, one of which would fall into the sea and mutate into Rodan. In addition to Rodan's inclusion, among Tomiyama's other requirements were the inclusion of a baby Godzilla for the sake of the female audience and also the outcome of the final battle being that Godzilla had to win since he had lost his previous two climactic battles (this, according to Tomiyama's book he wrote on the series).

Mechagodzilla's origins are brought down to earth as the creation of G-Force, rather than aliens from outer space. Screenwriter Mimura's storyline is well done, and the baby Godzilla is an excellent way to tie all of the film's story threads together. The script also never becomes convoluted with distracting side plots and an excess of characters as in Omori's scripts. These stellar results make *Godzilla vs. Mechagodzilla II* the best film of the Heisei series standing out as a creative masterpiece for many fans.

Akira Ifukube's work on the previous film received a Best Score nomination at the Japanese Academy Awards. But intending this film to be his swan song, it is Ifukube's grand themes here that truly deliver what is arguably the best score of his 1990's entries. Koichi Kawakita demonstrates a steady stream of impressive effects, without a turkey in the bunch despite the film's high ambitions. The tussle between Godzilla and Rodan provides a satisfying tooth and claw encounter while the battles with Mechagodzilla show off a bevy of computer-animated ray weapons. Godzilla's resurrection and subsequent red ray blasts (known in Japan as the "spiral ray") are the special effects crescendo of the picture. Keeping with Kawakita's love of transforming monsters, Mechagodzilla merges with Garuda to become Super-Mechagodzilla and Rodan mutates into the slightly differently-colored Fire Rodan complete with his own oral ray.

As for the actor inside the G-suit, Kenpachiro Satsuma gives the best performance of the monster to date here, though he would later top himself amidst Godzilla's agonizing death throes in *Godzilla vs. Destroyah* (1995). This film also marked a turning point for Godzilla in the Heisei series, who, after four straight films as an antagonist, is portrayed sympathetically.

Being the 20th entry in the series, the film contains several shots in homage to past classics like 1964's *Mothra vs. Godzilla* as well as the 1974 *Godzilla vs. Mechagodzilla*. Toho veteran Tadao Takashima (*King Kong vs. Godzilla, Son of Godzilla*) has a cameo in the film with his son Masahiro Takashima who plays the lead role of Aoki. Additionally, still fresh from a string of collaborative hits between he and Akira Kurosawa, rumor had it that Ishiro Honda had agreed to come back and direct this film, because—at the time—it was being planned as the "final" Godzilla movie. Whether this is true or not, unfortunately, Honda passed away on February 28, 1993, and Takao Okawara, whose *Godzilla vs. Mothra* was box office fire, would ultimately direct the film and establish himself as Godzilla's definitive director of the 1990s. His handling of the human cast, all of whom have some sort of link to the baby Godzilla is exceptional compared to other entries in the Heisei era.

Perhaps this is best exemplified by Megumi Odaka's Miki Saegusa character introduced in 1989's *Godzilla vs. Biollante*. After serving as little more than Godzilla radar in the previous two entries, Miki finally faces a moral dilemma as the one person who can operate Mechagodzilla's newest Godzilla-killing weapon, the G-Crusher. Because in Japan, women are still second-class citizens and despite her objections to her male superiors and affection for Godzilla and the baby, she is callously forced to pull the trigger that kills the Big G. Toho had pondered killing Godzilla to make way for TriStar Pictures' version of the character (at one time slated for a 1994 release) but decided against it at the last minute (when the TriStar film ran into serious delays) and Godzilla is revived from death by Rodan. Although its grosses didn't exceed that of its predecessor, it came close to equaling them and had far more success in the marketing of toys and other tie-in products.

Final Word This film serves as the gold standard for the second generation of Godzilla films and was such a creative success that the next year's release *Godzilla vs. Space Godzilla* was considered a critical failure, even if it was still a huge financial success.

KAMEN RIDER J

(TOEI/BANDAI)
Release Date: April 16, 1994

Directed by: Keita Amemiya **Special Effects by:** Hiroshi Butsuda **Screenplay by:** Shozo Uehara & Shotaro Ishinomori **Music by:** Eiji Kawamura **Cast:** Yuuta Mochizuki (Koji Segawa/voice of Kamen Rider J), Yûka Nomura (Kana Kimura), Rikako Aikawa (voice of Berry), Kyoji Kamui (Garai), Satoshi Kurihara (Agito), Maho Maruyama (voice of Fog Mother) **Suit Performers:** Jiro Okamoto (Kamen Rider J), Hideaki Kusaka (Garai), Yoshie Seki (Zu), Tomoyuki Tsuruyama (Agito)

Widescreen, Color, 47 Minutes

Koji Segawa is a nature photographer enjoying a camping trip with his little sister, Kana, when the duo are attacked by evil aliens. The group, led by Fog Mother, kills Koji and kidnaps Kana to serve as food for Fog Mother's hatchlings. Koji is resurrected underground as the Kamen Rider by the Earth Spirits. Koji returns to the surface with his insect guide, Berry, and together the duo take on Fog Mother's minions, dispatching them until only the giant Fog Mother ship remains. Kamen Rider grows in size to match the massive ship, and a battle ensues that the masked rider wins.

Background and Commentary In 1971, *Kamen Rider* debuted. It differentiated itself from its contemporaries like *Return of Ultraman* and *Spectreman* in that its transforming hero stayed human-sized. Oddly enough, this made Kamen Rider even more popular than his giant brethren, it is thought, because he was easier for children to relate to. However, in 1994, Kamen Rider finally joined his kaiju-sized counterparts for the theatrical release *Kamen Rider J*.

It should be noted that this was not the first Kamen Rider movie. There had been plenty of others before it, and that even included a 1975 Chaiyo Studios iteration where the Kamen Riders teamed with Hanuman à la *6 Ultra Brothers vs. the Monster Army* (1974). While that film had some giant monsters, it was not approved by Toei, and nor do the riders grow gigantic anyways, which is what sets *Kamen Rider J* apart from all the other iterations of Kamen Rider up to that point.

The film was notable for a few other reasons. For one, it wasn't derived from an existing TV series. This Kamen Rider was all new. It was also the last Kamen Rider property to have involvement from one of the original creators: Shotaro Ishinomori. It was co-written with Shozo Uehara, who also had a part in Kamen Rider's development back in 1971 (Uehara eventually left to focus on *Return of Ultraman*). At that time, there had been some debate amongst the developers as to whether or not Kamen Rider should be gigantic like Ultraman. Coincidentally, Kamen Rider almost didn't grow to kaiju-sized heights in the 1994 movie either—due to some hesitation on the part of Ishinomori. This aspect was only added into the very last draft. Another discarded idea had this Kamen Rider as an alien warrior from the stars, but the producers insisted that he be a normal human being to begin with.

Kamen Rider J gets off to an exciting start right in the middle of a burgeoning apocalypse. As such, we're treated to classic effects footage of volcanos, earthquakes, and other natural disasters. Running at less than 50 minutes, *Kamen Rider J* presents a straightforward story that runs at a brisk pace. If this were based upon a concurrent series, where the hero's origin is already established like the Ultraman movies, this wouldn't be anything unusual. What makes *Kamen Rider J* different is that it is an origin story that appears to be devoid of continuity ties to other entries. It's fairly remarkable that the film is able to cover enough ground that by only 13 minutes in, Koji has transformed into Kamen Rider for the very first time and is fighting an alien lizard. As in the original series, this battle occurs human-sized, the giant monsters don't come into play until the end.

The dai-kaiju aspects kick off with the giant Fog Mother ship engaging in some well-done miniature destruction, aided along by an exciting score from Eiji Kawamura. Kamen Rider's giant scenes are well staged. For instance, the moment he materializes, his feet immediately sink into the pavement. The framing of the scenes is also excellent, such as shots of his giant feet filmed through some trees on ground level. Scenes of the ship's full onslaught on Kamen Rider bring to mind Mechagodzilla's all-out assaults on Godzilla in the Showa Series.

While it's debatable whether this may have been a callback to *Godzilla vs. Mechagodzilla*, *Kamen Rider J* itself predates notable effects scenes from future tokusatsu films. Fans of *Mothra 3's* dinosaur scenes will be amused to know *Kamen Rider J* has a similar sequence in the form of a flashback where Fog Mother's offspring wipe out the dinosaurs. The quality of effects work is basically the same, despite the fact that this production predated *Mothra 3* by four years (and probably had a smaller budget). Another scene, where Kamen Rider punches his hand into the

Fog Mother ship to rescue his little sister, also predates a similar scene in *Gamera 3* (1999). Come to think of it; the giant insectoid Fog Mother ship brings to mind Legion from *Gamera 2* (1996) as well.

Kamen Rider J also exhibits how children's entertainment is a bit more hardcore in Japan as it's fairly violent. Koji gets punched through the stomach when he's still a normal human, and later, he punches out a lizard monster's eye as Kamen Rider. Though the aliens don't really have any major supernatural connotations, the interior of Fog Mother's ship has a very devilish design. Her offspring are also downright terrifying. Kana is dangled over the baby monsters in a cage in a scene that would terrify most children (the baby monsters are there to eat Kana, after all).

Kamen Rider J was released on a triple bill (hence its short runtime) with other TV to film adaptations of *Blue SWAT* and *Ninja Sentai Kakuranger*. As the last Kamen Rider production done with the involvement of creator Shotaro Ishinomori, fans consider this the end of the Showa Era of Kamen Rider. Though it didn't spawn a TV series or any direct sequels, the character of Kamen Rider J would return—giant stature and all—in future Kamen Rider team-up movies.

Final Word If you're a giant monster fan, but not a Kamen Rider fan, this short film is still worth checking out for the effects scenes because they definitely don't disappoint.

YAMATO TAKERU

(TOHO)
Release Date: July 09, 1994
Alternate Titles: *Orochi, the Eight-Headed Dragon* (U.S. home video) *Madra, the Eight-Headed Monster* (Germany) *The Eight-Headed Monster* (Thailand)

Directed by: Takao Okawara **Special Effects by:** Koichi Kawakita **Screenplay by:** Wataru Mimura **Music by:** Kiyoko Ogino **Cast:** Masahiro Takashima (Prince Osu/Yamato Takeru), Yasuko Sawaguchi (Oto Tachibana), Hiroshi Abe (Tsukiyomi), Hiroshi Fujioka (Kumaso Takeru), Saburo Shinoda (Keiko) **Suit Performers:** Kenpachiro Satsuma (Yamato no Orochi), Ryu Hariken (Kumaso God), Wataru Fukuda (Battle God of Outer Space), Yuji Saeki (Sea God Muba)

Widescreen, Color, 104 Minutes

Born under a bad sign and sentenced to death, Prince Osu is rescued by the White Bird of Heaven and taken to live with his aunt, where he trains under two mystical ninjas. When he returns home, he kills his twin brother in a fight and is falsely blamed for his mother's death. His father sends him on a mission of certain doom that he surprisingly survives and as a result, his enemy dubs him "Yamato Takeru." All the while, headed to earth is Tsukiyomi, an evil enemy the prince is destined to destroy. Together, Yamato Takeru and his love, Oto, a priestess, merge together into a giant warrior that battles Tsukiyomo on the moon when he transforms into Orochi the eight-headed dragon. After defeating Orochi, Yamato Takeru earns his father's blessing and returns to Earth to live in peace with Oto.

Background and Commentary In 1994, Toho finally released a giant monster film not starring Godzilla—or, rather, a mythological movie that featured kaiju at least. It was helmed by the same creative team that made *Godzilla vs. Mechagodzilla II* a hit, director Takao Okawara, special effects director Koichi Kawakita, scriptwriter Wataru Mimura, and star Masahiro Takashima. Mimura was approached to write a script around Yamato Takeru, a real historical figure with various legends surrounding him, by Shogo Tomiyama two years before he even began writing for the Godzilla series. This ambitious film had been in development since 1991

31

before production began in early 1994. It was also preceded by several other filmed versions of the Yamato Takeru legend, notably *The Three Treasures* (1959). The earlier Toho film starred Toshiro Mifune, was scored by Akira Ifukube, and the effects (including the dragon Orochi) were done by Eiji Tsuburaya (it was directed by Hiroshi Inagaki, who was one of Toho's premiere jidai-geki directors). The epic was considered a classic so plans came about to remake it with a big budget and a greater focus on mythical kaiju.

The tale gets off to a slow start due to its segmented nature and is also somewhat hard to follow as a result, but it eventually shifts into high gear and never lets up. Mimura's goal was to emulate Arnold Schwarzenegger's *Conan*. Mimura achieves his goal, especially in a scene where Yamato Takeru must battle the fiery Kusamo God. The film boasts many large sets, among the best a castle on the moon and a stony desert fortress. As a result, the lavish production was nominated for a Japanese Academy Award for Art Direction.

The film employs five monster suits/marionettes and there is also a full-sized Orochi dragon head and a White Bird of Heaven prop the actors ride upon. While the evil monsters have an earthy, organic look, the heavenly creatures have a more artificial almost mechanical appearance. Kawakita had an unabashed love of mechanical monsters in the Godzilla series, creating Mecha-King Ghidorah, Super-Mechagodzilla, and MOGERA (he even designed a Mecha-Mothra that was eventually aborted). In this film, Yamato Takeru's Battle God of Outer Space form may as well be called Mecha-Majin and the White Bird of Heaven could likewise be called Mecha-Giant Condor. Orochi the eight-headed dragon is undoubtedly the highlight of the film and the massive suit supposedly took two men, one of them Kenpachiro Satsuma, to operate at once (many other sources say it was only Satsuma, however). There is also an extraordinary amount of CGI utilized for this film, mostly for transforming/morphing affects.

The final battle is a gleeful experience for monster fans as the Battle God of Outer Space slices off Orochi's heads one by one. At one point, it is left with only three in a nod to King Ghidorah, who itself ironically owes its design to the mythical Orochi in the first place. Kiyoko Ogino's music that accompanies these battles is never unpleasant but is never quite grand enough to match the film's epic aspirations. However, the score was a very rushed affair, as Ogino didn't begin writing it until late May and composed it in June, only a month before the film's release. Okawara's direction is not as good here as it is in his G-films, though this is partly due to Mimura's script, which is too heavy on mythological exposition.

At the box office, the film (which had gone over its already high budget) bombed, putting an end to what was planned as a trilogy chronicling the other adventures of Yamato Takeru and Oto. Initially, Toho had hoped that the Yamato Takeru trilogy would be the summer equivalent of their "New Year's Blockbuster" Heisei Godzilla films, but it was not to be. The film was released straight-to-video in the U.S. by A.D. Vision in 1999 as *Orochi the Eight-Headed Dragon*.

Final Word One of Toho's most ambitious projects and one of its biggest disappointments. Still, most fans of the Heisei Godzilla series should be able to enjoy it for the effects work if nothing else.

GODZILLA VS.
SPACE GODZILLA

(TOHO)
Release Date: December 10, 1994
Alternate Titles: *Godzilla vs. Kosmogodzilla* (Poland)

Directed by: Kensho Yamashita **Special Effects by:** Koichi Kawakita **Screenplay by:** Hiroshi Kashiwabara **Music by:** Takayuki Hattori **Cast:** Megumi Odaka (Miki Saegusa), Jun Hashizume (Lt. Koji Shinjo), Zenkichi Yoneyama (Lt. Kiyo Sato), Akira Emoto (Akira Yuki), Towako Yoshikawa (Dr. Chinatsu Gondo), Yosuke Saito (Dr. Okubo), Akira Nakao (Commander Takaki Aso), Kenji Sahara (Minister Segawa), Koichi Ueda (Vice-Commander Hyodo) **Suit Performers:** Kenpachiro Satsuma (Godzilla), Ryo Hariya (Space Godzilla), Wataru Fukuda (MOGERA), Little Frankie (Little Godzilla)

Widescreen, Color, 108 Minutes

In late 1994, strange crystalized probes crash near Birth Island at the same time that G-Force arrives there with Miki Saegusa to study Godzilla and his son, now much bigger and known as Little Godzilla. Their goal is the "T-Project," a plan to telepathically control Godzilla using Miki's psychic abilities. Also stationed on the island is G-Force operative Yuki, who is determined to kill Godzilla with a special blood coagulator. The T-Project is interrupted by Space Godzilla, who arrives on earth after making short work of G-Force's new counter-Godzilla robot, MOGERA, in space. After a battle with his clone, Space Godzilla imprisons Little Godzilla in some crystals and flies off for Fukuoka with Godzilla in pursuit. In the meantime, Miki is kidnapped by her colleague, Dr. Okubo—secretly a member of the yakuza—who tries to use her ability to control Godzilla to sell to the highest bidder. Miki is rescued by a G-Force raid lead by the heroic Yuki and G-Force officer Shinjo just as Godzilla arrives in Japan. Together, Godzilla and MOGERA battle his evil clone in Fukuoka. After Godzilla manages to kill Space Godzilla with his red ray, he then destroys MOGERA as well. As Yuki watches Godzilla slip back into the ocean, he gives up on his vow to kill him. Miki telepathically shows Shinjo a happy and freed Little Godzilla learning to spit radioactive sparks on Birth Island.

Background and Commentary *Godzilla vs. Space Godzilla* is widely regarded as the worst offering of the Heisei series, though in the film's defense, it is the result of poor timing and bad circumstances. The film, following on the heels of the critically acclaimed *Godzilla vs. Mechagodzilla II* (1993), began ambitiously as *Godzilla vs. Astrogodzilla* in which a two-tailed, winged, albino Godzilla from space (spawned from the cells of Biollante) attacks earth and takes over the minds of both Miki Saegusa and Godzilla's son. In the climax, Godzilla frees the two and defeats his clone with the help of super-robot MOGERA (a robot originally from 1957's *The Mysterians*) and a returning Mothra. After the failure of Toho's big-budget opus *Yamato Takeru* in the summer of 1994, the sixth G-film's budget received a drastic cut initially resulting in the loss of MOGERA (to be replaced by the already-existing Mechagodzilla suit as a "Mechagodzilla II"), Mothra, and the more ambitious story elements. When the script was retooled yet again, Astrogodzilla became Space Godzilla, Mothra was downgraded to a brief stock footage cameo, and MOGERA was re-instated for marketing reasons (i.e. a new toy to sell as opposed to same Mechagodzilla figure from last year). Actually, it could be argued that the whole story was written from a marketing perspective: Space Godzilla for men, MOGERA for mecha-buffs, Mothra and a love-struck Miki Saegusa for the girls, and Little Godzilla for kids.

In certain respects, the finished film harkens back to the Godzilla entries of the late 1960s and early 1970s. This is most apparent with the first act being set on a tropical island, complete with a Little Godzilla who resembles Minilla more than a dinosaur. Supposedly Kawakita wasn't satisfied with the previous design and wanted to make him more monster than dinosaur, albeit a cute one. Even director Yamashita remarked in an interview with David Milner that, "I see Little Godzilla as a very bad omen because he is so cute." In regards to the new foe, Space Godzilla's design and alien origins would have fit well with the 1970s (right down to having a variation of Gigan's roar). Actually, Space Godzilla's finished design comes from the Super Nintendo video game *Super Godzilla*, wherein Godzilla sprouts spikes from his shoulders during the final stage when he transforms into the titular character. And, for the first time in the Heisei series, Godzilla has an ally (albeit an uneasy one) during the final battle in the form of MOGERA. That said, while the first two acts drag along, the climax in Fukuoka is exciting and well-executed. The most exciting battle of the film may well be MOGERA's one on one battle with Space Godzilla in Fukuoka (for this author at least). In any case, it was unusual to see two brand new monsters battling it out minus Godzilla in the Heisei series. This portion of the film is unfortunately marred by an earlier battle between MOGERA and Space Godzilla in an asteroid field, which may have looked fantastic on paper, but was too ambitious to actually pull off on film.

As for the cast, Megumi Odaka's Miki doesn't make for as intriguing a lead as people would think, and her forced love story with Jun Hashizume is especially weak. The film's standout character ends up being Yuki, played by Japanese action star Akira Emoto, who is obsessed with avenging the death of his best friend Colonel Goro Gondo, who Godzilla killed in *Godzilla vs. Biollante* (1989).

Toho, or rather specifically Toho president Yoshinobu Hayashi, made an odd choice for the film's director, Kensho Yamashita, best known for his teen-idol flick *Nineteen* (though it should be noted Yamashita did serve as an assistant director on 1975's *Terror of Mechagodzilla*). Akira Ifukube, having been told the previous movie would be the last one, turned down *Godzilla vs. Space Godzilla* flat. His replacement, the young, new composer Takayuki Hattori, was chosen by Yamashita. Though he comes up with a fairly rousing new march for Godzilla, his music naturally pales in comparison to Ifukube's. Thankfully, Yamashita decided to insert a few Ifukube tracks because he knew the audience expected to hear Godzilla's theme.

When filming wrapped after 55 days, Yamashita's first cut of the film ran 2 ½ hours but was edited down to 108 minutes by Toho. Most of the edits are bizarre and inexplicable. A scene of Godzilla failing to free Little Godzilla from his crystal prison (a scene which only seems to exist in stills now) was completely removed, while a sequence of Godzilla taking 10 minutes to land on Birth Island was retained. Other scenes included fleshing out the motives of the yakuza subplot as well as a fight between Godzilla and G-Force in Kagoshima Bay (cut down to a few seconds and mixed with two stock shots from *Godzilla vs. Biollante* and *Godzilla vs. Mothra* without Kawakita's permission). Another fight between Godzilla and G-Force in mainland Kyushu was removed, probably because it was exactly the same as a similar battle sequence in *Godzilla vs. Mechagodzilla II*, just with the new G-suit. Scenes of Godzilla and Little Godzilla frolicking on Birth Island were similarly excised. The final insult to the film came when it was critically beaten by the newest Gamera film several months later, though *Godzilla vs. Space Godzilla* was still the victor at the box office.

Final Word Though it has a few rousing battles and an excellent new enemy kaiju, unfortunately this film is regarded as something of a failure when compared to its predecessor and eventual sequel. However, on its own merits, *Godzilla vs. Space Godzilla* is a fun flick that deserves a better reputation.

GAMERA,
GUARDIAN OF THE UNIVERSE

(DAIEI)

Release Date: March 11, 1995

Alternate Titles: *Gamera: Giant Monster Mid-Air Battle* (Japan) *Gamera: The Protector of the Universe* (Greece), *Gamera: Guardian of the Cosmos* (Iran) *Gamera: Defender of the Universe* (Russia)

Directed by: Shusuke Kaneko **Special Effects by:** Shinji Higuchi **Screenplay by:** Kazunori Ito **Music by:** Ko Otani **Cast:** Shinobu Nakayama (Dr. Mayumi Nagamine), Tsuyoshi Ihara (Yonemori), Akira Onodera (Naoya Kusanagi), Ayako Fujitani (Asagi Kusanagi), Yukijiro Hotaro (Inspector Osako) **Suit Performers:** Naoki Manabe/Jun Suzuki (Gamera), Yumi Kanayama (Gyaos)

Widescreen, Color, 95 Minutes

Naval Officer Yonemori and insurance investigator Kusanagi team up to investigate a mysterious floating atoll in the Pacific. At the same time, ornithologist Dr. Nagamine is called to an island off the coast of Japan where a strange new species of large "bird" is sighted. The Japanese government deems the creatures an endangered species and attempts to capture them in Fukuoka Dome. Yonemori and Kusanagi find the atoll which turns out to actually be a giant turtle-like creature who makes his way to Fukuoka where the birds are being captured. It makes its way to Fukuoka Dome and kills all but one of the birds. At Kusanagi's home, Yonemori reads a translation of a slab they found on the atoll. It reveals the giant turtle is Gamera, a weapon created by the people of Mu to defeat the birds, another out-of-control creation called Gyaos. Kusanagi gives his daughter Asagi a curved jewel found on the atoll that glows when she touches it. She forms a strange link with Gamera and is compelled to follow him across Japan as he battles the Gyaos, sharing the wounds he accrues. Finally, a Gyaos grows into a much larger form and attacks Tokyo, building a nest atop Tokyo Tower. Gamera arrives from underground and engages in a final battle with Gyaos that transverses the sky, the ground, and even outer space! With the help of Asagi's connection, Gamera finally manages to blow Gyaos' head off with one *of his fireballs. As the Guardian of the Universe returns to the sea, Asagi proclaims that "Gamera will come again."*

Background & Commentary Comparing the new Gamera series to the old is a bit like comparing the Adam West *Batman* TV show to Christopher Nolan's *Dark Knight* trilogy. What was once unbelievably campy had become undeniably cool. Part of what helps is Gamera's new origin as a bioengineered weapon from the lost civilization of Mu (though it says Atlantis in the English dub, and Gamera was from Atlantis in the Showa series, in the 1995 film Mu is the lost continent of choice). Shusuke Kaneko, future director of hit films such as *Death Note*, insisted Gamera be treated in a serious manner. Not surprisingly this film was greenlit at the recently-revived Daiei due to Toho's renewed success with Godzilla. However, they were only able to allocate a fraction of those film's budgets at ¥600 million (roughly 6 million U.S. dollars. The Heisei Godzilla films were made for 10-13 million dollars). For this reason, Daiei thought the film could only be produced as a sort of parody until Kaneko convinced them otherwise.

Gamera and Gyaos' battles again make for spectacular aerial antics, which are made even better by the film's composer, Ko Otani, who proves himself to be the most talented kaiju eiga composer since Akira Ifukube. His rousing themes, all of which stand out, are original and easy to remember long after the film is over. While there are plenty of nods to past Gamera films—notably Gyaos' attack on a bullet train—Kaneko shows more reverence for Ishiro Honda than he does Noriaki Yuasa. One scene in the film even harkens back to a scene in *Mothra* involving rescuing a child on a bridge. That said, children are overall absent from the proceedings and are replaced by comely teenager Asagi, ably played by Ayako Fujitani, daughter of American action star Steven Seagal. In the lead is beautiful Shinobu Nakayama as Dr. Nagamine, who was nominated for a Japanese Academy Award for her performance. Interestingly, women provided the leads in all three of Kaneko's Gamera films, and here, Yumi Kanayama also makes history as the first female suit actor, playing the wicked Gyaos.

Special effects director Shinji Higuchi surpasses Toho's effects of the same era and does so with nearly half the budget, though they were allotted a fairly generous 101 days for shooting and 60 days for post-production (which is far more than Toho would allocate to the Godzilla crews, which were generally shot and edited in a couple of months' time). Working with smaller monsters and thus larger scale miniatures, his work is a near masterpiece with the illusion of size exemplified using low angle shots amongst the miniatures. To accomplish this, Higuchi built the suits with short-statured actors in mind. Unsurprisingly, Gamera's old flamethrower routine is done away with and the monster now fires CGI fireballs. Gyaos' new CGI ray is likewise stunning for Japanese films of the time and was every bit on par with concurrent American films. Higuchi deservedly won a Japanese Academy Award for his work on the film.

A co-production between Daiei, Nippon Television, and Hakuhodo, the film was distributed by Toho—who owns the largest theater chain in Japan—rather than Daiei themselves. The film—originally intended as a forgettable quickie matinee to capitalize on Toho's success reviving Godzilla—wound up critically and technically outdoing the most recent G-film, *Godzilla vs. Space Godzilla*. This film was ranked as #2 on the list of Top Ten Best Japanese-Made Films of 1995 and even American critics such as Roger Ebert had nice things to say about it when it went on a very limited U.S. theatrical run in 1997, something Godzilla hadn't accomplished in years. Despite the critical success of the film, the inferior *Godzilla vs. Space Godzilla* was still the victor at the Japanese box office.

Final Word Shusuke Kaneko, Shinji Higuchi, and Ko Otani emerge here as true successors to Honda, Tsuburaya, and Ifukube in what is arguably one of the best monster movies of the 1990s. This film would be followed by two stellar sequels and a reboot, *Gamera the Brave*, in 2006.

SUPER ATRAGON
PART I

新海底軍艦 滅亡への ゼロ アワー

(TOHO)
Release Date: 1995
Japanese Title: *New Undersea Warship: Zero Hours to Destruction*

Directed by: Kazuyoshi Katayama **Special Effects by:** Yasuhiko Komori, Manabu Maekawa & Akira Yamamoto **Screenplay by:** Nobuaki Kishima **Music by:** Masamichi Amano **Cast:** Tomokazu Seki (Go Arisaka), Junko Iwao (Annette), Kikuko Inoue (Avatar/Satomi Arisaka), Tetsuro Sagawa (Magane Hyuga), Koji Shimizu (Mitsugu Kageyama), Shinsuke Chikaishi (Kotaro Nishimura)

Widescreen, Color, 52 Minutes

During World War II, shortly after the bombing of Hiroshima, the Japanese undersea battleship Ra engages in a naval battle with a mysterious U.S. battleship piloted by Avatar, an enigmatic woman. On board the Ra is her counterpart, Annette, who manages to deter Avatar through a psychic connection. Annette and one of the commanding officers escape the ship. Fifty years later, a mysterious magnetic force is unleashed in the North Pole. An investigative team is sent to determine just what is causing the destructive phenomena. Among their numbers are a young man named Go and Ann (really Annette). It is revealed that an underground super race is behind the attacks, which are just a precursor to an even grander assault. When the ship Go is on is destroyed, he is rescued by the crew of the newly rebuilt Ra. To his shock, the captain of the Ra appears to be his long lost father...

Background & Commentary In 1963, Toho released *Atragon* to theaters as its "New Year's Blockbuster." It lived up to the hype, being one of Toho's biggest hits of the early 1960s. The film never got an actual sequel, though there was a quasi-remake in the form of 1977's *The War in Space,* which featured the Gohten fighting aliens. During the development of what became *Godzilla vs. Destroyah* in 1995, there was talk of integrating the Gohten into the story. That never came to pass, and that same year an OVA (original video animation) was released: *Super Atragon*. Though the credits proclaim that its "Based on the novel by Shunro Oshikawa," it's more so based upon Shinichi Sekizawa's screenplay for *Atragon*. The novel was set in 1899, nor did it feature an undersea empire, which was unique to *Atragon*.

Super Atragon does what any good retelling should do in keeping the basic concept but changing it up enough to be entertaining to people familiar with the story. Right off the bat, we are introduced to the ship, called the Ra in this iteration rather than Gohten or Atragon, during WWII. Though there were no scenes set during WWII in *Atragon*, the war was a huge part of the ship's backstory. The first real twist on the mythos for *Atragon* fans comes when we see a member of what appears to be the Mu Empire aboard the ship as an ally! The surprises keep coming as an American version of the sub, called the *Liberty*, then reveals itself. Both ships look the same, except the U.S. version has three drills rather than one. The exciting opening ends with both ships ramming into each other, their fates uncertain.

The estranged father/daughter relationship between Makoto and Captain Jinguji from *Atragon* is brought back here as a father and son relationship. In this case, Go's father vanished sometime in the 1980s, and when he boards the Ra, he suspects the unnamed captain is really his father, though the captain denies this.

As for the action and adventure elements, the story has the flare of an old Toho invasion picture like *The Mysterians* updated for the 1990s. The gravity bending ring weapons are fitting for the villains, which though modeled after the Mu, are never called such. The annihilation of an entire fleet of navy destroyers by the rings is quite a spectacle and would have been a blast to see in live-action tokusatsu.

The new Ra's entrance is a doozy. As the rest of the naval fleet is about to be destroyed, a massive iceberg drifts against the current coming towards the conflict. The iceberg is just a fake hull for the Ra, which literally explodes out of it to save the day. The ship's redesign is excellent. In fact, it might just be its best design period (it's definitely better than the *Godzilla: Final Wars* iteration).

Ultimately, Part I does what it should by providing some solid entertainment while also setting up several burning questions to be answered in Part II.

Final Word Don't expect any giant monsters, but if you're a fan of *Atragon,* then *Super Atragon* should probably be required viewing.

MIGHTY MORPHIN POWER RANGERS: THE MOVIE

(SABAN/TOEI)
Release Date: June 30, 1995

Directed by: Bryan Spicer **Screenplay by:** Arne Olsen & John Kamps (story) **Music by:** Graeme Revell **Cast:** Jason David Frank (Tommy Oliver/White Ranger), Amy Jo Johnson (Kimberly Hart/Pink Ranger), David Yost (Billy Cranston/Blue Ranger), Karan Ashley (Aisha Campbell/Yellow Ranger), Steve Cardenas (Rocky DeSantos/Red Ranger), Johnny Yong Bosch (Adam Park/Black Ranger), Paul Freeman (Ivan Ooze), Nicholas Bell (Zordon), Robert L. Manahan (voice of Zordon), Peta-Marie Rixon (Alpha-5), Paul Schrier (Bulk), Jason Narvy (Skull), Mark Ginther (Lord Zedd), Robert Axelrod (voice of Lord Zedd), Julia Cortez (Rita Repulsa), Barbara Goodson (voice of Rita Repulsa)

1.85 : 1, Color, 95 Minutes

6000 years ago, an alien being named Ivan Ooze ruled the world. He had just finished construction of two Ecto-Morphicon Titans, which would have extended his reign of terror except for he was stopped by an earlier incarnation of the Power Rangers. A construction crew in Angel Grove unearths his tomb, and soon after, Rita Repulsa and Lord Zedd come along to free Ooze, who they hope will kill Zordon. Ooze is happy to comply and goes to the Power Rangers command center to confront Zordon. Ooze leaves Zordon near death, imprisons Rita and Zedd, and takes away the Ranger's powers. Using the last of the command center's power, Alpha 5 sends the Rangers to a distant planet to train under the warrior Dulcea. The Rangers obtain new ninja powers and animal zords before returning to Earth. There they defeat Ooze's two Ecto-Morphicon Titans and then Ooze himself.

Background & Commentary In the mid-1970s, Toei began their Super Sentai franchise, which still runs to this day. In 1993, *Kyoryu Sentai Zyuranger* was brought to America as *Mighty Morphin' Power Rangers* and became a surprise hit. Like *Godzilla, King of the Monsters!* in 1956, new actors were hired to play the leads on the series, which was moved from Japan to Angel Grove, California. The new scenes of the American teenagers who transformed into the Rangers were light-hearted and in the vein of *Saved By the Bell*. When the teens transformed into the

Rangers, the Toei effects footage took over. *Power Rangers* proved to be such a phenomenon that it spawned an all-new feature film. You see, while the series used existing footage from *Zyuranger*, the $15 million film would consist of all new footage.

Though you'd think that big-budget American effects would be an improvement over the Toei TV footage, this is sadly not the case (at least not in the instance of the final battle). Even though a miniature city set was constructed for the end battle, the Zords and enemy monsters were all CGI. Back then, CGI was still relatively new... nor was it very good. Many a child, including this author, were puzzled by the strange new Zords, which looked like holographs. They were only a little better than video game CGI. Though this was forgivable at the time, repeat viewings of the film 25 years later are even more distracting because the CGI is so terrible. On the other hand, the Zords perform maneuvers in CGI that the suits would be incapable of (like the zippy outer space battle). A better compromise might have been to do suitmation effects within the city, and CGI in space.

Those quibbles aside, the battles are well choreographed, which still counts for something. The way the fight ends is also rather unique. As the gigantic Ivan Ooze envelops the new Megazord in a death grip, Aisha, the Yellow Ranger, suddenly has an idea. She breaks through some glass marked "Use Only in Case of Emergency" and pulls a special lever. What kind of secret weapon are they about to unleash? Well, it all turns out to be a joke as the Megazord knees Ooze in the groin. He releases them, sails through space, and collides with a fireball ending his reign of terror. It's quite funny, and as goofy as Power Rangers already was, if it took itself too seriously, it would've ruined the film.

As it is, the movie most resembles the live-action *Teenage Mutant Ninja Turtles* trilogy and Joel Schumacher's Batman movies (where Ivan Ooze would have been right at home). Ooze not only gave the audience a new villain, but he was also a more entertaining one than the previous villains. On that note, though Rita and Zedd are fun villains, it would've been a poor move to simply keep them as the main antagonists. Furthermore, Ooze imprisoning them both is a great way to make him more threatening.

If anybody gets the best moments in this movie, it's the villains. Paul Freeman absolutely dominates all of his scenes. In one, he pays Zordon a visit in the control room and laments all the horrible things he's missed since being imprisoned: the Black Plague, the Spanish Inquisition, the Brady Bunch Reunion (that last one was Freeman's adlib). One of the best moments has an imprisoned Zedd and Rita cheering on the rangers, even shouting, "Go! Go! Power Rangers!" There's also a mid-credits zinger with Goldar sitting on Zedd's throne and proclaiming himself the new ruler of the universe. In walks Rita and Zedd. "Uh oh!" Goldar shouts and then begins a pop song that also begins with "Uh-oh, we're in trouble..."

As a kid's film, *Power Rangers* is a quality production with solid pacing. Director Bryan Spicer was not familiar with the Power Rangers before this but did an excellent job of handling the characters. Spicer wanted the movie to have a journey/quest storyline and specifically wanted to give the movie the feel of *The Wizard of Oz*. He succeeds in this endeavor via the scenes set on the Planet Phaedos, where the Rangers spend most of the second act. Adding to the *Wizard of Oz* feel are Ooze's henchmen, the crow-like Tengu who bring to mind the flying monkeys of *Wizard of Oz*.

The film was a hit at the box office grossing around $66 million worldwide, which, of course, ensured a sequel...

Final Word If you were a kid who grew up watching *Power Rangers*, this movie probably holds enough nostalgia to warrant another viewing. If you're a serious tokusatsu connoisseur who dislikes things like the *Rebirth of Mothra* trilogy, then this is not a film you would enjoy.

GODZILLA vs. DESTROYAH

ゴジラVSデストロイア

(TOHO)

Release Date: December 09, 1995

Alternate Titles: *Godzilla vs. Destroyer* (Japan) *Godzilla vs. Destoroyah* (English copyrighted title) *Last Godzilla* (India) *Godzilla vs. Absolute Destroyer* (Greece) *Godzilla vs. Destructor* (Argentina)

Directed by: Takao Okawara **Special Effects by:** Koichi Kawakita **Screenplay by:** Kazuki Omori **Music by:** Akira Ifukube **Cast:** Yoko Ishino (Yukari Yamane), Takuro Tatsumi (Dr. Kensaku Ijuin), Yasufumi Hayashi (Kenkichi Yamane), Megumi Odaka (Miki Saegusa), Sayako Osawa (Meru Ozawa), Akira Nakao (Comnmander Takaki Aso), Saburo Shinoda (Mitsuru Kunimoto), Masahiro Takashima (Major Sho Kuroki), Momoko Kochi (Emiko Yamane), Shigeru Koyama (General) **Suit Performers:** Kenpachiro Satsuma (Godzilla), Ryo Hariya (Destroyah), Ryu Hariken (Godzilla Junior), Eiichi Yanagada (Aggregate Destroyah)

Widescreen, Color, 103 Minutes

In 1996, when a red-glowing Godzilla attacks Hong Kong, it is determined the monster king is in the process of a nuclear meltdown which has the potential to destroy the whole world. To stop the meltdown, G-Force develops a new set of freezing weapons and are able to successfully freeze Godzilla with the newly-created Super X-III. At the same time, a group of Precambrian life forms that were awakened by the use of the Oxygen Destroyer in 1954 have evolved enough to begin attacking Japan. When they come together to become a singular kaiju-sized monster and attack Tokyo, psychics Miki Saegusa and Meru Osawa use their powers to guide the adolescent and further-mutated Godzilla Junior to battle it. Though Junior is able to defeat the monster—dubbed Destroyer/Destroyah— he is helpless when it morphs into a gigantic final form and drops him from a great height into a building, killing him. Having just reunited with his son, an enraged Godzilla engages the gigantic Destroyah in battle as he enters the final stage of his meltdown. After Destroyah has been killed, Godzilla begins meltdown and is destroyed by the very power that gave him life. G-Force watches helplessly until something else begins to absorb the excess radiation. Junior, resurrected as a fully-grown new Godzilla, rises from his father's ashes.

Background and Commentary In 1992, DC Comics announced that they were killing off Superman and the news made headlines around the world. Perhaps Toho took notice of the media whirlwind, because in 1995, after exhausting many ideas that failed to gain any traction, they announced that Godzilla would kick the bucket in his next film. This move was also a result of their contract with TriStar. Toho had planned to kill Godzilla back in 1993's *Godzilla vs. Mechagodzilla II* to make way for TriStar's planned film, but changed their minds at the last minute when the TriStar film was delayed. But with the American film now "firmly" entrenched for a 1997 release date (which too would change), Toho decided now was the time to do the big guy in, and early versions of the script were actually titled *The Death of Godzilla*.

Preliminary ideas for the story featured everything from a Ghost Godzilla to time-traveling Juniors to Bagan to a reappearance of the Gohten, but the final version was decided to harken back to the 1954 original. The main characters are made up of members of the Yamane family and Momoko Kochi briefly reprises her role as Emiko. In addition to flashbacks from that film, even the enemy monster draws its origin from the Oxygen Destroyer. The idea of a living organism created from the Oxygen Destroyer is an interesting idea, but the monster's design—inspired a little too much by the *Alien* and *Predator* franchises—lacks the grace of foes like King Ghidorah. Then again, grace was probably not what Toho was going for when designing Destroyah which succeeds as a frightening looking kaiju.

Initially, the "Godzilla Dies" tagline was front and center in all advertising. To keep a little mystery to the film, the final stage of Destroyah was a highly-guarded secret. However, since merchandising was a huge part of the series, the Destroyah design was leaked when Bandai released toys of the monster early. Like past Heisei films, Destroyah is a transforming monster, going through more stages than any previous kaiju. A sequence where multiple man-sized Destroyahs do battle with a Japanese SWAT team is taken right out the *Alien* franchise, not surprising considering Kazuki Omori returned to write this film's script. Thankfully, this is the only big nod to American cinema in the film and the rest of the picture makes for some excellent Godzilla action.

As a way to both lend interest to the monster and also sell more toys, Godzilla's form in this film is known as "Burning Godzilla" for his red, patchy, glowing skin (the monster's ray is also now red rather than blue). His final battle with Destroyah is exhilarating right to the end. Many fans seem to misinterpret the ending as the military killing Destroyah instead of Godzilla, which is not the intention at all. Godzilla blasts away at Destroyah, even blowing off a chunk of his head. Realizing Godzilla's

46

about to kill him, Destroyah flees. As he flies into the air, the Super X-III and the freeze masers blast him with freeze rays, knocking him out of the air. In the Japanese dialogue, a member of the Super X-III crew remarks that even though Destroyah's falling onto him, Godzilla isn't moving. This is because Godzilla is holding his position and using his body to superheat the ground. When Destroyah hits the ground, this sudden change in temperature from freezing cold to blazing hot is what kills the evil monster. While Godzilla didn't kill Destroyah with violence, he did accomplish the feat with science.

As for the main event, Godzilla's death scene is touching, though perhaps a little exploitative due to its semi-gruesome manner. The moment that packs the biggest punch in the film isn't the death of Godzilla, but rather the unexpected killing of his son by Destroyah. As everyone is anticipating Godzilla's imminent demise, it's a real shock when Destroyah drops Godzilla Junior from high in the air, and the fall ends up killing him. Also touching are Godzilla's efforts to revive his son with bits of his life force, made all the more moving by Ifukube's music. The maestro truly turns in a powerhouse score, notably the opening and closing credits, the latter of which sounds becomes a funeral dirge.

Just as 1968's *Destroy All Monsters* was the final film to involve all four of the original "Godzilla Fathers," this film proved to be the final affair for the Heisei Era Godzilla filmmakers. It was the final score ever for Ifukube, the last Godzilla film produced by Tomoyuki Tanaka, and also the last collaboration between director Takao Okawara, writer Kazuki Omori, and special effects director Koichi Kawakita. Unsurprisingly, the film was as nearly a big hit as *Godzilla vs. Mothra* (1992) with an impressive attendance of 4 million people, making it the top-grossing Japanese-made film of 1996.

Final Word Much more than just a gimmick, *Godzilla vs. Destroyah* is one of the best films of the Heisei series and a fitting end to a fantastic era of special effects cinema.

ULTRAMAN ZEARTH

ウルトラマンゼアス

(TSUBURAYA PRODUCTIONS)
Release Date: March 9, 1996

Directed by: Shinya Nakajima **Special Effects by:** Shinya Nakajima
Screenplay by: Hideaki Nagasaka **Music by:** James Shimoji **Cast:** Masaharu
Sekiguchi (Katsuto Asahi), Yuka Takaoka (Toru Hoshimi), Takaaki Ishibashi
(Shinpei Okochi), Takeshi Kaga (Akuma Ogami/Alien Benzen) **Suit Performers:**
Keiji Hasegawa/Koichi Toshima (Ultraman Zearth), Toshio Miyake (Cottenpoppe),
Hiroyuki Okano (Alien Benzene)

Widescreen, Color, 51 Minutes

All across the world, gold is mysteriously vanishing, draining into
the very earth itself. The special team MYDO (Mysterious
Yonder Defense Organization) discovers the culprit is an
underground monster called Cottenpoppe. However, the team is
unaware that their lowest-ranking member, the inept clean-freak
Katsuto, is secretly the giant Ultraman Zearth—whose only weakness
happens to be dirt and grime. Controlling the gold-sucking
Cottenpoppe is Alien Benzen, who absorbs the gold's energy through
the monster. Benzen kidnaps Katsuto's love interest, Toru, and
Katsuto/Ultraman Zearth must overcome his fear of uncleanliness to
rescue her. When he confronts Alien Benzen and Cottenpoppe, he
uses the two beings' power against one another, defeating both.

Background & Commentary Instead of a straightforward film to
celebrate the 30th Anniversary of *Ultraman*, Tsuburaya Productions opted
for this send-up of the series. Thankfully, it is actually funny. Overall, the
story is a respectful and loving parody of the Ultraman series from its own
creators. The story concerns clean-freak Katsuto Asahi, the low man on
the totem pole at MYDO (which operates out of a gas station!). Ironically,
the team are all unaware that Katsuto is their most valuable player, the
heroic Ultraman Zearth (it is unclear if he is Zearth's human host or Zearth
in human form). Most humorously of all, Katsuto transforms into the
titular hero by using his electric toothbrush as his Beta Capsule. And
speaking of Beta Capsules, Susumu Kurobe, Hiroko Sakurai, and Akiji

Kobayashi all have cameos that are quite well done. Kurobe is a night watchman who, at one point, holds his flashlight in the air like a Beta Capsule. Sakurai is the only woman who ever seems to notice the MYDO team's ship leaving (it does so from a billboard at the gas station).

Being a comedy, the special effects don't need to excel, but for the most part, they are well done for mid-90s, low-budget standards. The film begins with an intriguing shot that appears to be on an alien planet that turns out to be the ocean floor of Earth. An old shipwreck is then floated into the sky in an interesting visual and later we learn this is the gold-hungry monster Cottenpoppe's doing. Though it appears in a spoof, there is nothing comical about Cottenpoppe, and the monster actually resembles a few of the designs considered for the title foe in the aborted *Mothra vs. Bagan*. The human/alien villain, Benzen, has a certain Hideyo Amamoto/ Dr. Who quality about him and serves the short story as well as he can.

Though the spoof elements would eventually be scrapped, *Ultraman Zearth* does start one trend in the theatrical vehicles in that its credits play over a digest/reprise of the whole film. Also, the film has a post-credits scene, though it is more of the *Ferris Bueller's Day Off* variety than the Marvel brand where sequels are teased. *Ultraman Zearth* proved to be enough of a hit to generate a sequel, and was released as part of Ultraman Wonderful World alongside *Revive! Ultraman* (an unofficial 40th episode of the original *Ultraman* series created by re-editing footage from the series and concluding with Ultraman killing Zetton this time) and *Ultraman Company*.

Final Word Brisk and energetic, *Ultraman Zearth* is short (and funny) enough to not wear out its welcome. Overall, it is a well-made spoof of the genre.

GAMERA 2
ADVENT OF LEGION

(DAIEI)
Release Date: July 13, 1996
Alternate Titles: *Gamera 2: Attack of the Legion* (U.S. home video) *G2: Gamera vs. Legion* (original international title) *Gamera 2: The Legion Attack* (Greece) *Gamera 2: A Guerrilla Army* (Iran)

Directed by: Shusuke Kaneko **Special Effects by:** Shinji Higuchi **Screenplay by:** Kazunori Ito **Music by:** Ko Otani **Cast:** Miki Mizuno (Midori Honami), Toshiyuki Nagashima (Colonel Yusuke Watarase), Mitsuru Fukikoshi (Obitsu), Tamotsu Ishibashi (Hanatani), Ayako Fujitani (Asagi Kusanagi), Yukijiro Hotaru (Osako) **Suit Performers:** Akira Ohashi (Gamera), Mizuho Yoshida/Koichi Tamura/Toshiyoshi Sasaki (Huge Legion), Tomohiko Akiyama/Yuji Kobayashi/Yoshiyuki Watabe/Akihiro Nakata (Legion Colony)

Widescreen, Color, 100 Minutes

When a meteor crashes in Japan, a mysterious hive of alien insects dubbed "Legion" (after the Bible verse) begin wreaking havoc. First, they create a huge seeding pod in Sapporo, which is destroyed by Gamera, though the giant turtle is soon overwhelmed by the smaller insect monsters. The Legion next attack Sendai with another huge pod, but this time when Gamera arrives to destroy it, he is stopped by a giant-sized Legion, and the pod destroys Sendai in a nuclear-esque explosion with Gamera at ground zero. Now more desperate to reproduce than ever, the Legion colony begins its advance on Tokyo while Gamera is seemingly dead in Sendai. Eventually, the hopes and well-wishes of children congregated around the monster's body manages to revive Gamera. He immediately jets off to the outskirts of Tokyo in a pitched battle where, with the help of the self defense forces (and the very earth itself), manages to destroy Legion.

Background & Commentary With *Gamera: Guardian of the Universe* racking up a great deal of critical praise (being voted the second-best made film in Japan in 1995), Daiei was quick to push a sequel into production. Early talks considered reviving another Showa creation Jiger and later, the space squid Viras, but a new alien foe was eventually decided upon for the sequel (likely at Kaneko's insistence). Surprisingly, this film manages to surpass its predecessor in almost every aspect, especially the special effects which were already quite good.

Instead of rehashing the previous picture's winning formula, *Gamera 2: Advent of Legion* deserves praise for exploring new territory with the Legion invasion instead. Among the script's interesting ideas are a gigantic Legion pod flower (inspired by a similar creation from *Ultra Q*), that jettisons seeds into space which will in turn spawn more Legions. An angular insectoid alien, Legion is certainly a monster for the 1990s with a heavy anime influence.

Gamera and Legion's final confrontation may be the most satisfying monster battle ever filmed. The fight begins in a country suburb outside of Tokyo and includes a bevy of interesting battle tactics right from the onset. Gamera enters the battle sliding across the landscape firing his fireballs at Legion, who deflects every single one with a force field of sorts. When Gamera tears off Legion's deflecting mandibles, things get worse when the alien flays Gamera with a new laser beam attack. To finally beat the invader, Gamera has to call upon a new power where he summons energy from the earth and then directs it through his torso. Although the scene surely sounds strange in written form, on film it is spectacular (even if what exactly was happening in this scene isn't fully explained until the sequel, though it's fairly easy enough to figure out).

Kaneko and effects director Shinji Higuchi were given more creative freedom this time around and were able to utilize some ideas nixed from the last film, such as Gamera sporting sea turtle-type fins when he takes flight. In a nod to the Showa films, Gamera sheds more blood this time and in the classic tradition, suffers a debilitating blow at the hands of his enemy when the Legion pod detonates in his face. After this, Gamera is revived by spiritual energy from a group of surrounding children. However, in an unexpected twist, Gamera severs his connection with Asagi and the rest of humanity upon waking (setting up an interesting mystery to be explored in the sequel). Another notable sequel set up happens in the film's epilogue, where the lead character warns a friend that Gamera may one day turn against humanity for their reckless exploitation of the earth.

Upon its release, the film grossed about the same amount of its predecessor. Even if its grosses weren't on par with Toho's films, the film's excellence was recognized when it won the award for Best Special Effects at the Japanese Academy Awards.

Final Word *Gamera 2: Advent of Legion* not only proved that Kaneko's success on the first film wasn't a fluke, but that he could also craft a wholly original storyline when given more creative freedom.

SUPER ATRAGON
PART II

メモリー・オーシャン

(TOHO)
Release Date: 1996
Japanese Title: *New Undersea Warship: Memory of the Ocean*

Directed by: Mitsuo Fukuda **Special Effects by:** Yasuhiko Komori, Manabu Maekawa, & Akira Yamamoto **Screenplay by:** Nobuaki Kishima **Music by:** Masamichi Amano **Cast:** Tomokazu Seki (Go Arisaka), Junko Iwao (Annette), Kikuko Inoue (Avatar/Satomi Arisaka), Tetsuro Sagawa (Magane Hyuga), Koji Shimizu (Mitsugu Kageyama), Shinsuke Chikaishi (Kotaro Nishimura)

Widescreen, Color, 46 Minutes

After a successful campaign against Avatar's forces, the Ra returns to its Ogasawara base for repairs and upgrades. While there, Go learns of Annette's hidden history as a member of an advanced race that lives below the surface. Annette is essentially a defector, as she was never supposed to aid the human race, while Avatar is accomplishing her purpose. Soon the U.S. navy comes to Ogasawara with orders for the Ra to surrender itself to them while at the same time Avatar's forces begin their final assault. Annette faces off with Avatar on the beach while the Ra launches to take on a "mother ship" beneath the waves. Ra seemingly destroys the orb-like ship, which breaks open to reveal a new version of the Liberty. Ra defeats the ship, which also dismantles all of Avatar's other weapons. With Avatar defeated, the Ra heads off on a new mission to the earth's core.

Background & Commentary Part II of the *Super Atragon* OVA begins with a flashback that immediately answers many of our burning questions from Part I. At the top of the list was how did the Japanese build such an advanced ship back in the 1940s? The flashback takes place in early 1930s Manchuria under Japanese occupation. There, a strange meteor has fallen from the skies, which we learn is what was used to create the Ra. Eventually, we learn that the U.S. also found a meteorite, hence the creation of their battleship Liberty. The "meteors" were advanced materials sent from the underground humans to test the surface dwellers.

If humanity used the material for peace, the subterranean super-race would let humanity live. If mankind used the meteor's materials to make war, the human race would be wiped out. Annette and Avatar were spies meant to observe humanity. But Annette developed compassion for humankind, and essentially cheated by explaining the rules of the game to the Japanese. Japan still makes a weapon out of the materials in the form of the Ra, as does the U.S. with the Liberty. Avatar then uses the Liberty as a way of attacking Annette, who she views as a traitor. Therefore the mysterious opening of Part I has been explained.

When we jump to the present, it's straight to the action. The giant rings are leveling cities and destroying battleships until the flying Ra joins the fight. Shots of the Ra's force field deflecting the lasers brings to mind some shots from *Godzilla: Final Wars*, so perhaps *Super Atragon* was the inspiration for them? Though some will be disappointed that there's still no monster equivalent to Manda in this story, a monster really wasn't needed. In its place is the rebuilt Liberty, and having the Gohten face off against an "evil twin," if it could be called that, is more interesting than a giant serpent.

As to references to *Atragon* in Part II, the island base where the Ra is kept originates from the film and the novel both. There's a visual callback to *Atragon*'s scene of Makoto and Jinguji having an important exchange next to a shimmering lake. Here, Go and Anne have an important conversation in a similar locale. The end battle between the Ra and the new Liberty is spectacular and has the Ra sink to the bottom of the ocean when it's damaged. To make matters worse, an undersea volcano erupts, threatening to consume the ship. The final maneuver is clever and well-staged. As Avatar launches all three drills at the Ra, it deflects them with some rockets anchors. With the Liberty's bow now unprotected without the drills, the Ra bores right through it.

Super Atragon doesn't end on a cliffhanger so much as it leaves a thread dangling for a sequel. Said thread is the question of whether or not the subterranean people will make peace with the surface dwellers. The film ends with the Ra crew preparing to go on a diplomatic mission to the earth's core with Annette. As to why no sequels were made, that is unknown.

Final Word If you were among those who lamented that a live-action Heisei era remake of *Atragon* never happened, this OVA is definitely the next best thing and would have made for a great live-action film itself.

THE ADVENTURES
OF GALGAMETH

(SHEEN COMMUNICATIONS)
Release Date: November 18, 1996
Alternate Titles: *Galgameth: The Monster of the Prince* (Germany) *Galgameth: The Dragon Apprentice* (France)
The Legend of Galgameth (Spain)

Directed by: Sean McNamara **Special Effects by:** David Allen **Screenplay by:** Michael Angeli, Turi Meyer, Al Septien, & Shin Sang-ok (as Simon Sheen) **Music by:** Richard Marvin **Cast:** Devin Oatway (Prince Davin), Stephen Macht (El El), Elizabeth Cheap (Periel), Lou Wagner (Zethar), Time Winters (Templeton), Sean McNamara (King Henryk) **Suit Performers:** Felix Silla (Small Galgameth), Doug Jones (Large Galgameth)

Academy Ratio, Color, 110 Minutes

When Prince Davan's father, King Henryk, is murdered by his first knight, El El, the young prince finds himself tossed out of the castle. His only friend is a small statue—given to him by his father—brought to life by his tears: Galgameth. Under the alias of John, Prince Davin and the constantly-growing Galgameth ally themselves with a group of rebels which includes the princess in hiding, Periel. As the rebels' faith in the gigantic Galgameth grows, they decide to feed their weapons to the monster so that he can grow even larger. The rebels, with Galgameth leading the charge, storm El El's castle. El El manages to capture Davin and takes him out to sea. As Galgameth can only be destroyed by that which brought him to life, the salt water of the sea begins to dissolve him as he wades into the water to rescue Davin. Galgameth rescues his young master even though it costs him his life, and the next morning on the beach, Prince Davin defeats El El in hand-to-hand combat. Davin is crowned the rightful king of his kingdom, and later while walking on the beach with Periel, he discovers a small statue of Galgameth washed up on the shore.

Background & Commentary The exact roots of this American remake of the notorious North Korean *Pulgasari* are something of a mystery. What is known is that after *Pulgasari's* (1985) director Shin Sang-ok escaped from North Korea, his name was taken off *Pulgasari's* credits. After he had established some clout as "Simon Sheen" in America with such films as *3 Ninjas Knuckle Up* (1995), Sang-ok managed to convince someone to remake *Pulgasari* as *Galgameth*—produced through his company, Sheen Communications, to get back at Kim Jong-Il for removing his name from the original *Pulgasari's* credits.

The remake moved the locale from feudal Korea to medieval Europe and was even filmed on location in Romania around Bucharest and Zarnesti. As a whole, this film is much lighter than *Pulgasari* and with its kid friendly tone, one could consider it a tonal combination between Shin's *3 Ninjas* movie and *Pulgasari*. For instance, though the monster still eats iron, instead of blood that brings the statue to life, it is the tears of Prince Davin. Galgameth does not turn on the villagers he once defended as in *Pulgasari* (though, more on that later). That said, the film still hits all of the same action notes from *Pulgasari*. The monster reveals itself by saving several innocents from an execution while it is human sized. There is a scene where the monster catches fire and glows (and in this case his body causes trees to catch fire). Galgameth is buried in a pit like Pulgasari. Finally, Galgameth storms the evil lord's castle while being beset upon by canon fire. As stated earlier, instead of ending with the iron-munching Galgameth eating up all the peasants' farming tools, this western version does away with *Pulgasari's* alleged communist message. Instead, this film's climax would seem to have borrowed from Daiei's *Return of Daimajin* (1966). Like that film's climax, Galgameth must pursue the villain into a stormy sea and uses a lightning strike to destroy the villain's boat. Though it is unknown if Shin wrote this scene, it was obvious that the director had a great deal of love for the Majin films in the original *Pulgasari*.

Overall, the effects work for Galgameth as a suitmation monster are stellar. The suit's face has a surprisingly wide range of expression and the composite shots of the giant Galgameth mixed in with live extras are near flawless. As for the monster's design, it still has hints of Pulgasari with its built-in body armor, but Galgameth is more dinosaurian than bovine. In fact, Galgameth looks a bit like the baby dinosaur Tasha from the 1991 *Land of the Lost* TV revival. *The Adventures of Galgameth* was released theatrically first in Spain on November 18, 1996 and in Japan on November 21st of that same year. It went straight to VHS in the U.S. through Trimark Home Video and was released on July 29, 1997. Today, it is mostly forgotten.

Final Word A well done—if not slightly par for the course—mid-90s adventure film for kids. As a western reimagining of *Pulgasari*, fans of that film will definitely find this one worth a watch.

REBIRTH OF MOTHRA

(TOHO)

Release Date: December 14, 1996

Alternate Titles: *Mothra* (Japan) *Mothra, the Queen of Monsters* (original international title) *Mothra Resurrection* (Finland) *Mothra: The Seal of Elias* (Germany) *The Renaissance of Mothras* (Greece)

Directed by: Okihiro Yoneda **Special Effects by:** Koichi Kawakita **Screenplay by:** Masumi Suetani **Music by:** Toshiyuki Watanabe **Cast:** Megumi Kobayashi (Moll), Sayaka Yamaguchi (Lora), Aki Hano (Belvera), Kazuki Futami (Taiki Goto), Maya Fujisawa (Wakaba Goto), Hitomi Takahashi (Makiko Goto), Kenjiro Nashimoto (Yuichi Goto) **Suit Performers:** Mizuho Yoshida (Death Ghidorah)

Widescreen, Color, 106 Minutes

On Infant Island, the aging monster Mothra spiritually creates an egg to replace her when she dies. In Japan, construction work in Hokkaido unearths the seal of Mothra's fairies, the Elias, which keeps the dreaded beast Death Ghidorah imprisoned inside of a mountain. Belvera, the evil sister of the Elias, and her mechanical dragon Garu-Garu obtain the seal but are intercepted by the Elias atop Fairy Mothra, a miniature version of the giant moth. The duo are unsuccessful in stopping Belvera and the wicked fairy unleashes Death Ghidorah, an armored, three-headed, quadruped beast who once killed all the life on Mars. Death Ghidorah begins his rampage anew by destroying forests, which have much stronger lifeforce than humans do. The Elias summon the aging Mothra into battle and she manages to hold her own, though is ineffective against the dragon. Sensing danger, Mothra's egg hatches prematurely and the larva swims to Japan to aid its mother. Both Mothras tag-team Death Ghidorah, but the space dragon still keeps an advantage in the battle. Mothra saves her offspring from the monster and flies it out to sea where it is given special instructions before the mother dies and sinks to the bottom of the ocean. The larva goes to Yaku Island and spins a cocoon around the ancient Yakusugi Tree and emerges as Mothra Leo with new and improved powers. Mothra Leo re-engages Death Ghidorah in battle then finally manages to seal him *underground again. Afterwards, Mothra Leo replenishes the burned forest while Belvera escapes to torment the Elias another day.*

Background & Commentary Toho had plans for a Mothra adventure as far back as 1990, the infamous *Mothra vs. Bagan*, though it was cancelled because of *Godzilla vs. Biollante's* (1989) poor performance at the box office. With Godzilla having died in 1995's *Godzilla vs. Destroyah*, Toho decided now would be a good time to try again at a solo Mothra film utilizing a few elements of the discarded *Mothra vs. Bagan* script—in fact, Bagan was considered as the villain briefly. The green-lighting of the production was also largely due to the huge success of 1992's *Godzilla vs. Mothra*, which was very popular with women, a big part of Japan's moviegoing audience. Initially, this film was meant to tie into the Heisei Godzilla series. The original foe was even to be the reanimated corpse of the same Ghidorah from 1991's *Godzilla vs. King Ghidorah* resurrected by Belvera's magic with a skeletal middle head. As this idea obviously tampered with that film's time-travel continuity and Mecha-King Ghidorah, it was dropped. The final film takes place in its own continuity even if Mothra sports the same basic design from *Godzilla vs. Mothra*.

Toho also changed the film's tone in an attempt to appeal to two demographics at once when *Rebirth of Mothra* was overhauled to become a children's feature. The film's juvenile approach alienates adult viewers but does offer a nearly constant supply of eye candy for its intended audience. One of the best set pieces involves the tiny Elias battling Belvera in a living room duel riding atop Fairy Mothra and Garu-Garu. While there is no city destruction of any sort, Death Ghidorah gets plenty of screen time destroying the forests of Hokkaido and is an impressive creation.

The film's battles exemplify the excessiveness of Koichi Kawakita's love of ray weapons. The newly-hatched larva (known informally as "Mothra Leo" but never referred to as anything other than "Mothra" in the films) has all sorts of new powers ranging from camouflage to a laser beam resembling Godzilla's that it just randomly starts firing out its neck! In his adult form, he has more tricks than can be listed here, even turning into a swarm of mini-Mothras to devastate Death Ghidorah. While visually stimulating, this anything-goes bag of trickery robs the battle of any suspense in the end. That said, the new Mothra's design is fantastic though. Whereas the old Mothra had a black, yellow, and white color scheme, this one is white, black, and green (the green coming from the fact that this Mothra spun its cocoon around an ancient tree).

The film is something of a milestone for Mothra's fairies who are no longer presented as identical twins that speak in unison. Moll and Lora each have their own personality, and one is older than the other. Thanks to this new dynamic, it enables the sisters to carry the film as characters rather than appear as just another special effect. While a dark Mothra called Battra was introduced in *Godzilla vs. Mothra*, here Toho cleverly concocts a wicked third sister to the fairies, Belvera, though we only learn the trio are related in a surprise reveal during the epilogue.

Although disdained by some fans, this film was reasonably profitable enough to continue with sequels. To be precise, *Godzilla vs. Mothra* grossed ¥2.22 billion, and this film ironically grossed ¥1.15 billion (about $10,277,550 in today's dollars), almost exactly half that amount. Furthermore, although many adult fans turn up their nose to this film, it was actually more financially successful than all three films in the superior Gamera trilogy. This film had a huge marketing push at the time of its release, while its two sequels were "sink or swim" affairs. Tomoyuki Tanaka died in 1997, making this his final production, even though he got an honorary credit on *Rebirth of Mothra 2*. *Rebirth of Mothra* would not make it to U.S. shores until it was released on VHS in August of 1999.

Final Word Like *All Monster's Attack* and other kid-friendly monster flicks, many adult fans may not love this film, but for kids—or people who at least saw it as a child initially—this is a fun film.

TURBO:
A POWER RANGERS MOVIE

(SABAN/TOEI)
Release Date: March 28, 1997

Directed by: David Winning & Shuki Levy **Screenplay by:** Shuki Levy & Shell Danielson **Music by:** Rick Hromadka & Shuki Levy **Cast:** Jason David Frank (Tommy Oliver/Red Ranger), Karan Ashley (Aisha Campbell/Yellow Ranger), Johnny Yong Bosch (Adam Park/Green Ranger), Catherine Sutherland (Kat Hillard/Pink Ranger), Blake Foster (Justin Stewart/Blue Ranger), Hilary Shepard Turner (Divatox), Amy Jo Johnson (Kimberly Hart), Austin St. John (Jason Lee Scott), Steve Cardenas (Rocky DeSantos), Paul Schrier (Bulk), Jason Narvy (Skull), Winston Richard (Zordon), Bob Manahan (voice of Zordon), Donene Kistler (Alpha-5), Richard Wood (voice of Alpha 5)

1.85 : 1, Color, 99 Minutes

Lerigot is a small, furry wizard living peacefully on a distant planet. The evil space pirate Divatox wants Lerigot to use his powers to open an interdimensional portal that will lead her to the fire demon Maligore. Lerigot escapes to Earth to find his old friends Zordon and Alpha 5, but lands in Africa by accident. In Angel Grove, Tommy and Rocky are practicing for a charity karate event as part of a fundraiser for an orphanage. Rocky hurts his back during practice and ends up in the hospital. Justin, a young boy who admires Rocky, eavesdrops when the Power Rangers pay their comrade a visit and learns their secret. Zordan summons the Rangers to come get Lerigot, stranded in Africa. Tommy and Kat (the new Pink Ranger) successfully acquire the wizard, but there's bad news. Divatox is now on Earth and holds Bulk, Skull, and former Rangers Kimberly and Jason hostage. A trade for the hostages doesn't go as planned, and Divatox ends up getting Lerigot. The Rangers must then set sail on a mystical sea to try and reach Maligore's island. Before setting sail, Zordon upgrades the Zeo Rangers into Turbo Rangers, and the young boy Justin replaces Rocky as the new Blue Ranger. The Rangers make it to the island, where they save their friends, and then form the new Megazord to defeat the giant Maligore. With the fire demon defeated, Divatox flees and vows vengeance on the Rangers.

Background & Commentary *Turbo: A Power Rangers Movie* is to the first film what *Rebirth of Mothra 2* is to *Rebirth of Mothra*. Like *Rebirth of Mothra 2*, released later the same year, *Turbo* is an inferior sequel largely based around the water that contains a furry McGuffin that's supposed to be cute, but if anything is just dull. Like Gogo, there's really no way to connect with Lerigot, who can't speak English. He's basically just there, and though the plot revolves around him, he's not very engaging or well designed.

Perhaps the biggest blow to this sequel was the lack of a good villain. The first film benefited tremendously from Paul Freeman's Ivan Ooze. The new villain, Divatox, has no charm to her whatsoever. Adding insult to injury is the fact that Grace Jones (*A View to a Kill*; *Conan the Destroyer*) was the original choice for the role. While Jones probably could have added fear and humor to the character (scary characters, especially, can be funny when played right), actress Hilary Shepard Turner isn't very memorable.

The first film made up for its extreme corniness by way of its humor, which occasionally worked pretty well. In that film, most of the laughs were generated by the villains. Ironically, in this film, the only laugh to be scored comes from a Rita Repulsa cameo! Divatox calls Rita up on the phone late at night to ask for advice as to defeating the Power Rangers, and it's quite amusing. The other comedic bits, left up to Bulk and Skull, fall completely flat. The duo's scenes reminded me of bad Italian slapstick from the 1970s.

Turbo does have one thing to its credit: it didn't try any CGI monsters this time around. Maligore is a suitmation creation, which brings to mind the fire monster from *Yamato Takeru* (1994). The new Megazord was also suitmation. However, the end battle between the two monsters was practically a non-event, wasn't very long, and didn't have any clever choreography to speak of.

The only other pluses in this film come from the return of Amy Jo Johnson as Kimberly and Austin St. John as Jason. Apparently, the director wanted all the original Rangers to come back, but it wasn't feasible for various reasons (and Johnson apparently only did so because she had already signed a contract for two movies).

Ultimately, audiences didn't take to this sequel and it flopped (though the Power Rangers popularity was no longer at a peak like it was back in 1995, either). Therefore, it's no surprise that no further sequels followed in theaters.

Final Word For completests and die-hard Power Rangers fans only.

ULTRAMAN ZEARTH 2

ウルトラマンゼアス

(TSUBURAYA PRODUCTIONS)
Release Date: April 12, 1997
Alternate Titles: *Ultraman Zearth 2: Great Superman War - Light and Shadow* (Japan)

Directed by: Kazuya Konaka **Special Effects by:** Kazuya Konaka **Screenplay by:** Kazunori Saito **Music by:** James Shimoji **Cast:** Masaharu Sekiguchi (Katsuto Asahi), Yuka Takaoka (Toru Hoshimi), Takaaki Ishibashi (Shinpei Okochi), Uno Kanada (Kagemi/Lady Benzene), Koji Moritsugu (Captain Ban Satsuma) **Suit Performers:** Keiji Hasegawa (Ultraman Zearth), Yutaka Kanezuka (Ultraman Shadow), Misato Suzuki (Lady Benzene alien form), Hiroyuki Okano (Darkler/Alien Benzen), Rikako Suzuki (Micron/Digital Kanegon)

Widescreen, Color, 66 Minutes

When Ultraman Zearth is defeated by a dark Ultraman called Ultraman Shadow at the South Pole, both humanity and Katsuto Asahi himself begin to lose faith in the giant hero. The evil mastermind behind the new Ultraman is Lady Benzen, the girlfriend of Alien Benzen bent on revenge. Katsuto begins taking karate lessons in hopes of learning a new move to defeat Ultraman Shadow. When the evil Ultra appears in Tokyo, Zearth sends his capsule monster Micron to battle him instead but Ultraman Shadow counters with his own capsule monster, Darkler. In the end, Zearth must muster his courage to travel to Lady Benzen's lair to vanquish Ultraman Shadow once and for all—in addition to saving a group of humans (Toru among them) from the alien's deadly mind control. As the world watches, Zearth defeats Shadow—which turns out to be a robot—and all are freed from Lady Benzen's mind control.

Background & Commentary Like many sequels, *Ultraman Zearth 2* is bigger, though not necessarily better, than the original. Not only is it longer than the first film with a more developed story, it also has even more cameos and monsters. There are three enemy monsters in total, the main one being the dark Ultraman Shadow—an evil robot version of Zearth. The Ultra's design is excellent, and in some ways is almost better (and certainly less cartoony) than Ultraman Belial who would premiere twelve years later in *Mega Monster Battle: Ultra Galaxy Legends* (2009).

The battles between the two Ultramen are well done, though there are a few shoddy CGI effects of the two flying that look like video game graphics. Zearth is even given a capsule monster this time around. However, this is more fan service than it is a plot point. The capsule monster (Micron, a reference to Miclas from *Ultra Seven*) appears once, as does Ultraman Shadow's capsule monster (Darkler), and then neither monster is seen again. The big bad is Lady Benzen, the girlfriend of the previous film's villain. There is even another good, human-sized monster, Digital Kanegon, that helps out around the MYDO base as well that is inspired by Kanegon from *Ultra Q*.

As for cameos, Susumu Kurobe is back with an even better cameo than last time, holding a spoon in the air as if it is a Beta-Capsule and threatening to teach Lady Benzen a lesson. Hiroko Sakurai gets the same cameo as last time, once again trying to snatch a picture of MYDO's secret gas station base in operation and *Return of Ultraman*'s Jiro Dan plays a newscaster. And, as Akiji Kobayashi had passed on, a character meant to be Kobayashi's fisherman character's son appears with a photo of Kobayashi in the background. Perhaps the best aspect of the whole film is Koji Moritsugu who gets a wonderful supporting role as the new MYDO captain, often breaking the fourth wall to call back to his Ultra Seven days (his character is even named Captain Ban Satsuma). Upon seeing Zearth's capsule monster, Satsuma exclaims, "Natsukashi!" which is a Japanese expression meaning someone is suddenly reminded of the old days. At the end of the film, Satsuma hints that he knows Zearth's human identity when he offers to teach Katsuto the "heel drop." However, these are some of the only truly funny scenes, and this entry is much less humorous than the first.

Though the novelty of Ultraman Zearth had already begun to wear off, the film was still a success financially and encouraged Shochiku to keep asking Tsuburaya Productions for more Ultraman movies.

Final Word Even though *Ultraman Zearth 2* has a more detailed story, the first film fares better and has more laughs.

REBIRTH OF
MOTHRA 2

(TOHO)
Release Date: December 13, 1997
Alternate Titles: *Mothra 2: Undersea Battle* (Japan) *Mothra 2: Battle Beneath the Sea*
(original international title) *Mothra vs. Dagarah* (Finland)

Directed by: Kunio Miyoshi **Special Effects by:** Koichi Kawakita **Screenplay by:** Masumi Suetani **Music by:** Toshiyuki Watanabe **Cast:** Megumi Kobayashi (Moll), Sayaka Yamaguchi (Lora), Aki Hano (Belvera), Hikari Mitsushima (Shidori Urauchi), Masano Shimada (Yoji Miyagi), Masaki Otake (Kohei Toguchi), Atsushi Okuno (Kotani), Hajime Okayama (Nagase), Maho Nonami (Princess Yuna) **Suit Performers:** Mizuho Yoshida (Dagarah)

Widescreen, Color, 100 Minutes

An underwater pyramid from the lost civilization of Nilai Kanai rises from the sea when a group of starfish-like creatures called Barem begin polluting the oceans. Go-Go, a furry creature from the pyramid, comes to the mainland for help and finds it in the form of three schoolmates, Shidori, Yoji, and Kohei. The trio are soon attacked by Belvera (riding a refurbished Garu-Garu 2) but rescued by the Elias. The children and the Elias make the journey to the giant pyramid. At the same time, a sea monster created by Nilai Kanai known as Dagarah destroys a submarine and begins trampling some seaside towns. Mothra Leo comes to intervene but is unable to beat Dagarah when he covers him with the Barem. Inside the pyramid, the Princess of Nilai Kinai appears and informs the youngsters that Go-Go is the fabled "treasure of Nilai Kinai." Making its way outside, Gogo— a water spirit—transforms into "magical water" and cures Mothra of the Barem. Able to fight again, Mothra transforms into an underwater form, "Aqua Mothra," to battle Dagarah. When Mothra defeats him, the Princess of Nilai Kinai calls Dagarah back to their lost civilization, and the pyramid transforms into water. Mothra reverts to his original form, albeit with rainbow-colored wings, which Go-Go lives on through.

Background & Commentary Much like they did with the Godzilla series, Toho announced *Mothra 2* at the end of *Mothra* (1996) before they even knew whether it was profitable enough to justify a sequel. It was, but just barely. Overall, *Rebirth of Mothra 2* presents an ambitious original story that is marred by subpar effects and too many shots and ideas that shamelessly copy American films. This is best exemplified in Aqua Mothra itself, a beautifully-designed creature on paper whom Kawakita's marionette cannot successfully represent. To add insult to injury, Aqua Mothra turns into a swarm of mini-Aqua Mothras that swim inside Dagarah and blow the monster up from the inside in a manner similar to the final Death Star scene in *Star Wars* (1977). As a result, the scene is comical rather than exciting. It should be noted, though, that years ago, Kawakita had planned to do a *Fantastic Voyage*-like scene for an aborted "Godzilla vs. Mechani-Kong" film in 1991, complete with giant starfish-like anti-bodies inside of Godzilla. This scene was not in the original script for *Rebirth of Mothra 2*, and perhaps knowing this was his final film as special effects director, Kawakita insisted on using the idea.

As for Dagarah, it isn't a well-designed monster when compared to Death Ghidorah, and perhaps not surprisingly, Bandai never made a full-sized figure to tie into the film either. (Bandai did make a smaller scale Dagarah figure, but it came in a set with *Mothra 2*-related Mothra figures. They didn't sell Dagarah on his own because their Death Ghidorah figures didn't sell well at all). Go-Go is a bit too stiff to ever bond with the audience and looks exactly like what it is: a toy. The human cast this time around caters even more so to children with no sympathetic adult characters at all, unlike the last film, which featured the children's parents as additional protagonists. The film does have one fun surprise, though, when Belvera saves her sisters from certain doom at the last minute, setting up interesting possibilities to be fully explored in the next entry.

Though some sources record that *Mothra 2* made ¥1 billion at the box office, the film was a financial and critical bomb both, and audiences were said to find it downright pitiful. To add insult to injury, Toho producer Tomoyuki Tanaka passed away in February of 1997, and the film was dedicated in his memory. Though the film's shortcomings were in no way Tanaka's fault, it's too bad the last movie he had a producer credit on had to be this one.

Final Word With better effects and less tipping of the hat to American films, this could've been a thoroughly entertaining and original monster/adventure film. Instead, it's an unfortunate soggy mess.

ULTRAMAN TIGA
AND ULTRAMAN DYNA

(TSUBURAYA PRODUCTIONS)
Release Date: March 14, 1998
Japanese Title: *Ultraman Tiga & Ultraman Dyna: Shining Star Warriors*

Directed by: Kazuya Konaka **Special Effects by:** Kazuya Konaka **Screenplay by:** Keiichi Hasegawa **Music by:** Tatsumi Yano **Cast:** Takeshi Tsuruno (Shin Asuka/voice of Ultraman Dyna), Ryo Kinomoto (Captain Hibiki), Toshikazu Fukawa (Koda), Risa Saito (Ryo Yumimura), Takao Kase (Kariya), Mariya Yamada (Mai Midorikawa), Mio Takaki (Captain Megumi Iruma), Yosuke Mitsuhashi (Susumu), Aya Sugimoto (Dr. Rui Kisaragi), Yasushi Manaka (voice of Ultraman Tiga) **Suit Performers:** Shunsuke Gondo (Ultraman Tiga), Keiji Hasegawa (Ultraman Dyna), Hisataka Kitaoka (Geranda), Hiroyuki Okano (Deathfacer)

Widescreen, Color, 68 Minutes

While battling the monster Geranda on the moon, Ultraman Dyna is saved by the TPC's (Terrestrial Peaceable Consortium) new superweapon, Prometheus. Back on their island base, Dr. Kisaragi expresses a disturbing lack of faith and hostility towards Ultraman Dyna. When an evil alien race, the Monera, attack the island, Dyna rushes out to combat them. Prometheus arises to join in the battle but it instead sides with the aliens and transforms into a fearsome robot, Deathfacer, and Dr. Kisaragi is revealed to be the aliens' puppet. Dyna is defeated and the Monera issue an ultimatum to mankind. Dyna and Super GUTS (Super Global Unlimited Task Squad) battle the Monera in Tokyo with the help of Captain Iruma of the original GUTS. Though Dyna defeats the Deathfacer, a new gigantic alien menace, Queen Monera, takes its place. It is only after the hopes of the people revive Ultraman Tiga that the two Ultramen defeat the alien invaders.

Background & Commentary In many ways, *Ultraman Tiga & Ultraman Dyna* is the first real Ultraman movie. The first ever Ultraman movie in 1967, and many of those that followed, were just compilation films. Though it included plenty of original footage, this even includes 1984's *Ultraman Story* as well. Or if it wasn't a compilation movie, it was some sort of off-shoot like *6 Ultra Brothers vs. the Monster Army* (1974) from

Thailand or the comedic *Ultraman Zearth* films. *Ultraman Tiga & Ultraman Dyna*, however, was the first all-original Ultraman movie made to tie in with a concurrent TV series, *Ultraman Dyna*, which ran from September of 1997 to August of 1998—with this film released in March of 1998 in the middle of the show's run.

The first Heisei Ultraman film gets off to an excellent start. After a long panning shot of the earth in space, a monster shoots into frame over the camera, and soon the audience is witnessing a battle between Ultraman Dyna and Geranda on the moon. This film was made in an era where CGI was first getting in vogue—though it was still in its infancy for lower budgeted films and often poorly done (see 1995's *Mighty Morphin' Power Rangers: The Movie*). This film, thankfully, mostly sticks to suitmation and real miniatures. That said, there are a few uses of primitive CGI in certain shots, but they aren't onscreen long enough to become obnoxious.

The film has four solid monster battles over the course of its scant hour plus run time. Of the monsters, scenes with the robot Deathfacer fare the best because of the machine's range of weaponry. In one scene, Deathfacer uses a machine gun-like weapon on its arm to blast a fleet of jet fighters out of the sky in quick succession. After Deathfacer's defeat and Ultraman Dyna flies towards the sky, a giant vine bursts from the ground in a surprising scene to grab the titular hero's leg. After that, the huge Queen Monera emerges from the ground. To this author's knowledge, Queen Monera is the first "supersized" kaiju to appear in live action to battle an Ultraman, and from here on out, most Ultraman films would end this way. In fact, this film also sets up the story pattern for all the Ultraman films to follow in many other ways as well. In addition to the "final boss battle," it also has a pre-credit outer space battle. It hinges heavily on a team-up with another Ultraman. Defeating the final monster requires some form of hope/goodwill-induced power-up. Lastly, a pop song plays over the end credits.

The film's main flaw is that it's not actually the team-up movie that its title implies. Though the original plan was to include *Ultraman Tiga* star Hiroshi Nagano as Daigo (the human host of Tiga on the TV series), the actor/musician was unavailable due to commitments to his band, V6. The story was tweaked and Tiga appears only for the last battle sans a human host. In Nagano's place is *Ultraman Tiga* cast member Mio Takaki returning as Captain Iruma. In a crowd-pleasing moment, Iruma joins in the final battle in her old GUTS gear to aid Super GUTS.

In an epilogue, the original GUTS crew (sans actor Kenichi Furuya and Hiroshi Nagano) cameos along with Daigo's new young daughter. Though heartfelt, the scene only makes Nagano's absence more conspicuous.

Final Word Though not a great team-up movie like the title implies, the film is noteworthy as the first real Heisei Ultraman movie and for establishing the subsequent formula of the series.

GODZILLA

(TRISTAR)
Release Date: May 20, 1998

Directed by: Roland Emmerich **Special Effects by:** Volker Engil **Screenplay by:** Roland Emmerich & Dean Devlin **Music by:** David Arnold **Cast:** Matthew Broderick (Dr. Niko Tatopoulos), Jean Reno (Philippe Roache), Maria Pitillo (Audrey Timmonds), Hank Azaria (Animal), Kevin Dunn (Colonel Hicks), Doug Savant (Sergeant O'Neal), Harry Shearer (Charles Cayman), Michael Lerner (Mayor Ebert), Vicki Lewis (Dr. Elsie Chapman) **Suit Performers:** Bruce Marrs/Kurt Carley (Godzilla)

Cinemascope, Color, 139 Minutes

A series of ship disasters at sea precedes the appearance of a gigantic, irradiated iguana—eventually dubbed Godzilla—in New York City. On the beast's trail is Dr. Niko Tatopoulos, his ex-girlfriend Audrey—now a fledging TV reporter—her cameraman Animal, and a group of French Secret Service agents whose country is responsible for Godzilla's creation. When a submarine strike is thought to have killed the monster, Dr. Tatopoulos warns that the monster likely left behind a nest though the U.S. military kicks him off the project. Joining with the French agents led by Philippe Roache, Dr. Tatopoulos finds the nest in Madison Square Garden, where Audrey and Animal are also investigating. After they alert the military of its existence, the group escapes as the eggs hatch, and the military blows the nest to smithereens. However, the parent Godzilla returns alive and gives chase to a taxi cab carrying the group through the streets of New York. When Godzilla becomes entangled in the wires of the Brooklyn Bridge, the military blasts him with missiles, killing the beast.

Background & Commentary In Japanese theaters in 1993, following *Godzilla vs. Mechagodzilla II* was a teaser trailer for a "dynamic" American version of Godzilla (which utilized the classic Japanese design) coming in 1994 from TriStar Pictures. Four years later, the film premiered that many fans to this day consider a complete abomination of the Godzilla legend. However, the film had respectable intentions in the beginning and featured a wonderful design for an updated Godzilla by Stan Winston. Winston's design, along with the original screenplay, were thrown out the window when then-director Jan De Bont (1994's *Speed*) requested a budget of $120 million, which the studio claimed was too high. After the success of 1996's *Independence Day*, that film's creative team, Roland Emmerich and Dean Devlin, were brought in to take over the fledgling American Godzilla by Sony. Sadly enough, TriStar shouldn't have balked at De Bont's projected budget; Emmerich's version ended up costing $10 million more, and De Bont's vision would have in all likelihood been superior to Emmerich's.

The main point of contention in the American *Godzilla* is the horrific redesign of the title monster. Slimmed down and turned into something more akin to a velociraptor, Godzilla runs away from the military rather than confront it and is eventually killed by six missiles once it is caught during the climax. To make matters worse, the horrific design was leaked to the public by, of all things, Fruit of the Loom underwear set to feature the monster. Not only that, but the producers denied that was their design for the monster!

The Toho brass didn't like the redesign of Godzilla either. In a meeting with Devlin and Emmerich, they presented their Godzilla to the Japanese businessmen who then voiced their objections. Devlin and Emmerich more or less told them "This is what we're doing. Take it or leave it." The men from Toho convened for a meeting and desperately wanting Sony's money, decided this may be the last time the American film would get made. The businessmen went out and gave the go-ahead to Devlin and Emmerich, but told them "You can keep your Godzilla, and we'll keep ours."

Though the monster did at least utilize Godzilla's classic roar and trademark dorsal plates (both heavily altered, though), it shockingly lacked fiery breath until it was added at the last second in post-production due to the heavy fan backlash. That's not to say the new Godzilla isn't interesting to look at (a scene of the monster crawling on all fours through a destroyed subway tunnel stands out), it's just the redesign itself was much too radical. On top of this, the film's two leads Matthew Broderick and Maria Pitillo effectively sink the human end of the storyline, and it's too bad someone more fitting, such as Jeff Goldblum, didn't play the lead scientist role. However, the supporting cast—particularly French superstar Jean Reno and the two *Simpsons'* alumnus Hank Azaria and Harry Shearer—are great fun. Another great casting gag is Michael Lerner and Lorry Goldman as Mayor Ebert and his berated assistant Gene, reportedly Emmerich and Devlin's revenge on the famous critical duo for giving *Independence Day* a "thumbs down" in 1996.

Flaws aside, there actually are plenty of good aspects to *Godzilla*. For instance, the buildup to Godzilla's appearance is fantastically handled. And Godzilla's thunderous footsteps bouncing cars off the ground on the streets of New York is iconic in its own right. Furthermore, the climax where the heroes dodge a swarm of Godzilla hatchlings is a fantastic piece of action (even if it is basically lifted from *Jurassic Park*). The uplifting music and performances of the actors after the hatchlings are destroyed in an explosion falsely leads the audience to believe the film is ending when suddenly Godzilla bursts from the ground. Following this is a cab chase with the monster through the streets of New York that is an absolute blast. This rousing climax comes to a pathetic end, though, when Godzilla becomes entangled in the Brooklyn Bridge and missiles from jet fighters kill him. The scene was so underwhelming apparently even the extras on set were shocked by its lackluster nature. This scene summed up the problem with the entire film: at the end of the day it just wasn't Godzilla.

Godzilla opened to more hype than any previous summer blockbuster, perhaps so much that the film would have still been doomed even if it had been better. The release was universally panned by critics and die-hard Godzilla fans despite a $55 million opening weekend. Essentially everyone wanted to see it when it came out... and then hated what they saw. The horrible word of mouth then soured the film's reputation starting with the opening weekend. In the end, the film managed a gross of just under $400 million worldwide (the third highest-grossing film of the year), but the critical backlash was so great the film was deemed a flop and the planned sequels never materialized. On the bright side, fans in the U.S. were treated to an avalanche of both new and classic Godzilla merchandise, which included the long-overdue U.S. releases of the Heisei Godzilla films on VHS.

Final Word Were this a lovingly-crafted tribute to all classic giant monster films, it could have become a cult-classic, but as a remake of *Godzilla*, it will forever live in infamy.

REBIRTH OF
MOTHRA 3

(TOHO)
Release Date: December 12, 1998
Alternate Titles: *Mothra 3: King Ghidorah Attacks* (Japan) *Mothra 3: Invasion of King Ghidorah*
(original international title) *Mothra III: King Ghidorah Returns* (Germany)

Directed by: Okihiro Yoneda **Special Effects by:** Kenji Suzuki **Screenplay by:**
Masumi Suetani **Music by:** Toshiyuki Watanabe **Cast:** Megumi Kobayashi (Moll),
Misato Tate (Lora), Aki Hano (Belvera), Takuma Yoshizawa (Shota Sonoda), Anhei
Shinozaki (Shuhei Sonoda), Ayano Suzuki (Tamako Sonoda), Atsushi Onita
(Yusuke Sonoda), Miyuki Matsuda (Yukie Sonoda), Koichi Ueda (Principal),
Sayaka Yamaguchi (Narrator) **Suit Performers:** Tsutomu Kitagawa (King
Ghidorah)

Widescreen, Color, 100 Minutes

In 1999, King Ghidorah arrives from space and begins destroying
Japan. Children begin to vanish in the monster's wake and a
mysterious dome appears at Mt. Fuji. Mothra and the Elias try to
intervene, but Mothra is easily defeated, and Lora is turned evil by
Ghidorah's mere glare. Shota, the sensitive older brother of two
missing children who stays home from school because he prefers
learning on his own, manages to track Ghidorah to the dome where
he holds the children prisoner. There, he meets Moll, who asks him to
rescue her sister to which Shota agrees. Moll crystalizes after she uses
the last of her energy to help Mothra travel 130 million years into the
past. Mothra's plan is to defeat Ghidorah when he was younger and
less powerful when he arrived on earth and tried to wipe out the
dinosaurs. Mothra battles the space dragon, who still is a force to be
reckoned with, amidst the dinosaurs. Mothra barely succeeds in his
mission by dumping the younger Ghidorah into a volcano... or so it
seems. Ghidorah's severed tail begins to regenerate while Mothra is
encased inside of a special cocoon by a trio of prehistoric Mothras.
Back in 1999, King Ghidorah suddenly disappears. Shota rescues his
siblings and also turns Lora back to the good side with help from
Belvera. But suddenly, King Ghidorah arrives on earth once again, and
kidnaps the children anew. Lora and Belvera hop onto Garu-Garu in a

feeble attempt to battle the space demon. Mothra suddenly emerges from his prehistoric cocoon just in time to battle Ghidorah in a new armored form. He kills the space monster, Moll is restored to life and reunited with her sisters, and Mothra transforms into yet another new form, "Eternal Mothra," before flying home to Infant Island.

Background & Commentary As *Rebirth of Mothra 2* ended its pitiful run in Japanese theaters, another sequel was announced in a teaser trailer. In truth, the sequel was announced out of a sense of stubborn pride in a way as 1996's *Mothra* had not been popular with moviegoers, and *Mothra 2* was even less so. This will sound incredibly odd, but Mothra's original opponent for the third film was not King Ghidorah, but her former ally Rodan, or, more specifically, a new version of Fire Rodan. What had happened was that initially, the enemy monster was going to be a brand new fire monster, and someone at the studio suggested Fire Rodan. In the proposed story, when Rodan proves too powerful to defeat in the present, Mothra travels back in time to the Edo Period (roughly the 1600s to late 1800s of Feudal Japan) to defeat a younger version of Rodan. Though this sounds like an internet rumor, at least one Toho produced book has actually confirmed this story!

Toho decided that Rodan wasn't popular enough to be a main opponent and replaced him with King Ghidorah, despite already having used a variation of the monster in the first film. Screenwriter Masumi Suetani also swapped the Edo Period for the Cretaceous, an ambitious move (and perhaps an unwise one, considering the film's budget). And due to Sayaka Yamaguchi's overcrowded filming schedule, she had to be replaced by Misato Tate as Lora, as the two actresses look vaguely similar. Also, Okihiro Yoneda, director of *Rebirth of Mothra* (1996), returned to the director's chair.

Rebirth of Mothra 3 easily emerges as the most ambitious of the trilogy, largely thanks to the return of the traditional golden-scaled King Ghidorah. The space dragon even engages in a few bouts of city destruction though technically, no elaborate miniatures are actually destroyed. Much of the new special effects work is CGI. Due to the film's time travel aspect, the film features two incarnations of King Ghidorah: the present-day Grand King Ghidorah and the prehistoric Cretaceous King Ghidorah. New special effects director Kenji Suzuki created a brand new Rainbow Mothra prop (with flimsier kite-like wings) as well as an armored battle Mothra for the final duel and after that, an "Eternal Mothra" more akin to the monster's appearance in the Showa Era. Sadly, by the time the numerous suits and marionettes had been built, there was little budget left to bring the dinosaurs and the prehistoric Mothra larvae to life. While the dinosaurs are mere tabletop puppets (based on *Jurassic Park* designs), the film still gets points for ambition (plus the puppets also make the monsters look bigger). Even with its flaws, the battle in the past between Mothra and Cretaceous King Ghidorah is the highlight of the film, climaxing with Mothra dragging the evil dragon into an erupting volcano.

When the film was released in December of 1998, it ended up being the lowest-grossing entry of the trilogy (hauling in only ¥850 million-- $7,620,250), likely due to *Rebirth of Mothra 2's* less-than-stellar reputation. Nonetheless, kaiju otaku were still pleased to see the return of King Ghidorah on screen and perhaps even more importantly, the return of the monster to toy shelves.

Final Word Despite its failure at the box office, this is still the best of the Mothra trilogy. Many fans preferred this to the same year's American-made Dean Devlin/Roland Emmerich *Godzilla* (though, that isn't saying much).

GAMERA 3
REVENGE OF IRYS

(DAIEI)
Release Date: March 06, 1999
Alternate Titles: *Gamera 3: Awakening of Irys* (Japan; simplified title) *Gamera 3: False God Irys Awakens* (Japan; full onscreen title) *GIII: Incomplete Struggle* (original international title)

Directed by: Shusuke Kaneko **Special Effects by:** Shinji Higuchi **Screenplay by:** Kazunori Ito and Shusuke Kaneko **Music by:** Ko Otani **Cast:** Shinobu Nakayama (Dr. Mayumi Nagamine), Ai Maeda (Ayana Hirasaka), Ayako Fujitani (Asagi Kusanagi), Senri Yamazaki (Mito Asakura), Toru Tezuka (Shinya Kurata), Yuu Koyama (Tatsunari Moribe), Yukijiro Hotaru (Inspector Osako) **Suit Performers:** Hirofumi Fukuzawa (Gamera), Akira Ohashi (Irys)

Widescreen, Color, 108 Minutes

In 1999, the Gyaos have returned and are being sighted all over the world. Meanwhile, in a small Japanese village, a young girl named Ayana (who believes that Gamera mercilessly killed her family in 1995) finds a strange egg in a cave. In Shibuya, no longer mindful of the humans in his wake, Gamera suddenly lands in the prefecture chasing after several Gyaos. Though he kills all three, he does severe damage to the city, and hundreds of people are killed. Ayana, witnessing this on TV, decides she will raise whatever's in the egg to kill Gamera. The hatchling turns out to be a new type of Gyaos, which she names Irys. As Irys grows larger, Nagamine and Asagi become concerned about Ayana's hatred of Gamera and her link with Irys. The monster, now larger than Gamera, flies to Kyoto where Ayana is being held by government agent Mito Asakura, who has her own agenda with the monsters. Gamera intercepts Irys and the two battle while Asagi convinces Ayana that Gamera fights for the survival of Earth and it is Irys that is evil. But it is too late; Irys attempts to merge with Ayana but Gamera intervenes. Losing his arm in the process, Gamera still manages to destroy Irys. Unbeknownst to the Guardian of the Universe, a huge swarm of Gyaos have congregated and are heading for Japan. The one-armed Gamera wades into the flaming Kyoto and prepares to battle once again...

Background & Commentary In the early 2000s, critics and most kaiju fans considered this to be the best Japanese monster film since the original *Godzilla*. Whether this was the case or not, it was arguably the greatest kaiju eiga of the 90s, featuring Shusuke Kaneko's best direction and Higuchi's best effects work. Ko Otani's themes are more subdued and less rousing than the previous two installments (even the Gamera theme is less stirring this go around), now slightly heavier and esoteric suiting the film's darker nature. The film also delves more heavily into the mythological origins of Gamera and Gyaos. While intriguing, it is also confusing. It is unclear why Asakura believes Gamera is evil, and Irys is meant to destroy him. As for Irys, Kurata leads the audience to believe the creature is a new Gyaos mutation, while an earlier scene with Ayana implied that Irys was an ancient guardian like Gamera who went bad because of her influence. Perhaps part of the film's enigmatic appeal is the many unanswered questions which can be more alluring than answers.

The film is again a female-driven affair with only the returning Yukijiro Hotaru and newcomer Yuu Koyama as something resembling male leads. As Ayana, Ai Maeda is sometimes too unsympathetic despite her tragic backstory. However, the concept of the one girl who can still connect with Gamera hating him makes for a fantastic dynamic with a satisfying payoff in the climax. Likewise, Ayako Fujitani shows off a new aspect to Asagi who has since lost her connection to the turtle monster due to events in *Gamera 2: Advent of Legion*.

On a technical level, the special effects sequences surpass the Millennium series of Godzilla films that would follow throughout the 2000s. Part of this is due to quality over quantity, as Gamera makes only two appearances. His first battle with the Gyaos in Shibuya is a stunning marriage of suitmation, CGI, and pyrotechnics. Gamera's new design is almost frightening and he has no regard for the humans in his path this time. He does save a child at one point, but it's unclear whether it's intentional or not, and it might have merely been a humorous nod to his roots, which he has firmly eschewed. The turtle's new image likely has its origins in two story concepts which Shusuke Kaneko eventually refused: Gamera battling an evil twin and a different story wherein Gamera turns on the human race.

In Gamera's second appearance, an aerial computer-generated battle between he and Irys provides the film's most exciting sequence while their ground-based suitmation conflict provides some bloody grappling, but seems to be far more interested in the fleeing humans than the battling monsters. The final bout manages to have the distinction of taking place inside a large structure, Kyoto Station, rather than outside it. Despite the cramped quarters, the game of strategy between the two kaiju is riveting with Gamera blowing off his own arm to free himself after Irys impales his limb to syphon off his energy. When Irys fires Gamera's own energy fired at him, he draws it into his cauterized stump, and forms a spiritual fist, which he uses to punch the false god into oblivion.

While some were initially disappointed by the film's open ending in which Gamera seems hopelessly outmatched against a Gyaos swarm, most have since come to embrace it. There is a great deal more to the ending of *Gamera 3: Revenge of Irys* than being a mere "cliffhanger." For starters, the film gives Gamera supernatural powers more akin to the Daimajin films. In the mid-90s, Kaneko noticed that many of the Japanese didn't believe in anything, old customs, or spirituality. He tried to address this with his Gamera films, loading them with more symbolism as they went along. In *Gamera 2: Advent of Legion*, a cross transforms into the middle part of Gamera's name. He is "dead" for three days and then resurrects. *Gamera 3* seems to imply that not only can Gamera utilize the power of his spirit to form attacks but also that he wields some sort of power over life and death (Ayana only comes back to life after Gamera lets out a roar).

As Gamera marches off to join forces with humanity's armies to save Earth from the Gyaos, the surviving characters believe in Gamera once again. The closing super of the movie reads *Gamera 1999: The Absolute Guardian of the Universe*. "Absolute," as in he's going to win the fight. While many westerners have long misinterpreted the ending as being apocalyptic in nature, Kaneko's intention was exactly the opposite. It didn't matter what you believed, just as long as you believed in *something*. As such, Gamera's victory over the Gyaos swarm is a matter of faith. Kaneko's position was, "Of course, Gamera's going to win, but I am not going to show it to you. You have to *believe* he's going to win." The trilogy concludes with an "incomplete struggle," but a happy one nonetheless.

Although it was the most critically-successful of the Gamera films, it was, unfortunately, the lowest-grossing entry at only one million admissions and Daiei slipped into bankruptcy once again. However, Kaneko had no intention of making a sequel, and the series had ended as he wished.

Final Word The best giant monster film of the 90s. To this day, it has a fervent band of defenders and detractors alike that argue its merits. Unlike the *Mothra* trilogy that paralleled its release, the *Gamera* trilogy comes close to perfection and even usurps *Daimajin* as the greatest kaiju trilogy of all time.

ULTRAMAN GAIA
THE BATTLE IN HYPERSPACE

(TSUBURAYA PRODUCTIONS)
Release Date: March 06, 1999
Japanese Title: *Ultraman Tiga, Ultraman Dyna, & Ultraman Gaia:*
Great Super Space-Time Decisive Battle

Directed by: Kazuya Konaka **Special Effects by:** Yuichi Abe **Screenplay by:** Keiichi Hasegawa **Music by:** Toshihiko Sahashi **Cast:** Takeshi Yoshioka (Gamu Takayama/voice of Ultraman Gaia), Gaku Hamada (Tsutomu), Mai Sato (Risa), Sei Hiraizumi (Chiba), Hiroyuki Watanabe (Commander Ishimuro) **Suit Performers:** Keiji Hasegawa (Ultraman Gaia), Shunsuke Gondo (Ultraman Tiga), Makoto Ito (Ultraman Dyna), Hiroyuki Okano (Satanbizor/King of Mons), Hisataka Kitaoka (Bajiris), Koichi Toshima (Scylla)

Widescreen, Color, 74 Minutes

In the real world, schoolboy Tsutomu is a huge fan of the TV series Ultraman Gaia, *though bullies at school make fun of him for it. One night, Tsutomu has a dream about a mysterious girl, Risa, whom he meets the next day at school. He also finds a mysterious alien orb that has the ability to grant wishes. Tsutomu wishes to meet Gamu Takayama, the human host of Ultraman Gaia. Gamu is then transported to Tsutomu's world. When one of the bullies steals the orb from Tsutomu, they use it to summon a monster, Satanbizor, who Gaia battles and defeats. Soon, the interdimensional effects wear off and Gamu is transferred back to his own world while in Tsutomu's world, the bullies create their own kaiju, King of Mons. Back in his own world, Gamu learns the alien orb is a supercomputer from another dimension that is linked to the girl Risa. He then uses an interdimensional vehicle from his world to travel back to Tsutomu's world and battles King of Mons. Tsutomu steals the orb back from the bullies and uses it to call Ultraman Tiga and Ultraman Dyna to aid Gaia. The three Ultramen defeat King of Mons, and Tsutomu wishes the orb out of existence.*

Background & Commentary After *Ultraman Tiga & Ultraman Dyna* proved to be a hit at the box office, Shochiku and Tsuburaya began plans to create another crossover movie revolving around the newest series,

Ultraman Gaia. Like the last film, though, it's not much of a team-up as Tiga and Dyna only show up for the climax minus their human hosts. Where this film differs from its predecessor is that it is aimed at children, with a young boy as the lead character. As Tsutomu, Gaku Hamada does a good job generating the audience's sympathy as he deals with the real-world issue of bullying. In an ingenious twist, just as it is Tsutomu who summons Gaia to his earth, it is the bullies that end up summoning the monsters.

The film's opening is intriguing as we watch all-new footage (and not stock footage from the TV series as is often believed) of Gamu Takayama in battle with Satanbizor. Then shockingly, right before Gamu is about to transform into Gaia, the TV turns off, courtesy of Tsutomu's mother revealing that in this world, *Ultraman Gaia* is just a TV show! In this sense, one could argue the film is the *Ultraman* equivalent of Arnold Schwarzenegger's action flick, *Last Action Hero* (in which a boy travels into his favorite Schwarzenegger movie via a magic ticket). However, the fish out of water aspect of Gamu in the real world is never quite allowed time to breathe and is cut short by the film's short run time. That said, there are amusing sequences of Gamu being mistaken for actor Takeshi Yoshioka in the real world. Ironically, the next time Yoshioka starred in an Ultraman film as Gamu/Gaia, a similar plot device would be used in *Superior 8 Ultra Brothers* (2008).

The film's action and special effects are very well done, particularly the destruction of a large city that draws comparisons to Teruyoshi Nakano's block by block destruction of Tokyo in *Terror of Mechagodzilla* (1975). The CGI fire mixed in with real miniatures is exemplary, though some other instances of CGI, notably a new mech piloted by Gamu, is still understandably primitive. The final monster, King of Mons, is well-designed and has an interesting origin in that it wasn't from a pre-existing series but was designed in the real world by the bullies who bring it to life. Eventually, the monster births two other monsters from its body, Bajiris and Scylla. Consequently, Tiga, Dyna, and Gaia each have their own monster to battle. As if that weren't enough, one battle takes place underwater, one in outer space, and one in the city. However, the huge monster battle is never mentioned by any of the story's adults in the epilogue, and one has to wonder if when Tsutomu wished away the supercomputer, it also somehow undid the events of the past several days? Then again, as an adult, I'm probably just overthinking things...

Final Word Though it faced stiff competition opening on the same day as the beloved *Gamera 3: Revenge of Irys*, this is still one Ultraman film that shouldn't be overlooked.

YONGGARY

(KOREA PICTURES/YOUNGGU-ART MOVIES)

Release Date: July 17, 1999 (original release); January 20, 2001 (rerelease)
Alternate Titles: *Great Monster Battle: Yongary* (Japan) *Reptilian* (U.S. home video) *Yonggary 2001: Yonggary vs. Cyker* (South Korean 2001 rerelease title) *Yonggary: The Space Monster* (Hungary) *Reptile* (Brazil) *Monster Yonggary* (Poland) *Resurrection of Godzilla* (China)

Directed by: Shim Hyung-rae **Special Effects by:** Ryu Hee Jung & Zero Nine Digital **Screenplay by:** Marty Poole **Music by:** Jo Sung-woo & Chris Desmond **Cast:** Donna Phillipson (Holly Davis), Harrison Young (Dr. Hughes), Dan Cashman (Lt. General George Murdock), Bruce Cornwell (Mr. Mills), Dennis Howard (Major General Jack Thomas), Brad Sergi (Bud Black), Eric Briant Wells (Captain Parker)

Widescreen, Color, 98 Minutes

In the southwest desert, the largest dinosaur skeleton of all time is unearthed. As the dig site is plagued by mysterious accidents, scientist Holly Davis encounters an eccentric old man, Dr. Hughes, who claims the skeleton is a prehistoric lifeform called Yonggary destined to rise again. Dr. Hughes turns out to be right when aliens resurrect the huge dinosaur and control it to destroy Los Angeles. With Holly and Dr. Hughes consulting for the U.S. military, the army does battle with Yonggary. When the alien controller is destroyed, Yonggary becomes peaceful and protective towards humanity. The aliens send their own monster Cyker to kill Yonggary, but the giant dinosaur emerges victorious and the aliens retreat. The military then airlifts the unconscious Yonggary to an island where he can live in peace.

Background & Commentary Back in 1967, during the great monster boom, South Korea decided to produce a Godzilla-type monster movie. The result was *Yongary, Monster from the Deep,* which, although a success in its homeland, never produced a sequel. Some thirty years later—apparently before the hype regarding the American *Godzilla* got into full swing—South Korea decided to do a remake of their homegrown monster, Yongary. Sadly, the resulting production is essentially the 1998 *Godzilla* in Yongary form.

Yonggary starts out promisingly enough with slick camera work, a nice cave set complete with well-done dinosaur skeletons—and then the cast speaks for the first time, and it's all downhill from there. The film's dialogue is some of the worst, most clichéd in the history of cinema and is crying out for a script doctor to fix it. The film has many similarities to the 1998 *Godzilla*; not only does it eliminate the monster's Asian origins (Korea is never even mentioned—nor are there any Asian characters), but it also relocates the action to a big American city (Los Angeles in this case), and drastically redesigns the monster. Not only that, it even copies certain scenes from the aforementioned 1998 film such as a helicopter battle with Yonggary. And when the monster is turned loose on Los Angeles, more damage is done to the city by the U.S. military's efforts to stop the monster just as was done to New York City in *Godzilla*.

Yonggary's best-remembered scene is probably the one where military men use jet packs to battle the monster, and one of them arrogantly quips that Yonggary "makes Godzilla look like a pussy." This statement is ironic as the movie is taking a dig at a film that it is itself copying, and poorly at that. In fact, the film is so bad that a bad scene intended to be funny... actually ends up being funny. Though it would have been groan-inducing in any other film, the scene consists of a busload of children narrowly avoiding death from the monster's fiery blasts, inexplicably jumping over a destroyed bridge and cheering as though they are on a rollercoaster. However, it should be noted that the film's director Shim Hyung-rae actually had a background in comedy so it's entirely possible that some of the film's "bad" scenes were entirely self-aware.

In any case, *Yonggary* doesn't begin to be any fun at all until the alien controller is destroyed, and Yonggary is set free. As it turns out, the monster is actually a friendly protector to humanity. Thankfully, the aliens send another monster, Cyker, to battle Yonggary. Though Cyker is also brought to life with CGI, the choreography is at least well done as the monsters toss each other into skyscrapers, limbs are torn off, and heads are severed. If not for the poor CGI, the final battle could have almost saved the film. Actually, early in the film, Yongary doesn't look too bad as its skeleton grows flesh and begins to form, but once it begins to move, what little realism it had is shattered.

On the other hand, the practical effects are quite good. The alien ship and the full-sized Yonggary skull are professional looking, as is the miniature city set that gets destroyed marvelously. What makes the proceedings truly sad is when chunks of the enemy monster are blown off using practical props and effects which are far superior to the flimsy CGI. Sadder yet, the first take on the special effects scenes were filmed with real Yongary and Cyker suits then replaced with CGI later on! How much better the effects scenes would have fared with practical suits isn't even debatable—the film should have been shot in suitmation. That said, supposedly, there are a few suitmation scenes in the film that eagle-eyed viewers have caught.

Like the original film with its lost original Korean version, the new Yongary has a similar convoluted history. It was initially released in 1999 and then re-released in 2001 with "upgraded special effects" and an altered storyline. The film was a big hit in South Korea and even spawned some Yonggary theme parks. It was slated for theatrical release in several other countries, but critical reviews of the film cancelled those plans. In the film's defense, it has merit from a historical perspective, and the subpar elements of the production were mainly due to the inexperience of the filmmakers trying to get on their feet. But because of this film, there were subsequent better Korean monster movies, namely *The Host* (2006) and *Dragon Wars* (2007).

Final Word Had suitmation been used to bring the monsters to life, the film wouldn't have been half as bad as it was. Due to its poor CGI and bad dialogue, *Yonggary* will forever live in infamy.

GODZILLA 2000

(TOHO)

Release Date: December 11, 1999

Alternate Titles: *Godzilla 2000 Millennium* (Japan) *Godzilla 2000: The Mutant Dinosaur* (Argentina) *Monster Godzilla* (Poland) *Godzilla vs. the Giant Squid* (Mexico) *Godzilla: Millennium* (Russia)

Directed by: Takao Okawara **Special Effects by:** Kenji Suzuki **Screenplay by:** Watura Mimura & Hiroshi Kashiwabara **Music by:** Takayuki Hattori **Cast:** Takehiro Murata (Yuji Shinoda), Naomi Nishida (Yuki Ichinose), Hiroshi Abe (Mitsuo Katagiri), Mayo Suzuki (Io Shinoda), Shiro Sano (Professor Shiro Miyasaka) **Suit Performers:** Tsutomu Kitagawa (Godzilla), Makoto Ito (Orga)

Cinemascope, Color, 107 Minutes

At the same time that the Godzilla Prediction Network (GPN) is tracking Godzilla when he comes ashore in Nemuro, a mysterious UFO is found on the ocean floor by the Crisis Control Information Agency (CCI). When the UFO is brought to the surface, it's suddenly reactivated by the power of the sun, and it flies off to find Godzilla, who has something in his body it wants. Godzilla attacks the UFO with his ray and is knocked into the sea by the alien craft. Flying off, the UFO perches itself atop a building in Shinjuku and hacks into the GPN's systems on Godzilla. When Godzilla appears in Tokyo, he and the UFO go to battle, and the UFO uses Godzilla's cells to create a new form for itself: Orga. Eventually, both the UFO and Orga are defeated by Godzilla. But then, the monster king turns his wrath on Tokyo...

Background & Commentary On July 11, 1998, TriStar's *Godzilla* was released in Japan to fairly high box office (due to curiosity) and negative perceptions. Disappointed with the American Godzilla (though they offered an official statement to the contrary), Toho was perhaps a little too hasty in prepping a new G-film for release. The earliest rumors in December of 1998 suggested the new film would utilize elements from 1957's *The Mysterians*—ironic considering Koichi Kawakita was trying to get Toho to remake said film around the same time. Furthermore, initially, the film was to pick up where *Godzilla vs. Destroyah* had left off, and the

50 meter Godzilla in this film was going to be a matured Godzilla Junior. But, for reasons unknown, Shogo Tomiyama decided to make a totally new Godzilla. And, while the Heisei films kept a strong continuity, Toho's eventual Millennium series was a set of unrelated adventures that only answered to the original *Godzilla* (1954).

The film is haunted by a lackluster feel throughout, made all the worse by Takayuki Hattori's score and the usually reliable Takao Okawara's uninspired direction. This feeling is evident in the very abrupt first shot of Shinoda setting up the GPN equipment. And, though Godzilla's reveal carrying a boat in his jaws was a wonderful idea on paper, it isn't executed properly and loses the element of surprise it so badly wants to convey. Sadly, that isn't the only missed opportunity. In the script, the UFO was to turn all of Tokyo against Godzilla, something that would have been interesting to see. Instead, all we get is the UFO using some fiber-optic lines to lasso Godzilla. The film's biggest faux-pas occurs during the climactic battle with Orga, when the mutated alien opens its mouth wide and Godzilla obliges by bending over and sticking his head into Orga's mouth. More than a few theatergoers were a bit confused by this scene, which badly needed some CGI tentacles to drag Godzilla into Orga's mouth. Actually, said tentacles curiously do exist in pre-production artwork. Other fans say Godzilla knew the only way to beat Orga was from the inside and that's why he stuck his head in Orga's mouth. Whatever the case, Orga then begins to take on some traits of the American Godzilla as he absorbs Godzilla's cells as a jab at the TriStar film. Toho often struggled to design monsters for the Heisei series that matched their Showa series predecessors. Destroyah was very emulative of the *Alien* and *Predators* series, and Orga is an even poorer creation that amounts to little more than a grey reptilian 'what's it?' in many ways.

Godzilla's new design is fantastic with a forward stance more akin to a dinosaur. The over-sized, spikey, purple dorsal plates on the back are the creature's most interesting new attribute, and furthermore, Godzilla's ray is changed to a more fiery orange in color. Also, Godzilla's two battles with the UFO arguably fare better than his battle with Orga.

The cast is likeable as well. Takehiro Murata, who had won numerous awards for his portrayal of salaryman Ando in *Godzilla vs. Mothra* (1992), is bumped up to the lead. Alongside him is the winner of the Nippon Award for Best Newcomer Naomi Nishida as feisty reporter Yuki, though the film's most interesting character just might be Katagiri, who at one point detonates a bomb to attack the UFO unconcerned that it will kill Shinoda. Katagiri was portrayed by Hiroshi Abe, who had appeared in 1994's *Yamato Takeru*, and shares a memorable death scene at the hands of Godzilla (literally).

Despite its flaws, the film was still the highest-grossing movie of the holiday releases in Japan, which caught the eye of Sony executives there at the time. They were impressed enough with the film's opening weekend crowds to consider it for release in America. Due to the American *Godzilla's* box office success—which still lacked a sequel—Sony decided to test the waters by releasing this film to American theaters on August 18, 2000. Unfortunately, it barely made it to the top ten on opening weekend, only grossing around $10 million, and dashing any chances for future releases.

Final Word Though Toho had hoped to show the world that their Godzilla was still the boss, in the end, this film is a somewhat uninspired attempt to revive the franchise.

ULTRAMAN TIGA
THE FINAL ODYSSEY

(TSUBURAYA PRODUCTIONS)
Release Date: March 11, 2000

Directed by: Hiromi Muraishi **Special Effects by:** Tsuyoshi Yagi **Screenplay by:** Keiichi Hasegawa **Music by:** Kazumi Yano **Cast:** Hiroshi Nagano (Daigo/voice of Ultraman Tiga), Takami Yoshimoto (Rena Yanase), Miyoko Yoshimoto (Kamila), Masaru Matsuda (Darramb), Tenmei Basara (Hydra), Mio Takaki (Captain Megumi Iruma), Shigeki Kagemaru (Tetsuo) **Suit Performers:** Shunsuke Gondo (Ultraman Tiga/Hydra), Keiji Hasegawa (Dark Tiga), Koji Nakamura (Darramb/Tiga Tornado), Toshi Nagino (Kamila), Hiroyuki Okano/Tsuyoshi Matsubara/Daisuke Terai (Super Ancient Warrior), Eiji Mori (Golza)

Widescreen, Color, 85 Minutes

Two years after his final battle as Tiga, Daigo has lost his ability to transform into the giant warrior and leads a peaceful life with fiancé, Rena. On an ancient Island, GUTS Captain Iruma leads a search party that unearths three giant statues of dark warriors called Kamila, Darramb, and Hydra. At the same time, Daigo is having strange visions of committing evil acts as Tiga under the influence of a mysterious woman. When the statues come to life, they reveal themselves to be evil former compatriots of Tiga, bent on luring Daigo to the dark side. When Kamila—Tiga's ex-love—gives Daigo the Spark Lens, she assumes he will turn into a dark version of Tiga on the island where the ruins were located. Instead, Tiga converts the dark energy into light, and uses it to destroy Hydra, and then Darramb. When it comes time to face Kamila in the ancient city, she transforms into a giant monster of darkness. To make matters worse, Tiga must also defend Rena's downed plane as he battles Kamila. At the last moment, the city's long dead Ultras release their light to Tiga, who absorbs it and uses it to destroy Kamila's darkness. The world safe, Daigo and Rena leave Earth for Mars to start a new life.

Background & Commentary For the next Ultraman movie, it was decided that rather than trying to tie into a new TV series at the same time—difficult from budgetary and continuity standards—to do a standalone movie instead. Or, standalone in the sense that you didn't have to be watching the current series to get the plot, though you did need to have seen *Ultraman Tiga*. As it was, the producers decided to aim at a slightly older demographic too as kids who watched *Ultraman Tiga* were now three years older. Kazuo Tsuburaya said on a radio interview that, "Even after the end of the TV series, Tiga's popularity was deep-rooted, but since the schedule was always busy for lead actor Hiroshi Nagano, we can now produce a theater version with Tiga as the main character." The series had been so popular there was even a fan petition for a movie version of *Ultraman Tiga*. Planning for the movie began before *Ultraman Gaia: The Battle in Hyperspace* wrapped, and the first draft was called *Ultraman Tiga: Light Forever*. The story had some differences with some of the ancient statues being found in Egypt, and one of the monsters emerging from the Arctic Ocean.

Like many films based off TV series, one needs to have at least some knowledge of *Ultraman Tiga's* mythology to follow the story and to a degree, only fans of the series can truly enjoy the film—and fans of said series should enjoy the film very much. As *Ultraman Tiga* had been off the air for three years at this point, the producers decided to give the film a darker tone in comparison to the last two kid-friendly entries. In a nightmare scene, Daigo dreams of pounding a small child into the ground with his fist as Tiga! The more mature tone works well, and one could consider this to be the *Superman II* of the Ultraman franchise. Not only does the story revolve around three supervillains that are the same race as Daigo/Tiga, but also, Daigo has lost the ability to transform into Tiga due to the events of the series finale. Furthermore, Daigo's quest to regain the ability to transform into Tiga jeopardizes his relationship with Rena, whom he is set to marry. In an interesting twist, the main villain is a female Ultra warrior who used to be Tiga's lover, and we even learn that Tiga was once evil himself!

Though he doesn't transform into Tiga until the climax, there are three spectacular battles, the first of which takes place among some underwater ruins. The next battle occurs in some type of alternate dimension in space, and the final battle with Kamila takes place in an ancient Ultra city. The drawback to the climax is that there is no clever method to defeat the villains. Predictably, Tiga beats the villains through the same old power-up move that so often plagues the Ultraman films. As was typical by this point, Kamila inexplicably transforms into a giant CGI monster.

However, the climax does have a delightful scene that is exciting and well-executed where the GUTS crew must fly their way out of a subterranean tunnel as the ancient island sinks beneath the ocean.

Thanks to the fact that Daigo is conspicuously absent from the movie *Ultraman Tiga & Ultraman Dyna*—set after the events of this film—there is an element of suspense during the final battle making Ultra fans wonder if Daigo will indeed make it out alive.

Final Word Thanks to its more mature tone, this is easily one of the better Ultraman movies based upon an existing TV series.

GODZILLA VS. MEGAGUIRUS

(TOHO)

Release Date: December 16, 2000

Alternate Titles: *Godzilla vs. Megaguirus: G-Eradication Strategy* (Japan) *Godzilla vs. Megaguirus: Command to Destroy* (Russia)

Directed by: Masaaki Tezuka **Special Effects by:** Kenji Suzuki **Screenplay by:** Wataru Mimura & Hiroshi Kashiwabara **Music by:** Michiru Oshima **Cast:** Misato Tanaka (Kiriko Tsujimori), Shosuke Tanihara (Hajime Kudo), Masato Ibu (Motohiko Sugiura), Mansaku Ikeuchi (Mima Kazuo), Yuriko Hoshi (Dr. Yoshino Yoshizawa), Masanobu Katsumura (Makoto Nikura) **Suit Performers:** Tsutomu Kitagawa (Godzilla), Minoru Watanabe (Megaguirus)

Cinemascope, Color, 105 Minutes

In 1954, Godzilla raids Tokyo and then disappears into the sea. With its capital destroyed, the Diet Building is rebuilt in Osaka a year later. In 1966, the monster returns to Japan, seeking its new nuclear power plants before disappearing once more. Afterwards, Japan does away with nuclear energy in favor of cleaner energy. Godzilla returns in 1996 and kills the commanding officer of Kiriko Tsujimori, who vows revenge on the monster. In 2001, she is a major in the G-Graspers, a military group dedicated to defending Japan against Godzilla. During testing of a new weapon they've developed called the Dimension Tide—which they believe will suck Godzilla into an artificial black hole—they inadvertently open a portal to the past, bringing the prehistoric insect monster Megaguirus to the present day. Eventually, swarms of dragonfly-like Meganulon attack Godzilla and use his energy to further gestate their queen, Megaguirus. Drawn to Tokyo by the Meganulon, Godzilla appears in Aqua City and is met by Megaguirus. After a pitched battle, Godzilla eventually kills Megaguirus with his ray. When the Dimension Tide begins to fall from orbit, Tsujimori must guide its targeting system to Godzilla manually as it falls from the sky. When Godzilla sees it coming, he blasts his ray at the Dimension Tide's black hole as well. When the smoke clears, a gigantic crater is where Godzilla once was and the G-Graspers assume

88

he has been sucked into the black hole. However, several months later, tremors are being detected in Tokyo...

Background & Commentary Back during the release of *Godzilla 2000* (1999), Toho had announced they were going to produce a trilogy of unrelated Godzilla movies. It once more fell to writers Hiroshi Kashiwabara and Wataru Mimura to develop a new universe for Godzilla to inhabit. Producer Tomiyama was tasked with making this new film on a smaller budget than *Godzilla 2000* as well.

Despite the previous film's title and American theatrical release, it is *Godzilla vs. Megaguirus* that best encapsulates the Godzilla films of the 2000s. It also represents the most far-fetched "otherworld" of the Millennium series with an elaborate backstory in which the capital has become Osaka (eliciting jeering laughs from Tokyo audiences in theaters) after Tokyo's destruction at the hands of Godzilla, who was never killed by the Oxygen Destroyer. Another interesting concept is the G-Graspers, an elite team with each member contributing or having a unique ability that specifically deals with Godzilla, which would seem to be lifted from the Ultraman franchise. The military scuffles with Godzilla make for some of the film's best scenes, notably the pre-credits scene in Osaka and later, an encounter with the monster king in the water in which Tsujimoro jumps onto his back and plants a tracking device.

The film features a rather out-of-place, unnecessarily violent attack by the Meganulon on a couple in Tokyo. In stark contrast to this is the end battle between Godzilla and Megaguirus, which has strange comical elements, unintentional though they may be. For instance, Godzilla performs a gravity-defying flying leap on his opponent and later, catches its tail in his mouth (in that case, we are meant to think that Megaguirus has impaled Godzilla somehow only to have the camera pivot around to show Godzilla caught Megaguirus' stinger in his mouth). This is on top of another scene where Megaguirus stabs Godzilla in his stomach. Due to these embarrassing maneuvers, the battle's main highlight is the miniature set of Aqua City, which is utilized well in the choreography. Megaguirus doesn't fare much better than Battra from ten years earlier (whom she looks suspiciously like), with stiff wings that don't look much better when they switch to CGI. In some respects, Megaguirus could be called the last original monster designed for the Millennium series (not counting Monster X which could be argued was just an alternate form of Keizer Ghidorah) and was in some ways itself a projection of the adult form of the Meganuron larvae from *Rodan* (1956).

As to a positive, new composer Michiru Oshima composes a new theme for Godzilla that is remarkably nearly on a par with Akira Ifukube's.

Final Word Though the film wasn't a big success, Toho had at least found a winning team for the Millennium series in the form of Tezuka and Oshima. The duo would collaborate on two more films in the series, more so than any of the other directors and composers of the era who only worked on one film each.

ULTRAMAN COSMOS
THE FIRST CONTACT

(TSUBURAYA PRODUCTIONS)
Release Date: July 20, 2001

Directed by: Toshihiro Iijima **Special Effects by:** Kazuo Sagawa **Screenplay by:** Satoru Kitazumi **Music by:** Toru Fuyuki **Cast:** Konosuke Tokai (Musashi Haruno), Hidekazu Akai (Yujiro Haruno), Taro Kawano (Captain Akatsuki), Ikkei Watanabe (Commander Shigemura), Mainomi Shuhei (Raiden), Hitomi Takahashi (Michiko Haruno), Daisuke Gori/Yukitoshi Hori (voice of Baltan) **Suit Performers:** Hiroshi Nekomata (Ultraman Cosmos Lunar Mode), Hidenori Ogino (Ultraman Cosmos Corona Mode), Tesshin Murata (Baltan/Neo-Baltan), Satoshi Yamamoto/Daisuke Terai/Hisataka Kitaoka (Don Ron the dragon)

Widescreen, Color, 90 Minutes

On a stormy night, a young boy named Musashi witnesses Ultraman falling to earth after an intense battle with the alien Baltan. Musashi revives the dormant Ultraman by reflecting light onto his body, putting him in the giant hero's debt. When Musashi tells his friends and family that he saw a real Ultraman, no one believes him except his father and members of the SRC (Scientific Research Circle). When a dragon called Don Ron emerges from the earth, the SRC goes to combat it. Don Ron was once peaceful but was riled into fighting by the alien Baltan, who wishes the earth to be a new home for his many children after they ruined their homeworld. Ultraman Cosmos shows up to battle the giant alien Baltan and defeats him. The Baltans decide to go back to their own planet but leave the children of Earth with a message encouraging them not to ruin their planet like the Baltans had. Ultraman Cosmos parts ways with Musashi and tells him they will meet again one day.

Background & Commentary Having witnessed one sequel after another, it's nice to return to a good old-fashioned Ultraman origin story in *Ultraman Cosmos: The First Contact*. And yet, when compared to *Ultraman Tiga: The Final Odyssey*, this film is something of a sad letdown considering this is the 35th anniversary Ultraman film. From a historical perspective, the film is of interest because it is directed by one of the original *Ultraman* TV series directors, Toshihiro Iijima, at the time 69 years old. Though set in another brand new continuity, the series producer Kiyoshi Suzuki requested the appearance of the classic villain Baltan for the film. Not coincidentally, Baltan had premiered in an episode of the original series directed by Iijima, and the whole film was based on a rejected story concept of Iijima's called *Ultraman: Baltan's Counterattack* from the early 1990s. Other bits of nostalgia include Susumu Kurobe's cameo in the film as a chief inspector as well as cameos from several other cast members from the 1960s and the SRC, who are meant to be reminiscent of the Science Patrol from the original series. The music sounds like it comes from the 60s at times, though this is intentional as an anniversary film.

For the era—not to mention the budget—the CGI in *The First Contact* is very well done, and shots of Ultraman and Baltan flying through the sky match well with their respective suits. *Ultraman Cosmos'* unique twist to the Ultra legacy is that most of the time, Cosmos tries to make peace with the enemy monsters. Cosmos has a blue-colored Lunar Mode, and a red Corona Mode for more intense fighting. The rather simplistic design of Ultraman Cosmos' all-blue Lunar Mode is more streamlined and better in many respects than the other Heisei Ultramen.

The 2001 version of Baltan fares well in both its CGI and suitmation forms and the slight upgrade to the design is superb. Naturally, Baltan "upgrades" itself during the final battle, taking on a more sinister, almost medieval look (it also sprouts a Gigan-like scythe from one of its arms). One of the film's most impressive scenes comprises of Baltan destroying a fleet of jet fighters on an asteroid and the best shot is undoubtedly one of Baltan watching as they crash around him in flames. However, this is followed by a strange, unfortunate scene where the SRC engage Baltan in the air and play music to put him to sleep! Another problem with this new Baltan is his motivations, which aren't always clear. At times, we are lead to believe that just maybe Baltan is peaceful—only looking for a new planet for his friendly children to call home. At other times, it seems certain that Baltan means only harm to the earth and its inhabitants. In the end, it isn't clear if the audience should feel sympathy or contempt for the alien race. The film's other giant monster, a dog-like dragon called Don Ron, also fares well and is reminiscent of that same year's rendition of Baragon from *Godzilla, Mothra, and King Ghidorah: Giant Monsters All-Out Attack*.

The film was originally scheduled to be released in March of 2001 before the TV series aired, but problems caused it to be rescheduled for July. Consequently, the film became something of a prequel rather than the first entry as the series began airing on July 6, 2001. This may have played to the film's favor as it works better as a prequel rather than an introductory film. This is because in the TV series, the audience meets Ultraman's host, Musashi, as a grown man while in this film, Musashi is an 11-year-old boy. It is a neat idea to showcase Ultraman bonding with his future host as a child. However, due to its longer running time, *Ultraman Cosmos: The First Contact* wears out its welcome somewhat. And after the dark mature tone of *Final Odyssey*, this kid's film is harder to swallow for adult fans.

Final Word Though it has its merits, overall *Ultraman Cosmos: The First Contact* is one of the less-enjoyable Ultraman films of the early 2000s.

GODZILLA, MOTHRA AND KING GHIDORAH:
GIANT MONSTERS ALL-OUT ATTACK

(TOHO)
Release Date: December 15, 2001
Alternate Titles: *Godzilla, Mothra, King Ghidorah: Giant Monsters All-Out Attack* (Japan) *Godzilla, Mothra, and King Ghidorah* (Bulgaria) *Godzilla vs. Mothra* (Greece) *Godzilla, Mothra, King Ghidorah: Giant Monsters Are Attacking* (Poland) *Godzilla, Mothra, King Ghidorah: Monsters Attack* (Russia)

Directed by: Shusuke Kaneko **Special Effects by:** Makoto Kamiya **Screenplay by:** Keiichi Hasegawa, Masahiro Yokotani, & Shusuke Kaneko **Music by:** Ko Otani **Cast:** Chiharu Niiyama (Yuri Tachibana), Ryudo Uzaki (Admiral Taizo Tachibana), Masahiro Kobayashi (Takeda), Shiro Sano (Kadokura), Hideyo Amamoto (Isayama), Kunio Murai (Secretary Hinogaki) **Suit Performers:** Mizuho Yoshida (Godzilla), Akira Ohashi (King Ghidorah), Rie Ota/Toshiyoshi Sasaki (Baragon)

Cinemascope, Color, 105 Minutes

In 2004, a missing U.S. submarine in Japanese waters leads Japan's self defense forces to believe that Godzilla has come back to life since destroying Tokyo in 1954. At the same time, Yuri Tachibana, a reporter for a low-rated cable network, is investigating the legend of the guardian monsters of Yamato. Mysterious events begin to plague Japan, from underground tremors to a giant cocoon that appears in a lake. Eventually, Godzilla returns and begins terrorizing Japan with an unholy vengeance. A strange old man connected to the monsters named Isayama tells Yuri that Godzilla has been resurrected by the spirits of the dead that perished in the Pacific during WWII and are punishing Japan for forgetting their role in said war. The first of the guardian monsters, Baragon, surfaces from underground to fight Godzilla but is killed. According to Isayama, only the 1,000-year-old dragon King Ghidorah, who is slumbering in an ice cave, can kill Godzilla. As Godzilla nears Yokohama, a final military strike is planned headed by Yuri's own father, Admiral Tachibana. Soon, Mothra hatches from the cocoon and (with Isayama's help) Ghidorah breaks free of the ice and the two guardians converge on Yokohama to battle Godzilla. After a pitched battle, these monsters also perish against Godzilla. It is Admiral Tachibana that delivers the killing blow to Godzilla by driving a mini-sub into the monster and exploding a new type of missile through his body. When Godzilla attempts to blast Yuri and her father with his ray, it causes him to explode. Father and daughter reunite happily, while on the ocean floor a single disembodied giant heart begins to beat...

Background & Commentary After two disappointments at the box office in a row, in a surprising move, Toho chose 90's *Gamera* director Shusuke Kaneko to helm the next Godzilla movie. The film's strange plot, concocted by Kaneko himself, is by far the most experimental of the Millennium films' many storylines and involves Godzilla being revived by the angry spirits of the WWII dead, a controversial topic during the film's release. Their previous two G-films had met with increasingly lackluster results so Toho went to the one man who had done the impossible and made Gamera cool to general audiences (though, Kaneko approached Shogo Tomiyama about directing a Godzilla film as far back as 1992).

As luck would have it, Kaneko does a splendid job with Godzilla—or rather his version of Godzilla, as the evil spirit beast he unleashes is one of the grimmer versions of the Big G ever conceived of. Kaneko goes for all-out nostalgia in the opening credits with various close-ups of the title monsters' body parts. Perhaps it's no coincidence the credits pay tribute to *Ghidorah, the Three-Headed Monster* (1964), as this film is a sort of bizarre inverse to that story where Mothra and Ghidorah team up to defeat Godzilla rather than the other way around.

For the first time ever, Godzilla is presented as being actually evil, something no other Godzilla before had been. With white eyes lacking pupils, he gets his big reveal when he emerges from the home port of the Lucky Dragon No.5. During a city rampage, he singles out a screaming old lady in a massive crowd. The scene cuts away to a mushroom cloud in the distance, the result of this Godzilla's ray. Later, a horrified woman lies helpless in a hospital bed (having survived a previous attack by Godzilla in the Bonin Islands) as Godzilla approaches and then passes her by unharmed. Just when the woman thinks she's safe, Godzilla's tail reenters the shot and smashes the hospital to bits. These are but a few of Godzilla's victims in the film, all of whom are deliberately personalized by Kaneko to evoke the horrors of his Godzilla.

Although the suit makers had good intentions with the G-suit, the results don't quite pay off. Godzilla was meant to have a Tyrannosaurus-like posture leaning over forward, but the logistics of such an idea made it impossible (there would be no way for the suit actor to maintain such a position underneath the heavy costume). As a result, the belly of the suit looks awkwardly large in its upright position. The King Ghidorah suit, made to enable the suit actor to manipulate two of the necks with his arms, is also unusually awkward. The creature is also given a smaller stature so that Godzilla could appear more threatening as the villain.

As for Mothra and Baragon, the two monsters fared quite well. Mothra (another male this time) enters the 21st century with flight scenes created with CGI rather than the stiff models that exclusively brought the character to life in the 1990s. Baragon, a fan favorite not seen since his cameo in *Destroy All Monsters* (1968), not surprisingly emerges as the film's favorite creation, and possibly its best-realized monster. Shusuke Kaneko actually wanted to utilize Anguirus and Varan, but Toho insisted upon the more marketable King Ghidorah and Mothra in their place. Baragon was the last vestige of the idea.

Rather than a forced romance between two leads, the film is anchored by the father/daughter relationship of stars Chiharu Niiyama and Ryudo Uzaki. Rounding out the rest of the cast (and directed in an over-the-top fashion) are *Godzilla 2000*'s Shiro Sano as Yuri's squid-chewing boss and Hideyo Amamoto (Dr. Who in *King Kong Escapes*) as Isayama, the old man connected to the monsters, who turns out to have been dead for 50 years all along! Yukijiro Hotaru, Inspector Osako in the *Gamera* trilogy, gets a cameo as does *Gamera 3*'s Ai Maeda and her sister as an in-joke reference to Mothra's fairies (or lack thereof). Ko Otani's esoteric supernatural-themed score doesn't manage to equal his work on the *Gamera* trilogy and Akira Ifukube's indefatigable Godzilla themes close the film on a high note to the visual of Godzilla's disembodied but still-beating heart perfectly.

The film ended up being the highest-grossing entry of the 2000s, though this honor was somewhat dubious as it was double-billed with an hour-long feature of the incredibly popular cartoon hamster *Hamtaro* (directed by *Gamera* special effects artist Shinji Higuchi). Actually, the movie wasn't an overnight success, but did well due to word of mouth. When it came out, the people who saw it told others "this one's actually good," which in turn made those people curious to see it and so on. Like *Godzilla 2000* before it, the film came close to getting a U.S. theatrical release from Sony TriStar but studio executives feared the film's lackluster suits wouldn't be taken seriously by American audiences. Specifically American executives from Sony watched a screening of the film at the American Film Market in 2002. They wound up walking out on the movie during the Godzilla vs. Baragon fight. The executives were heard complaining, "They're still using men in rubber suits!"

Final Word Despite a few technical flaws, it is generally considered the biggest financial and critical success in Toho's Millennium series.

ULTRAMAN COSMOS 2:
THE BLUE PLANET

(TSUBURAYA PRODUCTIONS)
Release Date: August 03, 2002

Directed by: Tsugumi Kitaura **Special Effects by:** Tsugumi Kitaura
Screenplay by: Keiichi Hasegawa & Hideyuki Kawakami **Music by:** Kazumi Yano
Cast: Taiyo Sugiura (Musashi Haruno), Miho Nishimura (Mari), Mai Saito (Shau), Masato Matsuo (Jin), Daisuke Shima (Captain Hiura), Kaori Sakagami (Deputy Captain Mizuki) **Suit Performers:** Keiji Hasegawa (Ultraman Cosmos Lunar Mode/Eclipse Mode/Space Corona Mode), Hidenori Ogino (Ultraman Justice/Ultraman Cosmos Skeleton Corona Mode), Satoshi Yamamoto/Shinya Iwasaki (Scorpiss), Yosa Saito (Reija), Nobuhiko Tanabe (Sandros)

Widescreen, Color, 75 Minutes

As Musashi Haruno explores what he hopes to be a peaceful new planet he can transport earth's monsters to, he instead finds the barren and destroyed planet Juran. There, he is attacked by the monster Scorpiss but saved by Ultraman Cosmos, whom he has since separated from. Back on earth, Musashi goes to a friend's wedding in Saipan. He and Mari spot a mermaid named Shou who turns out to be a member of the Gyashi, a friendly alien species living on earth under the ocean. She invites Musashi and Mari to her underwater world but their leader, Jin, is suspicious of Musashi. When a legion of Scorpiss attack earth, Shou and Jin use friendly underwater monsters called Reija to battle the Scorpiss. Musashi pleads for Cosmos to return to earth when the ruler of the Scorpiss, Sandros, arrives. Cosmos shows up and battles the powerful Sandros but does not defeat him. Ultraman Justice suddenly arrives to give his aid and together, he and Cosmos are able to defeat Sandros. Afterwards, the Gyashi depart from earth along with the two Ultramen.

Background & Commentary For this film, Tsugumi Kitaura, who served as an assistant director on the previous film, was promoted to the main director in addition to directing the special effects scenes. And, at the request of the Marianas Tourism Board, much of the filming was done on Saipan Island. However, due to the New York City terrorist attacks of September 11th, 2001, there was some hesitation on Tsuburaya's part to film in Saipan, which is a commonwealth of the U.S. But in the end, the producers decided to film there anyway and the tropical/aquatic theme is a welcome one. As a result, *Ultraman Cosmos 2: The Blue Planet* is a great travelogue for Saipan. The underwater footage, overseen by Ryuichi Ichino, is very well shot. Also fun is the new underwater stingray monster Reija, a good kaiju that can link with the benevolent aliens to aid in the fight against the enemy monster.

This film is a marked improvement over the previous entry in nearly all areas. The first scene in space not only sets up a great mystery of what devastated the planet Juran but great visuals as well as the planet is littered with monster carcasses across a barren landscape. The city destruction is well-done, and there is a spectacular shot of the Scorpiss destroying a large array of satellite dishes in a pyrotechnic spectacle. The Scorpiss are executed convincingly and are similar in design to Toho's Megaguirus, but are better executed than Megaguirus in their flying forms. They also bear a few similarities to the Legion from *Gamera 2: Advent of Legion* (1996), as does the final monster Sandros. To defeat Sandros, Ultraman Cosmos is aided by the brand new Ultraman Justice. Though it's always neat to see a new Ultraman, Justice arrives with hardly any setup or backstory. However, Ultraman movies, somewhat like entries in the Marvel Cinematic Universe, often exist to set-up/service future sequels and Ultraman Justice would be the focal point of the next film.

As was typical by this point, problems arose with the timing of this film's release due to the TV series. Originally, the film was supposed to be released after the series finished its run in June of 2002. Instead, the series was extended at the last minute to run until September of 2002, meaning this post-series finale movie would come out before the series finale itself. This move happened because series star Taiyo Sugiura had been arrested in June for possible involvement in an extortion and assault case. As such, Tsuburaya suspended the series until the matter was resolved and the charges against Sugiura were dropped. Other release dates were talked about, but in the end, it proved easier to release the film in August as originally planned, and the series began airing again in late July. It's possible the publicity may have helped the film though, as it grossed ¥200,000,000 more than its predecessor.

Final Word Thanks to its fresh feel and well-paced story, *Ultraman Cosmos 2: The Blue Planet* emerges as one of the better post-2000 Ultraman films.

GODZILLA
AGAINST MECHAGODZILLA

(TOHO)

Release Date: December 14, 2002

Alternate Titles: *Godzilla vs. Mechagodzilla* (Japan) *Operation Kiryu* (Greece) *Godzilla vs. Megagodzilla* (Bulgaria) *Godzilla vs. Mechagodzilla III* (Russia)

Directed by: Masaaki Tezuka **Special Effects by:** Yuichi Kikuchi **Screenplay by:** Watura Mimura **Music by:** Michiru Oshima **Cast:** Yumiko Shaku (Akane Yashiro), Shin Takuma (Tokimitsu Yuhara), Kana Onodera (Sara Yuhara), Akira Nakao (Prime Minister Igarashi), Ko Takasugi (Lt. Togashi), Kumi Mizuno (Prime Minister Tsuge), Koichi Ueda (Secretary Dobashi) **Suit Performers:** Tsutomu Kitagawa (Godzilla), Hirofumi Ishigaki (Kiryu)

Cinemascope, Color, 88 Minutes

In 1999, Godzilla comes ashore in Japan during a typhoon where he is confronted by the Anti-Special Creature Self Defense Forces. In the battle, Akane Yashiro accidentally causes an accident which costs many of her teammates their lives. Akane is haunted by the event for years, and when she learns of a robot called Kiryu, built over the original Godzilla's bones, she joins its pilot team. Its coup de grace weapon is the "Absolute Zero Cannon," a laser beam that freezes anything it hits. She also befriends a widower, Yuhara, who designed the robot's DNA computer, and his young daughter, Sara. In 2003, on Kiryu's first mission to battle Godzilla, the sea monster's roar triggers a memory in the mind of the 1954 Godzilla and Kiryu goes on a rampage until it finally runs out of power. Yuhara works hard to repair the glitch just in time as Godzilla resurfaces in Shinegawa. Godzilla battles the military and their maser tanks and causes great swaths of destruction until Kiryu arrives. There, Akane pilots Kiryu manually in a great fight between the two Godzillas. Akane tries to use the Absolute Zero Cannon, but the smarter Godzilla uses his ray to upend Kiryu, resulting in several skyscrapers frozen and annihilated. Utilizing energy from all over Japan, the pilots get Kiryu running again. The mechanical monster grabs Godzilla and the two tussle as they fly toward Tokyo Bay. When they hit the water, Akane fires the Absolute Zero Cannon, but apparently misses again and only causes the water *splash to freeze. The ice explodes, and Godzilla re-emerges, an eye and arm damaged. Seeing his enemy nowhere to be found, he turns and wanders back out the sea. Kiryu suddenly surfaces, but is inoperational, and the government decides it is a worthwhile weapon after all, should Godzilla return.*

Background & Commentary Coming off their first big success of the Millennium series, Shogo Tomiyama approached Masaaki Tezuka once more to helm the new film (Shusuke Kaneko was unavailable due to already being involved in his next production, *To Sing in Love*). An early draft of the script took place in the same world as *Godzilla vs. Megaguirus* (2000) until it was decided to place Godzilla back into the "real" Japan. This film's backstory encompasses not only the original *Godzilla* (1954), but *Mothra* (1961) and *The War of the Gargantuas* (1966) as well. Its best concept is its updated version of "Mechagodzilla", which is actually built over the bones of the 1954 Godzilla and has a DNA computer. As such, the monster isn't a true separate Mechagodzilla entity so much as the 1954 Godzilla RoboCop-ized (the Japanese title screen initially says "Godzilla vs. Godzilla" before transforming into "Godzilla vs. Mechagodzilla"). The resulting film, which runs at a brisk pace to better fit with another Hamtaro cartoon, ended up being one of the best entries of the new Millennium series.

The end monster battle, the meat of any kaiju eiga, is one of the greatest fights in the series' entire history balancing fantastic choreography with exemplary CGI ray blasts. Not only does the film have an exciting ending, but Godzilla receives one of the best entrances of his career in the film's opening scene set during a fierce typhoon. Hidden behind the rain, it's the best Godzilla ever looks in the Millennium series (and while the Millennium-style Godzilla design returns, he is back to his standard charcoal grey color with lighter grey dorsal plates).

Michiru Oshima's new Godzilla theme, first introduced in *Godzilla vs. Megaguirus*, blares nicely on the soundtrack and was so well-loved that no Ifukube music even appears in the film. The film's most fascinating moment comes when Godzilla's roar triggers a memory in Kiryu's DNA computer and the machine goes berserk and begins rampaging through Tokyo while Godzilla dives back into the sea. While there is an interesting opportunity here to have Godzilla become the film's hero, it doesn't go down that path. Instead, Kiryu is repaired and emerges a hero in the climax and the notion of his restless bones is addressed in the next year's sequel. Furthermore, the redesign is the best the mecha has ever looked, and takes much of its inspiration from early designs of the 1993 Mechagodzilla.

Oddly, this film recycles the same exact plot of *Godzilla vs. Megaguirus* with another female defense officer out to avenge her commanding officer when he is killed by Godzilla (however, it is much better handled in this film). Even the Anti-Special Creature Self Defense Force (bizarrely called the "Anti-Megalosaurus Force" in Toho's export version) is just another version of G-Graspers—and before it G-Force—which again makes one wonder why Toho felt the need to constantly reboot despite using the same concepts over and over again. The film had decent grosses thanks to being double-billed with another Hamtaro cartoon, drawing in 1.7 million attendees resulting in a gross of ¥1.9 billion ($17,084,940).

Final Word *Godzilla Against Mechagodzilla* proved to be one of the best films in the Millennium series, but just like its predecessor, *Godzilla vs. Mechagodzilla* from 1974, it was already too little, too late.

ULTRAMAN COSMOS VS. ULTRAMAN JUSTICE: THE FINAL BATTLE

(TSUBURAYA PRODUCTIONS)
Release Date: August 02, 2003

Directed by: Tsugumi Kitaura **Special Effects by:** Tsugumi Kitaura
Screenplay by: Keiichi Hasegawa & Hideyuki Kawakami **Music by:** Kazumi Yano
Cast: Taiyo Sugiura (Musashi Haruno), Kazue Fukiishi (Julie/voice of Ultraman Justice), Miho Nishimura (Mari), Hidekazu Ichinose (Fubuki), Daisuke Shima (Captain Hiura) **Suit Performers:** Keiji Hasegawa (Ultraman Cosmos Lunar Mode/Ultraman Cosmos Space Corona Mode/Ultraman Cosmos Eclipse Mode/Ultraman Cosmos Future Mode/Ultraman Legend), Hidenori Ogino (Ultraman Justice), Daisuke Terai (Ultraman Cosmos Eclipse Mode/Don Ron), Shinya Iwasaki/Kazunori Yokoo (First Form Gloker), Satoshi Yamamoto (Second Form Gloker), Nobuhiko Tanabe (Third Form Gloker), Yoshiyuki Yamazaki (Borgills), Tomohiro Nagata (Golmede), Hiroyuki Okano (Lidorias)

Widescreen, Color, 77 Minutes

As Musashi plans to implement his lifelong dream of transporting earth's monsters to another planet via the spacecraft Noah, evil aliens show up and use robots, called Gloker Pawns, to stop the launch. Musashi calls on Ultraman Cosmos, who comes to his aid. However, Cosmos is confronted by his old ally, Ultraman Justice, who has allied itself with the aliens. The aliens have looked into earth's future and deemed humanity too dangerous to live, and they are to be exterminated. Justice seemingly kills Cosmos, and as the aliens prep for the eradication of humanity, Justice wanders the earth in its female human form, Julie. As Musashi's friends and family search for him, Julie sees both the good and bad in humanity and decides to abandon the mission. Ultraman Justice battles the Gloker Bishop until Musashi is revived by his friends and transforms back into Ultraman. Cosmos and Justice defeat the Gloker Bishop together and then fly into space to stop the Giga Endra—the aliens' doomsday device which will reset all life on earth. When they are unable to defeat the device, they merge together into Ultraman Legend and destroy the machine, which drives the aliens away for good.

Background & Commentary As the year 2003 lacked an ongoing Ultraman TV series, Tsuburaya Productions put out yet another sequel to the *Ultraman Cosmos* series towards the end of the summer. Using the same production team as the last film, *Ultraman Cosmos vs. Ultraman Justice: The Final Battle* effectively served as the grand finale to the *Ultraman Cosmos* story (even though the character naturally returned for other series and movies down the road). The film expands upon the more mature tone that was set up in the last film, and even the music score is more mature—and somewhat reminiscent of Isao Tomita at times. In one dark scene, after Cosmos is defeated, a group of rappers celebrate the end of the world and his death in the streets with a song!

As it turns out, very little of the film actually concerns Cosmos battling Justice as the title bout occurs very early in the film. After that, Musashi/Cosmos disappears for most of the film until the climax with the bulk of the film focusing on Justice's human form, Julie. Initially, Justice was imagined as a "beautiful young man" but at some point, the producers decided to make Justice's human counterpart a woman. This is somewhat confusing, as previous female Ultras were usually designated as Ultrawoman Beth and so on. Also, the Ultra Mother and Yullian, the female Ultra from *Ultraman 80*, clearly have breasts. However, the producers stated that they switched Justice to having a female host but with a male Ultra form as a way of showing that the character was "gender neutral." Along those same lines, early episodes of *Ultraman Ace* featured a man and a woman joining rings to transform into Ace so it wasn't totally unprecedented.

As for Ultraman Justice's design, it is overall very good and elements are evocative of Ultra Seven. As an evil—though morally ambiguous is a better term—Ultraman, Justice might be better than Ultraman Belial as the character has far more depth while Belial is fairly one-dimensional. The best scenes come from Julie/Justice walking the streets and interacting with humanity, both good and bad. She confronts the rappers who celebrated Ultraman Cosmos' death and begrudgingly befriends a little girl and her dog, "Cosmos." One of the film's other best scenes has past monsters that Cosmos had aided showing up to defend the earth, such as Don Ron, the dragon from *Ultraman Cosmos: The First Contact* (2001), and an updated version of Lidorias showing up to fight the Gloker Pawns. The Gloker Pawns' designs seem to anticipate those of the MUTOs from the 2014 *Godzilla*. Likewise, Ultraman Legend resembles the succeeding Ultraman that would be seen in the next film, *Ultraman: The Next* (2004).

There are several callbacks not only to the TV series, but the past two films as well. Shou and Jin reappear from *Ultraman Cosmos 2: The Blue*

Planet and Justice blames itself for not destroying Sandros from that same film. Notably, the park where Musashi first met Cosmos in the first prequel film is where Musashi is rediscovered after he goes missing. Even the child Baltan returns. The film ends with another post credit scene, this one showing Musashi finally accomplishing his mission of transporting the monsters to a new world. As he does so, dialogue from the first film plays from Musashi as a boy. Not as successful as the last film, this one grossed ¥500,000,000 ($4,482,500), the same amount as *Ultraman Cosmos: The First Contact*.

Final Word As the grand finale to the *Ultraman Cosmos* saga, it's safe to say the series goes out with a bang rather than a whisper.

GODZILLA
TOKYO S.O.S.

(TOHO)
Release Date: December 13, 2003
Alternate Titles: *Godzilla vs. Mothra vs. Mechagodzilla: Tokyo S.O.S.* (Japan) *S.O.S. for Tokyo* (Poland)
Godzilla, Mothra, Mechagodzilla: Save Tokyo (Russia)

Directed by: Masaaki Tezuka **Special Effects by:** Eiichi Asada **Screenplay by:**
Masahiro Yokotani & Masaaki Tezuka **Music by:** Michiru Oshima **Cast:** Noboru
Kaneko (Yoshito Chujo), Miho Yoshioka (Azusa Kisaragi), Hiroshi Koizumi (Shinichi
Chujo), Akira Nakao (Prime Minister Igarashi), Chihiro Otsuka (Shobijin Hio),
Masami Nagasawa (Shobijin Mana), Koichi Ueda (Secretary Dobashi) **Suit
Performers:** Tsutomu Kitagawa (Godzilla), Motokuni Nakagawa (Kiryu)

Cinemascope, Color, 91 Minutes

4 3 years after his involvement with Mothra and her fairies,
Shinichi Chujo and his nephew Yoshito are visited by the
Shobijin, who warn that the original Godzilla's bones—held
within Kiryu—must be returned to the sea where they can rest in
peace. They doubly warn that if mankind will not do this, Mothra will
have to become their enemy. Chujo takes this information to his
friend, Prime Minister Igarashi, who rejects the idea because Mothra
had attacked Japan back in 1961. The corpse of a giant turtle monster
washes ashore and an American nuclear sub goes missing, both are
determined to be the actions of the reactivated Godzilla. When
Godzilla surfaces in Tokyo—now sporting a huge scar on his chest—
Mothra shows up to face him. Igarashi is hesitant to send out Kiryu
until he sees the aged Mothra fighting a losing battle against Godzilla,
so he orders the machine out to back her up. Elsewhere, two Mothra
larvae hatch from an egg on Ogasawara Island and head to meet their
mother for battle. When Godzilla kills the adult Mothra and damages
Kiryu, the Shobijin and Yoshito work together to repair Kiryu to defend
the enraged larvae. Yoshito manages to get Kiryu up and running
again. The two Godzillas battle once again, completely annihilating the
Diet Building. Kiryu manages to incapacitate Godzilla by slicing his scar
open and drilling into his stomach. The Mothra larvae subsequently
spin a cocoon around Godzilla, rendering him helpless. However, when
the Japanese government orders Kiryu to kill Godzilla, the machine

finally transforms spiritually back into the 1954 Godzilla and refuses. The machine-monster picks up Godzilla and flies them both away from Tokyo with Yoshito still trapped inside. Yoshito manages to escape with help from his fellow pilots and Igarashi vows to let Kiryu rest in peace. The Mothra larvae take the Shobijin back home to Infant Island and the two Godzillas peacefully sink into the depths of the Pacific. However, in a government facility somewhere, a chamber has DNA material from the original Godzilla and other monsters...

Background & Commentary After four unrelated Godzilla adventures, *Godzilla: Tokyo S.O.S.* marks the first direct in-continuity sequel in the history of the Millennium series. Shogo Tomiyama had stated in the early 2000s Toho wanted to explore their options until they found a suitable timeline to settle into. After exploring four very unique universes, Toho finally decided on the one created in Masaaki Tezuka's *Godzilla Against Mechagodzilla* (2002). Actually, even before that film's release, there was already planned to be a follow-up (presumably one of the reasons why Kiryu and Godzilla both survive the ending of that film). If Takao Okawara and Akira Ifukube were the dream team of the 1990s, this film cemented Tezuka and composer Michiru Oshima as the director/composer team of the 2000s. Unfortunately, it was already too late, and by the next sequel, Toho would once again create a brand new universe, and Tezuka and Oshima got the boot.

Despite sporting the best special effects of the Millennium series, *Godzilla: Tokyo S.O.S.'s* storyline somehow manages to make the whole thing feel like a direct-to-video sequel. A sequence where Godzilla attacks a U.S. nuclear submarine plays like an Asylum mockbuster version of a similar scene from *The Return of Godzilla* (1984). The film even feels a little similar to 1972's *Godzilla vs. Gigan* in that the end monster battle begins taking place about halfway through the film's paltry storyline at the forty-minute mark. Perhaps this isn't surprising as the film mostly existed to keep Godzilla alive until his 50th anniversary the next year (though this movie does take place 50 years after the first Godzilla's appearance). In fact, the story would seem to have been concocted from a mostly commercial and financial perspective more than any past entry. The Kiryu and Godzilla suits were reused because they were still in working condition and in a fiscally creative move—for the sake of selling new toys—Godzilla is given a chest scar and Kiryu a new drill hand. Mothra's presence was specifically requested by the distribution department to draw in the female audience and it was also dictated that the Diet Building and Tokyo Tower should be destroyed. To draw interest from the old-school fans, for the first time since *The Return of Godzilla*,

Hiroshi Koizumi returns to the franchise actually reprising his role from 1961's *Mothra*.

Despite the lackluster story, the film has some standout moments. Mothra's death defending her two larvae is quite touching as are the final scenes regarding Kiryu/Godzilla '54, who manages to generate some audience sympathy itself. The film's final sequence is spectacular and frankly, it's the sort of scene every Godzilla fan deserved to see in the new Millennium series. In it, Yoshito Chujo is trapped inside Kiryu as it takes off with intentions of sinking Godzilla and itself in the Japan Trench. Realizing Chujo (who loves the machine) is trapped inside, the robot remarkably aids in his escape and even gives him a "sayonara" message on the computer monitor. Chujo hurtling in between Kiryu's metal dorsal plates in mid-air is hands down one of the most amazing shots in the Godzilla franchise. Sadly, this creative sequence couldn't save the film. Again double-billed with a Hamtaro cartoon, *Ham-Ham Grand Prix*, *Godzilla: Tokyo S.O.S.* had an attendance of just over 1 million people with a poor gross of 1.3 billion yen ($12,000,000), more or less the same amount of money as its budget.

Final Word Unable to truly stand on its own merits, *Tokyo S.O.S.* is difficult to judge as a standalone film and is best viewed back to back with *Godzilla Against Mechagodzilla*. Together the two films make a very entertaining whole.

GODZILLA
FINAL WARS

(TOHO)
Release Date: December 04, 2004
Alternate Titles: *Godzilla - Final Battle* (Brazil) *Godzilla: The Last Wars* (Bulgaria) *Godzilla: The Final War* (Greece) *Godzilla: The Last War* (Poland) *Godzilla: The Final Wars* (Russia)

Directed by: Ryuhei Kitamura **Special Effects by:** Eiichi Asada **Screenplay by:** Wataru Mimura, Shogo Tomiyama (uncredited), Isao Kiriyama, & Ryuhei Kitamura (uncredited) **Music by:** Keith Emerson **Cast:** Masahiro Matsuoka (Shinichi Ozaki), Rei Kikukawa (Miyuki Otanashi), Don Frye (Captain Douglas Gordon), Kazuki Kitamura (Xilien Commander), Maki Mizuno (Anna Otanashi), Kane Kosugi (Kazama), Akira Takarada (Secretary General Daigo) Kumi Mizuno (Commander Namikawa), Masato Ibu (Xilien Controller) **Suit Performers:** Tsutomu Kitagawa (Godzilla), Motokuni Nakagawa (Monster X/King Seesar/half of Keizer Ghidorah), Naoko Kamio (Rodan/Minilla), Kazuhiro Yoshida (Gigan/Hedorah), Toshihiro Ogura (Anguirus/Ebirah/half of Keizer Ghidorah)

Cinemascope, Color, 124 Minutes

I n 20XX, a branch of mutant humans—known as the M Agency— has arisen to use their powers to defend the earth. Inexplicably, giant monsters suddenly appear all across the globe. Anguirus attacks Shanghai, King Seesar raids Okinawa, Zilla invades Sydney, Kamacuras appears in Paris, and Rodan assaults New York. The monsters disappear mysteriously, followed by the appearance of the Xiliens, a group of seemingly benevolent aliens claiming to have done away with them. They also warn of a giant star on a collision course with earth and convince the governments of the world to fire all their nuclear weapons at the star. Now devoid of nuclear weapons, the aliens attack earth and unleash the monsters that were under their command all along. A young, friendly monster appears at Mt. Fuji that a young boy stops his grandfather from shooting. The boy names it Minilla. A band of humans and mutants led by Captain Gordon of the flying battleship Gotengo fly to the Arctic to unleash Godzilla, buried there many years ago. A cyborg called Gigan arrives just as the Gotengo releases Godzilla from his icy prison. The monster king blows Gigan's head off but is then beset upon by other monsters as he heads to Japan. He makes easy work of Zilla, Kumonga, and Kamacuras *before the Xilien Commander sends King Seesar, Rodan, and Anguirus to attack him near Mt. Fuji. Victorious again, Godzilla continues on his trek to Tokyo where the mother ship is. There, he and Mothra sort-of team up to battle a revamped Gigan and the mysterious Monster X while Gotengo's crew tackles the mothership. Mothra manages to destroy Gigan once again, while Monster X morphs into the three-headed abomination Keizer Ghidorah which easily overpowers Godzilla. After the aliens have been wiped out, the Gotengo crew gives Godzilla an energy boost, and he manages to kill Keizer Ghidorah. Godzilla stands before the humans, unable to forgive them for creating atomic weapons. Before the two sides can begin fighting, a larger-sized Minilla shows up and convinces him to go away peacefully. Godzilla complies, and the two monsters head out to sea.*

Background & Commentary With Toho paying homage to the 1960s G-films throughout the 1990s, perhaps it was inevitable they would begin mirroring the 1970s films in the 2000s. Godzilla battles alien invaders in *Godzilla 2000* (1999) and performs a flying leap in *Godzilla vs. Megaguirus* (2000). Further down the road were a pair of Mechagodzilla films in 2002 (*Godzilla Against Mechagodzilla*) and 2003 (*Godzilla: Tokyo S.O.S.*). *Godzilla: Final Wars*, the most polarizing entry in the series since *Godzilla vs. Hedorah*, represents the final revenge of the 1970s G-films. Rather than the perennial darling *Mothra vs. Godzilla*, the young, hotshot director Toho courted to helm the film, Ryuhei Kitamura, claimed to love the G-films of the 1970s, specifically the 1974 *Godzilla vs. Mechagodzilla* (behind closed doors he supposedly admitted he had little if any love for the series though). Though the mechanical titan makes no appearance in the film, his Masaru Sato theme and two co-stars Anguirus and King Seesar make their first appearances in thirty years. For that matter, so do Gigan and Hedorah, sight unseen since the 1970s. The film tips its hat not only to the Godzilla series, but also Toho sci-fi classics such as *Atragon* (the Atragon battles Godzilla in the prologue and later, the Gotengo battles Manda) and *Gorath* (the star about to collide with earth) almost making itself more of a 50th Anniversary tribute to Toho tokusatsu films in general.

Toho had high hopes of the movie being a big international success (particularly in America), which is why they hired Ryuhei Kitamura—a director almost universally reviled in his home country but popular with the younger crowd in America, particularly his slick action film *Versus* (2000)—and gave him carte blanche, as well as the highest budget of the series, $18 million dollars. Unfortunately, the director blew most of it on superfluous things, rather than the film itself. In addition to himself,

Kitamura spent his enlarged budget on Masahiro Matsuoka, a pop idol (who was contractually not allowed to be shown in the trailers for the film!), Rei Kikukawa, a model-turned-actress, Kyle Cooper, a main title designer, Keith Emerson, a musician best known for his rock group Emerson, Lake, & Palmer, and Sum 41, a Canadian rock band.

Kyle Cooper (*Se7en*, *Superman Returns*) designed the choppy main title sequence and Keith Emerson (*Nighthawks*, *Inferno*) wrote the score. Despite the novelty of having the legendary Emerson as a composer, his music is hit and miss (mostly miss) and would've been more appropriate for a video game. Toho was so dismayed with what he delivered, they hired two additional composers, Nobuhiko Morino and Daisuke Yano, to composed better tracks for the film (Emerson's covers of the Godzilla theme and the Monster Zero March went unused). *We're All to Blame*, a hit single from Canadian band Sum 41, blares more effectively over the soundtrack during the fight between Godzilla and Zilla.

Don Frye, a popular pro-wrestler and UFC fighter, steals the show despite his relative inexperience as Captain Douglas Gordon. Masahiro Matsuoka, singer and drummer for the band Tokio, plays the lead role of Ozaki, who is more or less an expy for Neo from *The Matrix* films. He is one of many new faces that are joined by Toho stalwarts. In addition to large roles for returning favorites Akira Takarada and Kumi Mizuno, a cameo role was given to Kenji Sahara for his thirteenth G-film appearance and twenty-third Toho special effects picture overall. 1990s regulars Akira Nakao and Koichi Ueda cameo in the opening prologue as well. Shiro Sano has the best cameo as a cloaked character inspired by the original inception of Dr. Yamane, who tries to assassinate Takarada's Secretary Daigo.

Kitamura's film was controversial even before it was released as rumors leaked of a profanity-laced sequence set in New York inspired by American cable television. Although filmed with full profanity, it was redubbed minus the swearing before release resulting in some mismatched dubbing and corny lines. Nodding its head to *Star Wars*, *The Matrix*, and even the *X-Men* series, the film tries to be too many things at once and, as a result, descends into total madness though it never collapses. It is undeniably fun if nonsensical, perhaps a statement on the flaws of 21st century genre filmmaking. Some scenes come out of nowhere; Minilla's appearance is especially jarring and at one point, the human-sized kaiju tries to take the steering wheel of a truck.

Godzilla's nuclear origins are glossed over in his 50th anniversary film, though during a break in the fighting as Godzilla stomps a village, the grandfather explains to his grandson that Godzilla is attacking humanity because he hates them for creating and using atomic weapons. Minilla seems to understand as he hangs his head with sadness. Elsewhere in the movie—for lack of a more eloquent word—Godzilla is a badass throughout the proceedings, easily dispatching his foes with little to no difficulty. Some battles last less than a minute, though all are amusing enough.

Although everyone agreed the special effects weren't great, to some it didn't matter. Stranger still, some enjoyed the film because of it. The bad effects and monster suits are the results of Kitamura's wasteful spending. Special effects director Eichi Asada had to make this film with its 15 monsters on the exact same effects budget he had for *Godzilla: Tokyo S.O.S.* with its four[ish] monsters (not a single extra yen of the 18 million budget went to the effects department). If anyone in this production exemplifies Eiji Tsuburaya's "we can do it; we will do it" spirit, it's Asada.

Godzilla's 50th anniversary film managed to premiere in late November at the Grauman's Chinese Theater in Los Angeles, though it never did get a U.S. theatrical release as hoped, nor did it do well at home. Though Toho had a huge publicity push for it, including garnering Godzilla a star on the Hollywood Walk of Fame, the Grauman's premiere was a disaster, with many attendees (infamously including Steven Seagal with his daughter Ayako Fujitani) walking out on the film midway through. The word of mouth spread about the film through Hollywood overnight, squashing any hopes for a wide American release right then and there. When the film premiered in December back in Japan (where they by and large hate Kitamura's movies), it managed to dethrone *Terror of Mechagodzilla* (1975) to become the biggest bomb of the series, earning ¥200 million ($1,790,000) opening weekend and only pulling in $13 million when all was said and done. Toho had announced this would be the final Godzilla movie for at least ten years before shooting even began, and the end result cemented that Toho would not be going back on their word this time.

Final Word Whether you love it or hate it, *Godzilla: Final Wars* is worth sitting through just to see Godzilla trounce his 1998 CG American imposter in all of twelve seconds.

ULTRAMAN:
THE NEXT

(TSUBURAYA PRODUCTIONS)
Release Date: December 18, 2004
Japanese Title: *Ultraman*

Directed by: Kazuya Konaka **Special Effects by:** Yuichi Kikuchi **Screenplay by:** Keiichi Hasegawa **Music by:** Tak Matsumoto **Cast:** Tetsuya Bessho (Shunichi Maki), Kyoko Toyama (Sara Mizuhara), Kenya Osumi (Takafumi Udo/voice of Beast the One) **Suit Performers:** Keiji Hasegawa (Ultraman), Satoshi Yamamoto (Beast the One- Reputiria/Bezerubua), Junya Iwamoto (Beast the One - Idorobia)

Widescreen, Color, 97 Minutes

Strange alien lights from the sky have very different effects on two men in the JSDF. The first, Takafumi Udo, is attacked by a bizarre light under the sea and metamorphoses into a monster. The next is fighter pilot Maki Shunichi, who is set to retire so he can spend time with his ill son. After his encounter with the alien light, he is sequestered by the government under the watchful eye of Sara Mizuhara, who fears he will become a monster like her fiancé, Takafumi, whom they now call The One. Instead, Maki transforms into the benevolent alien Ultraman when he is attacked by The One. During a battle in Tokyo, Maki as Ultraman with the assistance of the JSDF defeats The One. Ultraman separates himself from Maki, who returns to his wife and son.

Background & Commentary The Ultraman franchise's first film came out in 1967 as a double-bill for *King Kong Escapes*. Though intended as an all-original feature, it ended up being comprised solely of clips from the TV series. In later years when the franchise appeared on the big screen, the offerings were almost always continuations/tie-ins with the various TV series. On top of that, they didn't really clock in at feature length. For these reasons, 2004's *Ultraman: The Next* registers itself as not only the first standalone Ultraman film but also a bigger-budgeted feature-length reimagining. The film has a certain quality to it that makes it reminiscent of 1995's excellent *Gamera, Guardian of the Universe*.

The whole film has an undeniable 1990s feel to it, right down to the score and its end rock ballad "Never Goodbye" by Jack Brace, and this isn't a bad thing at all. Adding to this feel is the casting of 90s heartthrob Tetsuya Bessho as Maki, who was cast in 1992's *Godzilla vs. Mothra* specifically due to his popularity with female audiences. He does a solid job and carries the entire film as a likeable lead with an excellent emotional arc. His storyline, giving up the job he loves to be with his sick son, gives the picture a solid core. The same can be said for the arc of Kyoko Toyama's character Sara, who we learn is the ex-fiancé of Takafumi Udo (The One) infected by the monstrous alien. The film's title comes from Sara's character when Maki asks her, "If you call him the One, then what am I?" She replies to him, "The Next."

The relationship between Ultraman and his host Maki is well-crafted and they even have a face-to-face exchange during the climax. Ultraman's redesign in the film is somewhat radical, but is nonetheless a fantastic departure from what tokusatsu fans had seen before. The One, which has the ability to absorb various animals, looks impressive in its final winged form, but the face has an unfortunate, almost goofy quality to it at times. The end battle between the two in the skies over Tokyo is spectacular and though the CGI effects used to bring their fight to life can't be on par with big-budget U.S. fare, it holds up quite well and is the highlight of the film.

Overall, because this film has no ties to previous TV shows and doesn't have to play itself off as a sequel beholden to lots of continuity, it emerges as what is quite possibly the best Ultraman film ever made. Serving as a sort of new origin for the franchise, the plot was meant as a modern, more realistic take on the pilot episode of the original *Ultraman*. Actually, the whole film was originally meant to be dark and gritty but was changed to be more family friendly in the end. Reportedly, the tone of the finished film was inspired by the *Spider-Man* movies of the 2000s.

Ultimately, the box office take was disappointing at only ¥150 million ($1,347,300, though DVD sales were reportedly higher than usual). The planned sequel, *Ultraman 2: Requiem*, was scrapped and Tsuburaya Productions would take the series down a more traditional path in the future.

Final Word If Ultraman ever gets the Hollywood treatment in America, this film should be considered the blueprint.

THE GREAT YOKAI WAR

妖怪大戦争

(DAIEI)

Release Date: August 06, 2005

Alternate Titles: *The War of the Yokai* (France) *War of the Demons* (Germany) *The War of Ghosts* (Italy) *Great Goblin War* (Russia)

Directed by: Takashi Miike **Special Effects by:** Yoshinari Dohi, Tomo Hyakutake, Pierre Suda & Yuya Takahashi **Screenplay by:** Takashi Miike, Mitsuhiko Sawamura, and Takehiko Itakura **Music by:** Koji Endo **Cast:** Ryunosuke Kamiki (Tadashi Ino), Hiroyuki Miyasako (Sata), Chiaki Kuriyama (Agi), Etsushi Toyokawa (Kato Yasunori), Seiko Iwaido (Kawahime), Masoami Kondo (Shojo), Sadao Abe (Kawataro/Kappa)

2.35 : 1, Color, 124 Minutes

After his parents' divorce, young Tadashi moves to a rural town where, during a local festival, he is ceremonially chosen to be the Kirin Rider—a mythical protector of all that is good. Though Tadashi thinks of this as nothing more than tradition, he soon finds that he literally is the Kirin Rider when he is targeted by the evil yokai, Kato. Kato, who has allied with another evil yokai named Agi, has a vendetta against the people of Japan, whom he hopes to annihilate through a new fusion of yokai and machinery called Kikai. One of the captured yokai, Sunekosuri, escapes Kato's grasp and befriends Tadashi. Together, they journey to Sakaiminato where they ally themselves with other yokai. When Sunekosuri is captured by Agi and turned into one of the Kikai, Tadashi and thousands of yokai—who mistakenly believe they are going to a party—storm Shinjuku where Kato has established a fortress. Though Tadashi is forced to kill Sunekosuri in its Kikai form, Agi and Kato are defeated and balance is restored to Japan.

Background & Commentary In November of 2002, shortly after Kadokawa Publishing had acquired the again bankrupt Daiei Motion Picture Company, magazine writer Miyuki Miyabe wrote a piece on the original yokai films that stirred the new Kadokawa/Daiei's interests in a reboot. However, this new incarnation wouldn't be based on the classic

Daiei films but would have other influences, chief among them the novel *The Tale of the Imperial Capital* by Hiroshi Aramata (published in 1983 by Kadokawa Shoten). That story's antagonist, Kato Yasunori, is even the villain of the completed film.

In the previous version, the yokai rid the land of a foreign demon from the Middle East. In this version, due to the influence of Aramata's novel, instead of foreign invaders, the clash is meant to represent a clash between traditional Japan and modern culture with the villain's yokai that have been converted into machines. The new film would also pay homage to the works of Shigeru Mizuki, the manga artist who popularized yokai. In fact, the real-life museum in Sakaiminato dedicated to his work acts as a location in the story when Tadashi goes to research yokai there.

As the 60th anniversary Kadokawa film, it had a very healthy ¥1.3 billion ($11,659,700) budget. Filming began in July 2004 and wasn't without incident. In November, a fire occurred that burnt down part of the set. Filming completed in January 2005 in time for it to be released during the summer ghost season in August. The movie starts with intriguing, well-done imagery of a reddened apocalyptic city (which turns out to be Tadashi's dream) which sets the tone for the fantastic imagery to come. In particular, fans of the classic Daiei yokai trilogy will find much delight in a scene where Tadashi meets reimagined versions of yokai like the water Kappa (here called Kawataro). The CGI update to classic characters like the long-necked woman are excellent, and for a 2005 Japanese film, the CGI is top-notch. There is plenty of humor in the film too. In one scene where the Kappa flies over the city, a man casually states, "It's only Gamera." Also humorous is the fact that the thousands of yokai (an update of the march in 1968's *Spook Warfare*) that appear to aid in the battle for the climax only do so because they mistakenly think they are going to a party. Needless to say, the ensuing battle is humorous and exciting.

The heart of the film is undeniably the little yokai Sunekosuri. The little ghost is forced to become one of Agi's machine minions, whom Tadashi tragically has to fight and mortally wound in a heartbreaking scene. Sadder yet, after defeating the final villain, the film has an epilogue with an adult Takashi being followed around by a resurrected Sunekosuri. The ghost can see Tadashi but Tadashi has lost his ability to see the yokai. As a tearful Sunekosuri watches Tadashi ride off on his bike, the villainous Kato casts a shadow over the little yokai, setting up a sequel that never materialized.

Final Word An excellent reimaging of Daiei's yokai series set in modern times.

NEGADON

THE MONSTER FROM MARS

(STUDIO MAGARA/COMIX WAVE INC)
Broadcast Date: October 16, 2005
Japanese Title: *Giant Planet Monster Negadon*

Directed by: Jun Awazu **Screenplay by:** Jun Awazu **Music by:** Shingo Terasawa **Voice Cast:** Dai Shimizu (Ryuichi Narasaki), Takuma Sasahara (Seiji Yoshizawa), Akane Yumoto (Emi Narasaki), Masafumi Kishi (TV Announcer/Narrator)

Cinemascope, Color, 25 Minutes

In the year 2025 during the Mars terraforming project, a large cocoon found in some Martian ruins is brought to earth. It crashes in Japan on the way there and the alien monster, dubbed Negadon, hatches and begins destroying the city. An elderly professor dusts off an abandoned project, his giant robot, to battle the monster. The fight takes them all the way into space where Negadon is defeated by the professor piloting the robot.

Background & Commentary *Negadon: The Monster from Mars* is a lovingly-crafted CGI-animated short film inspired by Japanese sci-fi of the late 1950s and early 1960s. In the very first shot, a space station that looks nearly identical to the one seen in Toho's 1959 classic *Battle in Outer Space* can be glimpsed. The next shot, of a mushroom cloud on Mars (due to a terraforming experiment), is obviously meant to evoke the nuclear tensions of the era. The film is even tinted with a vintage look as various "scratches" occasionally flash across the screen. It's reminiscent of a CGI Max Fleischer cartoon. Even though it is set in 2025, the short is clearly a 1950s version of the future. In classic Toho tradition, the film is anchored by a scientist and his daughter Emi, who was killed when a test on his giant robot went awry. Like Dr. Serizawa and other tortured scientist characters of the past, the professor dies in a heroic sacrifice, killing Negadon in space.

Negadon's design is a strange juxtaposition of old-school 1950s alien bug monsters and newer anime-style kaiju. Though it should be noted this film predates 2013's *Pacific Rim*, the giant robot Maroku II in this short film greatly resembles a Jaeger. The short film was produced by director Jun Awazu's Studio Magara and co-produced with Comix Wave Inc. for broadcast on the Animax anime network in Japan. Production started in 2003, with hopes of finishing in time for Godzilla's 50th Anniversary in 2004, though the film wasn't ready for broadcast until 2005.

Final Word An extraordinary and excellently-executed short film for kaiju enthusiasts.

SUPER FLEET SAZER X: THE MOVIE

(TOHO)
Release Date: December 17, 2005
Japanese Title: *Super Star Fleet Sazer X: Fight! Star Warriors*

Directed by: Kazuki Omori **Special Effects by:** Koichi Kawakita **Screenplay by:** Toshiyuki Tanabe **Music by:** Hiroshi Takagi **Cast:** Ryosuke Takahashi (Takuto Ando/Lio-Sazer), Manabu Shindo (Ad/Eagle-Sazer), Ryosuke Miura (Kane/ Beetle-Sazer), Tatsuya Isaka (Date Shota/Riser Glen), Shiori Kanzaki (Yuka Sanada/Riser Kageri), Shunya Isaka (Chinya Hiraga/Riser Gant), Toru Minegishi (Captain Jinguji), Oribito Kasahara (Riki)

Widescreen, Color, 70 Minutes

At the same time as a mysterious ghost ship from space approaches Earth, a young alien boy named Riki appears before the Sazer X crew, a group of time-traveling superheroes. As it turns out, Riki is an alien refugee sent to spy on the Sazer X crew and retrieve some powerful energy orbs located on earth. The giant mechanical ape monster Bulgario manages to absorb one of the orbs after a battle with Sazer X, and Riki eventually steals the rest. This leads to the resurrection of the giant two-headed dragon, Bosquito. With the combined efforts of Atragon, plus the many different forms of the Granziers, Bosquito is destroyed, and Riki and his family peacefully return to space.

Background & Commentary In the early 2000s, Toho began a Sentai series, *Super Star God GranSazer*, for the new Millennium. Like *Zone Fighter* of the 1970s, it had several interesting ties to the Godzilla franchise (though none in terms of continuity). Several of the monsters that appeared throughout the series were more or less revamped Toho kaiju with different names, and one kaiju was even constructed from the *Godzilla: Final Wars* (2004) Hedorah suit. The series spawned two sequels (*Phantom Star God Justirisers* and *Super Star Fleet Sazer-X*), resulting in a trilogy of tokusatsu TV series from Toho. And though not set within any previous Toho movie continuity, the three series featured everything from

118

Gorath to Atragon and even had an appearance from Hiroshi Koizumi as Dr. Chujo to tie in with the release of *Godzilla: Tokyo S.O.S.*!

Sazer X: The Movie (the culmination of all three series) has too much backstory and too many characters crammed in its 70-minute run time to feel like an actual feature film. If one isn't a fan of tokusatsu or the related TV series, there really isn't anything to recommend in it for the average viewer. That said, Toho tokusatsu fans unfamiliar with the show will find the film of interest for several reasons. Firstly, though he "retired" after *Rebirth of Mothra 2* (1997), all three series plus this film's special effects were directed by Koichi Kawakita, who reteamed with director Kazuki Omori. And thanks to Kawakita, this film (not to mention the whole series) is chock full of nods to the Godzilla canon. For starters, Atragon reappears, complete with the classic Akira Ifukube theme from *Atragon* (1963) every time it goes into action (which, sadly, does wear out its welcome by the end). The ship is even piloted by Captain Jinguji (played here by Toru Minegishi, Goro Gondo of *Godzilla vs. Biollante*)!

The robot ape monster Bulgario is a thinly-veiled version of Kawakita's dreamed-of Mechani-Kong, which he tried and failed (due to legal issues) to bring to the big screen to fight Godzilla in 1991. Enemy monster Bosquito is basically an armed, two-headed version of King Ghidorah. Not only does the monster birth itself in a fiery King Ghidorah manner, but its backstory is that of an outer space destroyer of worlds. The battles are full of the ray blasts that Kawakita excels at, including an underwater one with Bulgario. The final battle between the Sazer X fleet of Megazord-like robots and Bosquito plays out like the climaxes of many of the modern Ultraman feature films, with Bosquito dwarfing the heroes until it is defeated in a typical, predictable power-up move.

Final Word Fans of *Atragon* (1963) and the Heisei Godzilla series will find this film worth watching for the sake of checking out the Atragon in action one more time, along with several of the film's Godzilla-inspired villains. Otherwise, it's no different than every other made-for-kids Super Sentai movie.

GAMERA THE BRAVE

(DAIEI)
Release Date: April 29, 2006
Alternate Titles: *Little Braves: Gamera* (Japan) *Gamera the Heroic* (France)

Directed by: Ryuta Tazaki **Special Effects by:** Isao Kaneko **Screenplay by:** Yukari Tatsui **Music by:** Yoko Ueno **Cast:** Ryo Tomioka (Toru Aizawa), Kaho (Mai Nishio), Kanji Tsuda (Kosuke Aizawa), Shogo Narita (Katsuya), Kenjiro Ishimaru (Professor Amemiya) **Suit Performers:** Toshinori Sasaki (Gamera/Toto), Mizuho Yoshida (Zedus)

Cinemascope, Color, 96 Minutes

Toru, a young boy, who has recently lost his mother, discovers a strange egg at the spot where Gamera died thirty three years earlier battling a swarm of Gyaos. The egg hatches a turtle that he names Toto, which soon begins exhibiting odd behavior such as flying and flame-breath, though Toru hopes the turtle won't grow up to be another Gamera as he fears he too will die in combat. Soon the monster Zedus surfaces in Toru's village and begins wreaking havoc until a nearly full grown Toto comes to the rescue. The battle ends in a draw with Zedus falling into the ocean and Toto being captured by the government and taken to a facility in Nagoya. Zedus eventually attacks Nagoya, and in the chaos Toto, now a fully grown Gamera, is broken free from the lab. Toto battles Zedus with his full powers and emerges victorious. He is surrounded by the Japanese government, but the children of Nagoya form a barrier between the government and Toto. Toru tells Toto to fly away, calling him "Gamera" for the first time, and the turtle monster obliges.

Background & Commentary When Toho announced that Godzilla was going into a semi-retirement in 2004, Kadokawa took it as a good sign to try their hand at Gamera again even though 1999's *Gamera 3: Revenge of Irys* was only a moderate financial success. Perhaps in response to this, the studio decided to reboot Gamera back to his more child-friendly origins (that, or from a legal standpoint, it was easier not having to worry about the Heisei series' creators and continuity). While this may have sounded like a bad idea, the results don't alienate the adult audience. The idea of a child raising a baby Gamera was an inspired idea (possibly originating from a 1993 script by Kazunori Ito simply titled *Gamera* in which a group of children raises Gamera as a juvenile). Additionally, the film has a fairly engaging human storyline told from a child's perspective. The main character, Toru, has recently lost his mother and fears the baby tortoise will grow into Gamera. Also in the mix is his next door neighbor Mai, who is on the verge of having a life-altering operation. As a result, the film is far superior to the comparable Mothra trilogy of the late 1990s.

The film's magnificent opening scene features flawless effects and exciting music as an adult Gamera battles a swarm of Gyaos while Toru's father, a child himself in 1973, looks on. The sequence whets the appetite for what's to come, though it is never equaled. That said, the special effects are on par with the 1990s Gamera films, which is saying a lot. One of the film's main publicity aspects was its full-scale Toto prop, which is used frequently throughout the film while a real African spurred tortoise was used to play the juvenile Toto. Strangely, this Gamera lacks his classic roar and instead cries stock dinosaur roars from the Tyrannosaurus of *The Land Unknown* (1957), the 1976 *King Kong*, and the shark in *Jaws: The Revenge* (1987), as well as many more. As for Zedus, he makes for an interesting departure from Irys and Legion, being more down-to-earth and something of a throwback to the 1960s. With the lizard-like kaiju's tongue weapon, Kadokawa might have been wise to simply make Zedus an updated version of Barugon, the Gamera foe this creature is most comparable to.

With several dangling story threads—chiefly, a scientist obsessed with studying Gamera—it is clear Kadokawa was planting seeds for sequels, but due to the film's lukewarm reception, they would never materialize. The film, which had a high budget, sold even fewer tickets than the Heisei Gamera films though it had a strong opening night performance.

Final Word Though the story never quite lives up to its ambitious opening, it is still a wonderfully realized children's film.

SINKING OF JAPAN

(TBS/TOHO)

Release Date: July 15, 2006

Alternate Titles: *Japan Sinks* (Japan) *Doomsday: The Sinking of Japan* (U.S. home video) *The Fall of Japan* (Bulgaria) *The Submersion of Japan* (France) *2012: Death of the Empire* (Hungary)

Directed by: Shinji Higuchi **Special Effects by:** Makoto Kamiya **Screenplay by:** Masato Kato **Music by:** Taro Iwashiro **Cast:** Tsuyoshi Kusanagi (Toshio Onodera), Ko Shibasaki (Reiko Abe), Etsushi Toyokawa (Dr. Tadokoro), Mao Daichi (Saori Takamori), Mitsuhiro Oikawa (Shinji Yuki), Mayuko Fukuda (Misaki Kuraki), Akira Emoto (Professor Fukuhara), Koji Ishizaka (Prime Minister Yamamoto)

Cinemascope, Color, 135 Minutes

In Numazu, submersible pilot Toshio Onodera awakens in the aftermath of a devastating earthquake and does his best to save a small girl, Misaki, wandering through the wreckage. Both are saved by female firefighter Reiko Abe. The trio keeps in touch after the incident as authorities investigate the earthquake under the leadership of Dr. Tadokoro. It is soon learned through Tadokoro that Japan will sink into the ocean in less than a year's time, though the government covers this information up. When a devastating earthquake strikes Kyushu, killing the Prime Minister, the government has no choice but to reveal Japan's fate to the public. Dr. Tadokoro comes up with a way to save Japan by strategically placed bombs that will separate Japan from the megalith pulling it into the ocean. As the Japanese evacuate their homeland, Onodera receives an offer to take a job in England and beseeches Reiko and Misaki to come with him but Reiko declines, wanting to save as many people as she can in Japan. When the first attempt to plant the explosives fails via submersible pilot Yuki, Onodera mounts a last-minute mission in an antiquated submersible to finish the job. He plants the explosions and the whole of Japan is separated from the tectonic plates pulling it under. However, Onodera dies during the operation, leaving behind a heartbroken Reiko.

Background & Commentary Ever since the release of the original *Submersion of Japan* in 1973, Toho promised a sequel throughout the 1970s that never came to be. Shochiku also pledged a Kazuki Omori-helmed remake in 1998 that failed to materialize. Finally in 2006, the former effects director of the Heisei Gamera films, Shinji Higuchi, made his directorial debut with a remake of Sakyo Komatsu's classic novel. Higuchi has stated the original *Submersion of Japan* was his inspiration to get into filmmaking (specifically mentioning the film's miniatures reflected places that he knew). Despite this, or perhaps out of respect for it, Higuchi wanted to adapt the book for modern times more so than remake the original movie. This makes sense as there are plenty of differences to both the movie and the book. That said, the new film does pay homage to the original in the form of the Wadatsumi 2000 (the Wadatsumi 1 in the original), an antiquated sub that saves the day in the end.

One of the film's main themes would seem to be the survival of Japanese culture over that of the Japanese people themselves. Or rather, the question seems to be what is more important: preserving Japanese culture or as many of the Japanese themselves? This is best exemplified early in the film when a large boat is used to transport Japanese treasures out of Japan over the people themselves. As in his Gamera films, lauded for their realism in terms of military and government portrayal, Higuchi shows how the real Japan would react in such a crisis. The populace's reaction to the news that they are all doomed is realistic too as the poorer class, knowing they likely won't be among those saved, brush off the news with jokes as a way to deal with the tragedy.

Naturally, like any good disaster film, the story has several tragic death scenes, notably submersible pilots Yuki and Onodera in their respective submersibles. Onodera is given much more depth in this version and overall Tsuyoshi Kusanagi (from the boy band SMAP) does a good job as a more fleshed-out version of the character. In the original, Onodera does little more than search for his love interest Reiko in the climax, but in this film, Onodera actually saves Japan and sacrifices his life in the process. The character of Reiko, fairly uninteresting in the original, is given a major overhaul as a female firefighter in this version. An orphan of the Kobe earthquake, Reiko has grown up believing her adoptive grandfather to have been a firefighter. In a surprise twist, it was all a story her grandmother told her. The Prime Minister, prominent in the original, is given less to do here but is poignant nevertheless. In one scene, he tells Saori Takamori that the best option he has heard to save his country is to simply die with it. A few scenes later, the Prime Minister is killed when his plane flies over a volcanic eruption in Kyushu, one of the film's greatest special effects scenes. A POV shot above the plane as the land below erupts is one of the film's best shots by far.

This version actually has more special effects set-pieces than the original, though naturally, the destruction is mostly CGI rather than miniatures. And like the original film, the score is very much a sign of the times and is a bit jazzier than one would expect.

With this film's production, Toho was more or less the distributor and the real powerhouse behind the film was TBS [Tokyo Broadcasting System], who invested ¥2 billion ($17,928,000) in the production. The investment paid off as it grossed over ¥5 billion ($44,825,000) and even saw a healthy international release too. This film was so highly anticipated in Japan that Minoru Kawasaki managed to release a spoof, *The World Sinks Except Japan*, within months of this film's release.

Final Word Shinji Higuchi's *The Sinking of Japan* has enough similarities and differences to the original to make this a truly well-rounded remake. In fact, it's better done than contemporaries like *The Day After Tomorrow* (2004).

ULTRAMAN MEBIUS AND ULTRA BROTHERS

(TSUBURAYA PRODUCTIONS)
Release Date: September 16, 2006

Directed by: Kazuya Konaka **Special Effects by:** Ichiro Itano **Screenplay by:** Keiichi Hasegawa **Music by:** Toshihiko Sahashi **Cast:** Shunji Igarashi (Mirai Hibino/voice of Ultraman Mebius), Aiko Ito (Aya), Ouga Tanaka (Takoto), Susumu Kurobe (Shin Hayata/voice of Ultraman), Koji Moritsugu (Dan Moroboshi/voice of Ultra Seven), Jiro Dan (Hideki Go/voice of Ultraman Jack), Keiji Takamine (Seiji Hokuto/voice of Ultraman Ace) **Suit Performers:** Keiji Hasegawa (Ultraman Mebius), Kenya Soma (Ultraman), Katsuhiko Watanabe (Ultra Seven), Akeshi Kajimoto (Ultraman Jack), Keizo Yabe (Ultraman Ace), Shun Kobayashi (Ultraman Taro), Daisuke Fukuda (Zoffy), Tomohiro Nagata/Hiroaki Nakamura/Hiroshi Suenaga/Makoto Ito (various monsters and aliens), Hidenori Ogino (Fake Ultraman Mebius)

Widescreen, Color, 93 Minutes

After battling the dread monster U-Killersaurus on the moon, Ultraman, Ultra Seven, Ultraman Ace, and Ultraman Jack seal the defeated monster in Kobe Bay. However, in doing so, the four superheroes lose their ability to transform and are stuck in human form. Twenty years pass and a conclave of evil aliens come to earth to resurrect the monster but are opposed by the new Ultraman, Mebius. When Mebius is unable to defeat the aliens, the four Ultra brothers decide to transform one last time to save him. Though the aliens are defeated, U-Killersaurus, controlled by the evil alien Yapool, is revived bigger and more powerful than ever. The five Ultramen are aided by Zoffy and Ultraman Taro and all six veteran Ultramen channel their powers into Mebius, who manages to defeat the monster.

Background & Commentary In the mid-2000s, Tsuburaya Productions' once great Ultraman franchise was in something of a slump and in need of a shot in the arm for the series' looming 40th anniversary in 2006. Rather than try to reinvent it—as was done with *Ultraman: The Next* (2004)—the studio decided to go back to their roots. Their new TV series, *Ultraman Mebius*, would be placed in the continuity of their old Showa era series that had run from *Ultraman* (1966-1967) to *Ultraman*

80 (1980-1981). Developed alongside the new series was also this 40th anniversary film. The film was shot before the series and was released in September of 2004, just around the time the 24th episode was airing on TV.

At its core, *Ultraman Mebius and Ultra Brothers* is a reunion film and brings six classic—and one new—Ultramen together on the big screen. This concept was nothing new in the TV series and crossovers like this had been occurring since *Return of Ultraman* back in the early 1970s. Fans don't have to wait long for their favorites either; the film gets off to a spectacular start with a battle on the moon involving the first four classic Ultramen and it may well be the film's best scene. That's not to say the rest of the film isn't good, just that the opening battle really is that great. From there on, the film balances itself between servicing nostalgic adult fans and children alike—the only overly childish instance for adults is a subplot involving a young boy and his dog, though it doesn't wear out its welcome.

Some of the CGI is a little clunky, but it's so fast and frenetic that it doesn't detract from one's enjoyment of the movie. The miniature set of Kobe looks good at least, as is the U-Killersaurus's design and suit. The four invading aliens which include Temperor, Zarab, Guts, and Nackle are a bit too goofy-looking to be threatening, but this is because they are accurately recreated from the original TV series from the 60s and 70s. The real joy of the film is the reunion of the veteran Ultramen actors Susume Kurobe (*Ultraman*), Koji Moritsugu (*Ultra Seven*), Jiro Dan (*Return of Ultraman*) and Keiji Takamine (*Ultraman Ace*). The foursome's scenes together when they interact with newcomer Shunji Igarashi are great, as is the scene where they decide to transform one last time even if it costs their lives. Absent are the other two Showa era Ultramen: Ultraman Leo and Ultraman 80 (though both get guest spots on the TV series later).

Shochiku again distributed this film for Tsuburaya Productions and it grossed a healthy ¥680 million ($6,096,200) which was considered a success. Tsuburaya Productions had effectively rejuvenated their Ultra series for the foreseeable future ensuring many more sequels would be produced for the big and small screens alike.

Final Word A great reunion film that fans of tokusatsu TV series and Ultraman are sure to love.

BIG MAN JAPAN

(SHOCHIKU)
Release Date: May 19, 2007
Alternate Titles: *Big Japanese* (Japan) *The Big Japanese* (Austria)
The Giant of Japan (Brazil) *Very Large Japanese* (Greece) *The Biggest Japanese* (Hungary)
Japanese Giant (Russia)

Directed by: Hitoshi Matsumoto **Special Effects by:** Hiroyuki Seshita
Screenplay by: Hitoshi Matsumoto & Mitsuyoshi Takasu **Music by:** Tei Towa
Cast: Hitoshi Matsumoto (Masaru Daisoto/Big Man Japan), Riki Takeuchi
(Haneru), Ua (Manager Kobori), Taichi Yazaki (Daisato's grandfather), Tomoji
Hasegawa (Director)

Widescreen, Color, 113 Minutes

A documentary film crew follows the day-to-day life of Masaru
Daisoto, otherwise known as Big Man Japan. Daisato is part of
a long line of special men that have the ability to grow to
gigantic proportions when charged with electricity and for generations
have defended Japan against monsters. However, Big Man Japan has
fallen out of public favor in Japan. Daisato isn't very enthusiastic—or
good—at his job, which causes numerous disasters after he is beaten
by one of the monsters. During a rematch with the red monster that
beat him, Big Man Japan loses consciousness and hallucinates he is
part of a TV show similar to the Ultraman franchise. In his dying
moments Big Man Japan watches as the superhero family kills the
kaiju and then invites him to come home with them.

Background & Commentary Filmed as a low-key documentary on a
real individual, *Big Man Japan* has a long drawn out opening with a very
dry sense of humor and this actually works to the film's favor once one
accepts the pacing. There's a certain Peter Sellers/Inspector Clouseau
quality to actor/director Hitoshi Matsumoto's character Daisato, and his
timing is also slightly reminiscent of the *Pink Panther* films. Most of the
humor is generated by Daisato's given-up-on-life attitude and the fact his
female agent is clearly screwing him out of any profits he could be
making. Daisato is paid so little by the government that he actually has

to have advertisements painted on his body by sponsors. Over a lunchtime meeting, his agent actually tells him, "I found a sponsor for your chest. Try not to fold your arms from now on [when fighting monsters on TV]." Another of the funnier scenes occurs when Daisato's grandfather zaps himself with electricity and then goes on a dementia-fueled rampage across Japan.

The monsters Big Man Japan faces are also humorous but aren't traditional kaiju. All are humanoid and most are comparable to yokai. The monster battles are a little too slow to be entertaining, but are humorous nonetheless. For a Japanese film, the special effects are excellent and its ¥1 billion ($8,965,000) budget is apparent on screen. Of course, the effects still aren't much compared to Hollywood CGI, but for 2007 they're pretty spectacular. The old newsreel footage is especially well-created.

The otherwise excellent film is derailed by its ending; in the final "reel," the film switches from CGI to a spoof of 1970s suitmation. This switch happens at a pivotal moment during the climax where Big Man Japan is being badly beaten by a devilish crimson-colored monster. Suddenly Daisato (now suitmation not CGI) finds himself in the middle of a miniature city set with the same red monster, only showing up to aid him are a family of superheroes clearly meant to parody the Ultraman franchise. Stranger still, Daisato refuses to participate in the battle and the superhero family kills the monster. They then invite Daisato to fly off with them to their lair and the film ends. The bizarre ending is open to interpretation and it's possible the red monster has killed Daisato and this is a death dream. That's not to say the scene isn't funny—it's actually one of the funniest scenes in the film—it's just so jarringly inserted into the proceedings and robs the story of any resolution. It would have been far more satisfying to see Daisato's story come to a fitting conclusion. However, some people actually love the ending and think it's brilliant. Either way, everyone has their own theory as to what it means.

Big Man Japan, which was Matsumoto's directorial debut, was distributed by Shochiku and made ¥1.16 billion ($10,399,400; only slightly more than its budget) at the Japanese box office. The film was well-received in America, where Roger Ebert gave it three and half stars out of four, and the film had a limited theatrical release.

Final Word Of all the monster parodies that would follow, this one still stands head and shoulders above the rest. Of the sub-genre, it is arguably the best.

DRAGON WARS

(YOUNGGU ART MOVIES)
Release Date: August 01, 2007
Alternate Titles: *D-War* (South Korea) *D-War: Dragon Wars* (U.S. opening title) *Fury of Dragons* (Argentina) *Dragon War* (Croatian) *The Dragon War* (Greece) *Naga Mystery Forest* (India) *Dinosaur War* (Russia)

Directed by: Shim Hyung-rae **Screenplay by:** Shim Hyung-rae **Music by:** Steve Jablonsky **Cast:** Jason Behr (Ethan Kendrick), Amanda Brooks (Sarah Daniels), Robert Forster (Jack), Craig Robinson (Bruce), Chris Mulkey (Frank Pinsky), Elizabeth Pena (Linda Perez), Aimee Garcia (Brandy)

Widescreen, Color, 90 Minutes

TV reporter Ethan Kendrick learns that he is the reincarnated guardian of the Yuh Yi Joo—a woman who has the power to transform an Imoogi (Korean Dragon) into a Celestial Dragon. Ethan finds the new Yuh Yi Joo in the form of Sara, a young woman with no family living in Los Angeles. Pursuing Sara are an evil Imoogi, Buraki, and his army of followers comprised of humanoid soliders and sundry dragons. The army descends upon L.A. and Ethan does his best to protect Sara. In the end, they are captured and taken to an ancient city somewhere in the Orient. There, just as all hope seems lost, the good Imoogi arrives to battle Buraki, but is only able to defeat the evil dragon after Sara sacrifices her lifeforce to turn the good Imoogi into a Celestial Dragon.

Background & Commentary Shortly after the rerelease of *Yonggary* (2001), director Shim Hyung-rae announced plans for a new, more ambitious monster movie entitled *Dragon Wars*. The film went before cameras with a high-profile American cast in 2004. However, production on the extensive special effects went on for over two years. The film's effects were good enough to score a U.S. release through Freestyle Releasing in September 2007. There are conflicting reports on the film's budget with the initial estimate set at $35 million. Later, it was rumored that the budget climbed to heights of up to $75 million or $100 million.

Either way, it was the highest-budgeted South Korean film of all time, and also the highest-grossing at a reported $75-100 million worldwide.

And what of Shim Hyung-rae's second Korean monster film? Whereas the problem with *Yonggary* was the acting, story, and special effects, here it is only the rudimentary scriptwriting that hinders the film. Everything else is more or less Grade-A filmmaking. The problem with *Dragon Wars* is that it tries too hard to appeal to the American market. Conversely, had the film been set in South Korea with South Korean actors/characters, the story probably would have fared somewhat better. Anytime foreign films try too hard to carry an American feel, they almost always come across as clichéd instead. Take the previous year's Korean monster movie *The Host* (2006) for example. It was set in South Korea, used South Korean actors, and was much less clichéd, better-received, and did better in the U.S. In *Dragon Wars*, the situations and dialogue are very stilted and clichéd—not to the extent of something as bad as *The Room*, but still distractingly bad. This was likely why the film was panned so badly in America because the action and special effects scenes are spectacular. They just need a better storyline to set them up.

The battle in Los Angeles has the film's best scenes, notably when Buraki slithers his way through a main street causing traffic to explode all around him. Buraki's crawl up a skyscraper is also a fantastic visual and the helicopter battle with an army of flying dragons is probably the film's second-best scene. The best scene, naturally, is the end battle between Buraki and the good Imoogi. Though one wouldn't think a battle between two cobra-like monsters sans limbs could be so interesting, it is actually very exciting. The good Imoogi also transforms into a traditional Chinese dragon (and is very Manda-like) for the battle's final act when he finally defeats Buraki with fireballs.

The cast for *Dragon Wars* is also top-notch. The problem is their characters aren't very interesting and you know there's a problem when the sidekicks outshine the leads—in this case a pre-stardom Craig Robinson. Jason Behr (best known for TV's *Roswell*) is a good enough actor but the idea that an ancient, martial arts-proficient guardian has been reincarnated as a TV reporter is a bit silly. The same can be said for Amanda Brooks' character Sara, also a reincarnated ancient guardian who can help the good Imoogi fully develop its powers. Also reincarnated as a Caucasian is their master, Robert Forster (*Alligator*, *Jackie Brown*), who gives the best performance in the film.

As noted, the American cast didn't do the film any favors at the American box office, where it only earned around $10 million dollars.

Sequels have been rumored since the film's release, and in 2016, *D-War II: Mysteries of the Dragon* was announced. Time will tell if it ever sees the light of day.

Final Word Though the storyline is still a little too derivative of other films, the special effects have come a long way since *Yonggary,* and this is a much better film overall.

REIGO
KING OF THE SEA MONSTERS

(INDEPENDENT)
Release Date: May 10, 2008
Alternate Titles: *Deep Sea Monster Reigo* (Japan) *Reigo vs. Yamato* (Germany)
Reigo: Monster from the Depths (Czech Republic)

Directed by: Shinpei Hayashiya **Special Effects by:** Shinpei Hayashiya
Screenplay by: Shinpei Hayashiya & Keita Toriumi **Music by:** Keiichiro Kitazono
Cast: Yukijiro Hotaro (Officer Noboru Osako), Taiyo Sugiura (Ensign Takeshi Kaido), Susumu Kurobe (Captain Yamagami), Mai Nanami (Chie)

Widescreen, Color, 81 Minutes

*I*n September of 1942, Captain Yamagami and his crew pilot the legendary battleship Yamato to rendezvous with the Japanese fleet in Micronesia. Along the way, they stop near the Truk Islands, where the disbelieving officers are warned of monsters lurking in the depths. True to the locals' words, the next night, the ship spots a strange creature in the water which they shoot and kill. Soon after, the ship is ravaged by giant man-sized "Bonefish" who kills several of the crew. Not far behind them is the giant sea monster Reigo, who engages in a titanic struggle with the Yamato. A plan created by ensign Kaido, wherein the ship's ballast tanks will be intentionally flooded to angle the ship's cannons downward, is implemented (the cannons are aimed too high to hit Reigo). The maneuver works, and the ship strikes a killing blow to Reigo.

Background & Commentary In 2003, the fan film *Gamera 4: Truth* by Shinpei Hayashiya was released. That film attempted to resolve *Gamera 3: Revenge of Irys*'s many (to Hayashiya) unanswered questions. Two years later, Hayashiya surprised the world with this low-budget, yet well-crafted and original film.

The storyline is brought to life with various kaiju eiga stars. In the lead is Taiyo Sugiura of *Ultraman Cosmos*, while at the helm of the ship is none other than the original *Ultraman*, Susumu Kurobe. Along for the ride is Yukijiro Hotaro, better known as Inspector Osako from the Gamera films (a role he even reprised for *Gamera 4: Truth*). His character in this film is even named after Osako (and in the film's epilogue, it is hinted that his son will grow up to be the Inspector Osako from the Gamera films). Each of the three leads is driven to survive for varying reasons: Osako to return to his pregnant wife, Ensign Kaido for his sweetheart, and Captain Yamagami just hopes to keep the men under his command alive.

Due to its limited budget, *Reigo King of the Sea Monsters* is not a film to be judged harshly. The Reigo puppet is fantastic in its design and many fans call it a cross between Godzilla and a shark (or if nothing else, a better version of Dagara from *Rebirth of Mothra 2*). Also frightening are the man-sized bonefish, for which one full-scale prop was created.

The CGI for Reigo itself is mostly OK for the time period and budget in which it was constrained to, but the CGI Yamato is probably the film's poorest creation. As far as good CGI goes, there are some truly wonderful shots of Reigo leaping from the water and sailing over the battleship. The main money shot is pulled off well, in which Reigo is blasted midair by a cannon creating a red mist of blood.

Though filmed and completed in 2005, it was not officially released in Japan until 2008. The film was officially released in the United States on DVD in 2019.

Final Word Held back by only its budget, *Reigo King of the Sea Monsters'* excellent story deserves to have a big-budget remake one day.

MONSTER X STRIKES BACK: ATTACK THE G8 SUMMIT

(SHOCHIKU)
Release Date: July 26, 2008
Alternate Titles: *Guilala's Counterattack: Lake Toyo Summit Crisis* (Japan)
Monster X vs. the G8 Summit (Germany)

Directed by: Minoru Kawasaki **Special Effects by:** Hiroshi Butsuda **Screenplay by:** Masakazu Migita **Music by:** Yasuhiko Fukuda **Cast:** Natsuki Kato (Sumire Sumidagawa), Kato Kazuki (Sanpei Toyama), Jon Heese (President Burger), Hide Fukumoto (Prime Minister Sanzo Ibe), Yosuke Natsuki (Narumi Secretary), Susumu Kurobe (Kimura Secretary), Yuri Morishita (Traitor Translator) **Suit Performers:** "Beat" Takeshi Kitano (Take-Majin), Ryu Hariken/Yuichi Okada (Guilala)

Widescreen, Color, 98 Minutes

During the 2008 G8 Summit in Japan, a meteorite crashes in Sapporo, releasing the space monster Guilala. As he advances towards the G8 Summit, the world leaders (for their own individually selfish reasons) decide to stay and come up with a plan to fight the monster. At the same time, two journalists investigate the story of a monster called Take-Majin, prophesied to battle Guilala. Every one of the world leaders' increasingly inane schemes to kill Guilala fails. But as a North Korean nuke heads for the monster, Take-Majin appears. After a pitched battle, the god-actor-monster manages to kill Guilala.

Background & Commentary A sequel to Shochiku's 1967 *The X From Outer Space* starring the monster Guilala had been bandied about for over ten years before this film finally came to fruition. Originally, it began life in 1995 as a serious story where Guilala would returned from space (though contrary to rumors, the monster was never set to battle Gappa, from Nikkatsu's *Gappa the Triphibian Monster* [1967]).

Monster X Strikes Back: Attack the G8 Summit is directed by Japanese parody-favorite Minoru Kawasaki, director of such fare as *The World Sinks Except Japan* (2006). Though Guilala is correctly presented in a comic context, *Monster X Strikes Back* is never terribly funny, though it does have some great moments sure to delight fans familiar with the genre. The best occurs when a little boy literally appears out of nowhere in the military planning session to tell them to give the monster a name (he likes "Guilala" because it reminds him of a Gila monster he saw at a zoo) and is promptly thrown out. Also humorous are the motivations behind the various political figures for fighting the monster, namely the U.S. president who just wants to boost his ratings in the polls and the French prime minister trying to get his beautiful Japanese interpreter (who turns out to be a North Korean spy) into bed. The English-speaking actors never master the accents of the nations they are representing though, making the Japanese version a confusing affair for English-speaking viewers. In the film's defense though, it wasn't filmed with English speaking people in mind, and to the Japanese audience the scenes are obviously a bit different in that respect.

Worst of all, nearly all of the Guilala footage in the film is stock-footage from the original 1967 *The X From Outer Space*! The new footage mostly consists of Guilala tooling about on a set dealing with nonsensical ways to destroy him and battling his opponent, Take Majin. The latter makes for an amusing—if not overly crude— sequence in which Take Majin saves Japan from a nuclear missile attack by catching it with his butt.

The film was shown at various film festivals and not surprisingly was a dud in Japan. The film saw its American premiere at G-Fest, a Godzilla convention held in Chicago, where most fans were fairly happy with it.

Final Word Overall, *Monster X Strikes Back: Attack the G8 Summit* is a good idea that never lives up to its premise.

SUPERIOR ULTRAMAN 8 BROTHERS

(TSUBURAYA PRODUCTIONS)
Release Date: September 13, 2008
Japanese Title: *Great Decisive Battle! Super 8 Ultra Brothers*

Directed by: Takeshi Yagi **Special Effects by:** Takeshi Yagi **Screenplay by:** Keiichi Hasegawa **Music by:** Toshihiko Sahashi **Cast:** Hiroshi Nagano (Daigo/voice of Ultraman Tiga), Takeshi Tsuruno (Asuka/voice of Ultraman Dyna), Takeshi Yoshioka (Gamu/voice of Ultraman Gaia), Shunji Igarashi (Mirai Hibino/voice of Ultraman Mebius), Susumu Kurobe (Shin Hayata/voice of Ultraman), Koji Moritsugu (Dan Moroboshi/voice of Ultra Seven), Jiro Dan (Hideki Go/voice of Ultraman Jack), Keiji Takamine (Seiji Hokuto/voice of Ultraman Ace) **Suit Performers:** Hideyoshi Iwata (Ultraman Tiga), Daisuke Fukuda (Ultraman Dyna), Tatsunari Fukushima/Daisuke Terai (Ultraman Gaia), Hideyoshi Iwata/Sanshiro Wada (Ultraman Mebius), Kenya Soma (Ultraman), Satoshi Yamamoto (Ultra Seven/King Silvergon), Shinya Iwasaki (Ultraman Jack/King Pandon), Koji Maruyama (Ultraman Ace), Kazunori Yokoo (King Gesura), Ro Nishimura (King Goldras), Hiroshi Suenaga (Super Alien Hipporito)

Widescreen, Color, 97 Minutes

I n an alternate universe, three boys named Daigo, Asuka, and Gamu, who watched the original Ultraman series on TV in 1966, have grown up to become businessmen in Yokohama and have lost sight of their childhood dreams. One day, a mirror city appears in the sky then mysteriously vanishes. After this, Daigo begins having dreams that he is Ultraman Tiga and also that several men he knows are also secretly Ultramen. The real Ultraman Mebius manages to jump dimensions and eventually convinces Daigo of his secret abilities. Daigo in turn convinces this world's versions of Shin Hayata, Dan Moroboshi, Hideki Go, Seiji Hokuto, and also his two friends, that they are Ultramen as well. All seven Ultra Brothers transform to save Mebius and the city of Yokohama from an evil alien intent on destroying it.

Background & Commentary Much like the previous year's *Ultraman Mebius and the Ultra Brothers*, *Superior 8 Ultra Brothers* continues the generational crossover that began in the aforementioned film. In a move similar to *Star Trek Generations* (1994), this is the first Ultraman movie to mix the Heisei and Showa continuity Ultramen together for one film. It features the main stars of *Ultraman, Ultra Seven, Return of Ultraman, Ultraman Ace, Ultraman Mebius, Ultraman Tiga, Ultraman Dyna,* and *Ultraman Gaia*. It also features many of their love interests, such as Yuriko Hishimi from *Ultra Seven* and Hiroko Sakurai from *Ultraman*. The idea that young, alternate-world versions of Tiga, Dyna, and Gaia grew up watching the original Ultramen on television is an inspired concept. However, this same concept could also make the film confusing for non-fans. Apparently, all of the Showa timeline Ultra TV series exist in this universe (including *Ultraman Mebius*), just not the Heisei Ultramen such as *Ultraman Tiga*, etc.

The film also has a fun fish out of water aspect in that the else-world Ultramen are unaware of their powers. Though his role here is brief, actor Shunji Igarashi gets some great scenes as the "real" version of Mirai, who crosses universes and then gets mistaken for "Shunji Igarashi" by a group of child fans who recognize him from TV. The most delightful scene happens when Mirai runs from Ultraman to Ultraman, with none of them recognizing him. The best occurs when he asks Ultraman Ace to combine his rings with his wife (in the first episodes of *Ultraman Ace*, a man and woman clicked their rings together to jointly transform into the titular hero) so that they can transform. Naturally, they have no idea what he is talking about and think he is crazy.

It is scenes like these that make most of the film's enjoyment, but the same can't be said for the action. This film lacks a high-octane opening like many of the other Ultraman films, and the first two monster battles are sub-par. Furthermore, the end battle is one of the weaker ones of the franchise, and the main thrill mostly comes from seeing the Heisei and Showa Ultramen together for the first time. The climax also moves into supernatural territory like *Ghostbusters* (1984) or *Raiders of the Lost Ark* (1981) when a bunch of monster spirits combine into one giant being. Sadly, the resulting villain is one of the series' poorer CGI creations even though the design itself is excellent.

Though it can come off as so nostalgic it's corny to some, for fans who actually grew up just like the three protagonists watching the original series, it is a heartfelt experience. This certainly rang true at the box office. Over the course of only one month, it managed to earn $8 million U.S. dollars, making it the most successful Ultraman film of all time.

Final Word Even though it lacks thrills in the action department, the film stands out amongst the pantheon of Ultraman movies as one of the most endearing of the entire series.

GEHARA:
THE DARK AND LONG-HAIRED MONSTER

(NHK)
Broadcast Date: February 24, 2009
Japanese Title: *Giant Long-Haired Monster Gehara*

Directed by: Kiyotaka Taguchi **Special Effects by:** Kiyotaka Taguchi **Screenplay by:** Jun Awazu **Music by:** Shingo Terasawa **Cast:** Shiro Sano (Dr. Murakami), Ken Osawa (Hideo Akihara), Jiji Bu (Doctor), Mark Chinnery (Dr. Anderson), Hiroyuki Watanabe (Self Defense Force Commander), Mina Fuji (Momoko)

Widescreen, Color, 17 Minutes

When a fishing boat at sea is attacked by a hairy monster, the lone survivor inexplicably loses all of his hair. Dr. Murakami believes the beast to be from Japanese folklore: the Keukegen specter. A reporter then investigates a forest shrine dedicated to the spook and finds a group of bald followers. They reveal that the seal which keeps the monster imprisoned has been broken. The hairy monster, dubbed Gehara, marches on Kanazawa and when attacked by the self defense forces, begins emitting a noxious gas. Gehara is then combated with a new invention, the Gas Vortical Device "Fujin."

Background & Commentary A TV Short from NHK's PAPHOOO! program, *Gehara the Dark and Long-Haired Monster* is an affectionate parody of kaiju eiga from the 1950s and 60s. Notable scenes recreate shots from *Ghidorah, the Three-Headed Monster* (1964) and *Varan* (1958). Despite being the star of what amounts to a spoof, Gehara is still well-executed and sometimes quite frightening. The project was the brainchild of none other than Shinji Higuchi, special effects director of the Heisei Gamera films.

The cast is composed of many stars of recent kaiju eiga, among them Shiro Sano (*Godzilla 2000*; *Godzilla, Mothra, and King Ghidorah: Giant Monsters All-Out Attack*), Kanji Tsuda (*Gamera the Brave*), and Hiroyuki Watanabe (*Godzilla, Mothra, and King Ghidorah: Giant Monsters All-Out Attack*). The film's story hits all of the usual beats—as it should being a tribute film—with the monster being introduced through a mystery attack at sea, being investigated by a reporter and a professor, and finally being confronted by the military via a very creative plan. The short TV film ends with a teaser for a nonexistent sequel entitled *Gehara: Monster Martial Law*.

Final Word Perhaps due to its short length, *Gehara: The Long and Dark-Haired Monster* amounts to one of the best and most lovingly crafted spoofs of the genre.

DEMEKING
THE SEA MONSTER

(JOLLY ROGER)
Release Date: March 7, 2009
Japanese Title: *Demeking*

Directed by: Kotaro Terauchi **Special Effects by:** Tsuyoshi Kazuno
Screenplay by: Takashi Imashiro **Music by:** Chika Fujino **Cast:** Takeshi Nadagi
(Nakajima), Kohei Kiyasu (Kameoka), Sato Panch (Kenji), Ryoma Ito (Masaru),
Amane Niaki (Hiro)

Widescreen, Color, 99 Minutes

Set in 1970, Nakajima is a loner who works at Mamahama Marine Park. A group of misfit boys led by Kameoka, who call themselves the Explorers Club, are intrigued by Nakajima and his sailboat containing samurai armor. Nakajima tells them it is to battle the monster Demeking, prophecized to invade earth in 2019, and sets them off on a mad scavenger hunt before leaving for Tokyo. The kids wonder if the tale of Demeking was all just a wild story Nakajima made up before leaving. That night, Kameoka dreams of Demeking, and afterward decides to write a novel about the prophecy not coming true. Eventually, Kameoka loses sight of his dream and gives up.

Background & Commentary If one doesn't know what to expect when going into *Demeking, the Sea Monster*, it's a sure bet they'll hate it. Actually, even if they do know what to expect, chances are they may still hate it. The best way to describe the film is a character study akin to Richard Linklater's *Boyhood* (2014) with a giant monster dream sequence thrown into the mix.

The scene begins with a fighter jet crashing dramatically into a bay. After that, what appears to be a floating meteorite coursing with electricity glides through the skies ominously. When it finally touches down, the titular monster, which looks something like a giant slug that can shoot a fiery atomic ray, emerges from it. Despite its silly design, the beast is surprisingly well-executed. Much like the 1970s Godzilla films, Demeking spectacularly sets fire to an oil refinery in the bay. Demeking then glides through the city, laying a multitude of eggs in his wake while Kameoka follows snapping pictures. The scene lasts for a whole ten minutes before it is finally revealed to be Kameoka's dream.

It is only after the dream scene is over that the film's themes begin to be fully explored, and they certainly aren't about giant monsters. The film's tone becomes more melancholy right away as Kameoka decides to disband the Explorer's Club, perhaps signaling childhood's end. The film may also be trying to make a statement about a generation oversaturated by TV monsters who wish for excitement, and in this sense, makes for an interesting and depressing inverse to 2008's uplifting *Superior 8 Ultra Brothers*.

As Kameoka struggles with his existence, he decides to write a novel based on himself, his friends, and the fictional kaiju Demeking. Perhaps it is his way of coping with the disappointment of normal, boring life. Kameoka is certainly presented as someone who has trouble coping with reality. He is clearly several years older than his younger childish friends, is bullied by his peers, and believes he will take over his family's business, and therefore needn't worry about doing well at school. But after a year and a half time jump, it is apparent this is likely no longer the case as the business is fading away due to the changing times. Likewise, his novel, which he believes will win a sci-fi prize, will most likely never catch on. The final shots show Kameoka working on said novel, his desk littered with crumpled pages. At one point, he looks at a bum wandering the beach, and one has to wonder if he is looking at his own future. Later, we see the same desk minus the writing tablet, implying Kameoka has given up on his novel. Following that is a shot of Demeking's asteroid hurtling through space. Is it a fantasy or reality? The last shot is particularly Linklater-esque, with the character of Nakajima eating his breakfast alone in Tokyo when the credits abruptly begin to roll.

The film was directed by Kotaro Terauchi, who also helmed similar offbeat fare such as *Shaolin Grandma* (2008). It was inspired by the 1991 manga Demeking (or "bug-eyed king") by Takashi Imashiro. The film had a limited theatrical release in Japan via Jolly Roger Inc. and was released to DVD in America fairly quickly.

Final Word *Demeking, the Sea Monster* can be a good film when viewed with the proper expectations, just so long as those expectations aren't actually a giant monster film.

RAIGA
GOD OF THE MONSTERS

(INDEPENDENT)
Release Date: August 15, 2009
Alternate Titles: *Raiga: The Monster from the Deep Sea* (Japan)

Directed by: Shinpei Hayashiya **Special Effects by:** Shuichi Kokumai **Screenplay by:** Shinpei Hayashiya **Music by:** Keiichiro Kitazono **Cast:** Yukijiro Hotaru (Hajime), Miyu Oriyama (Matsuri), Mao Urata (Hibari), Manami Enosawa (Akari), Makoto Inamiya (Commander Kito)

Widescreen, Color, 80 Minutes

60 years after the monster Reigo sunk the battleship Yamato, a new version of the monster, called Raiga, surfaces in Asakusa Japan. The first man to see the monster is Hajime, who begins selling t-shirts and trinkets based upon the kaiju after its appearance. The defense forces endure several failed attempts to kill the monster as Raiga ravages Asakusa. Just when they think they've killed the beast, it revives when a second Raiga shows up. The two creatures battle and the second Raiga is destroyed, leaving a crater in the center of Asakusa.

Background & Commentary If you loved *Reigo, King of the Sea Monsters*, it's debatable how you'll feel about *Raiga, God of the Monsters*. Whereas *Reigo* was a straight monster movie, this one is a spoof of the genre, and a good one at that.

Whether you can get on board with the spoof angle or not, one thing's for sure: *Raiga* doesn't skimp on the monster action for a low budget feature! *Raiga* begins with a monster fight right off the bat between Raiga and a giant bonefish on the ocean floor. It has no bearing on the story, but it's certainly fun to watch. In the very next scene, a horde of bonefish kills two fishermen, and if you're a fan of the first film, it's interesting to see the creatures in a modern setting. Soon after this we meet our lead played by Shusuke Kaneko/Shinpei Hayashiya stock player Yukijiro Hotaru. He is not playing a descendant of his character from *Reigo* (not that I can tell at least) and portrays a widowed father of three young women. He's really just an observer, though; a sort of avatar for the audience while a small defense force decides how to battle the monster.

Raiga's first scenes are not only a hoot, they are also fun to watch from a classic tokusatsu perspective. In an age of CGI monsters, Raiga is still brought to life via suitmation. While Reigo was more of a shark-like version of Godzilla and lacked anthropomorphic features, Raiga looks very much like a more ocean-centric version of Godzilla. The monster resembles a bipedal version of Reigo with flipper-like arms, and the dorsal plates on the back are very similar both to Godzilla's and those of a shark. The monster doesn't fire any oral rays, though, and instead manipulates lighting blasts either from its dorsal plates or its hands.

There are many funny scenes of people evacuating Asakusa as Raiga attacks. These scenes probably fare better with Japanese viewers who can get all the nuances, but many of the jokes still translate for western viewers. One has the police trying to hurry along three drunks—one man and two women. The women eventually get with the program and run off, but the man is oblivious and keeps staggering along at a slower pace. "I'll catch you at the next bar!" he shouts after them. Meanwhile, in the monster control room, a spoof scene relatable to monster fans occurs. Ever since *Godzilla Raids Again* (1955), the Japanese military has often placed crude monster figures atop tabletop maps to show where the monster is. That idea is spoofed here when one of the gruffer looking soldiers places a small baby doll on the table. "Doesn't look very menacing," one of the bureaucrats complains. The soldier explains that they didn't have time to make a monster figure and that this will have to do. Back on the streets, Hajime and his two Japanese friends are joined by two Caucasian onlookers who mistake Raiga for Godzilla. Hajime and his friends very sternly correct the men in what I interpret to be a nod to Toho's overzealous lawyers. In a scene soon after, the three men appear to perish after a military onslaught drives away Raiga. The men, in their apparent death throes, lament not being able to eat their favorite Japanese dishes one more time, crying out the names of each. When Hayashiya pans over to the two Americans they cry out the names of Burger King and McDonalds, and one even gasps, "I'm loving it!" (the McDonald's slogan).

But Hajime and his friends aren't dead, as we cut to two months later where Hajime is selling t-shirts and trinkets based upon the monster. Raiga soon returns to attack Asakusa a second time, and Hajime excitedly exclaims that he'll be a millionaire! Even if one doesn't appreciate the comedy, the effects scenes are undeniably fun to watch as Raiga gets a great deal of screen time trouncing the city. A second Raiga even shows up to battle the first, though the battle maneuvers are a bit limited. The two monsters collide their electric beams midair à la *Godzilla vs. Mechagodzilla* (1974/1993). This creates a massive explosion that decimates the town and kills the new Raiga. The original Raiga then proceeds to bend over and urinate all over the city to mark its property. The monster then returns to the sea.

The film ends strong from a comic perspective by spoofing the epilogues of monster movies like *Godzilla vs. Hedorah*, *Gamera vs. Zigra* (both 1971), and many others. In those films, the characters lament the dangers of pollution as the monsters wander off. While in those two films the scenes were warranted by the story's themes, many other movies, like *Godzilla vs. Space Godzilla* (1994), seemed to insert rather arbitrary moments about environmental pollution. As Raiga's characters stand atop a hill, one of them randomly proclaims that Raiga came to teach them all about global warming! "Yes, that's it," adds Hajime as one of his daughters ponders how exactly the monster did this.

Final Word If you enjoy the spoof aspect along with the effects, then *Raiga* should have double the appeal to you. But if the effects are all that interest you, the film is still worth watching for those alone too.

MEGA MONSTER BATTLE: ULTRA GALAXY LEGENDS: THE MOVIE

(TSUBURAYA PRODUCTIONS)
Release Date: December 12, 2009
Japanese Title: *Giant Monster Battle: Ultra Galaxy Legends*

Directed by: Koichi Sakamoto **Special Effects by:** Hajime Koyasu **Screenplay by:** Junya Okabe & Tatsuro Yuji **Music by:** Mike Verta **Cast:** Shota Minami (Rei), Shunji Igarashi (Mirai Hibino/voice of Mebius), Susumu Kurobe (Shin Hayata/voice of Ultraman), Koji Moritsugu (Dan/voice of Ultra Seven), Hiroyuki Miyasako (voice of Belial), Miyano Mamoru (voice of Ultraman Zero) **Suit Performers:** Masaki Onishi (Ultraman Zero/Ultraman Taro/Ultraman Mebius/Zoffy/Ultraman Max/Ultraman Powered), Hirokazu Iwagami (Belial/Ultra Seven/Ultraman Leo/Gomora/Dada/Babarue), Hiroyuki Inomata (Ultraman/Ultraman Ace/Reimon), Jun Yamashita (the Ultra Mother, Yullian, Ultrawoman Beth), Namihei Koshige (Pigmon), Hideyoshi Iwata (Mobutraman), Makoto Ito (the Ultra King)

Widescreen, Color, 96 Minutes

When the evil Ultraman Belial is freed from Ultra prison, he steals the light from M78 causing the entire planet and its Ultra denizens to freeze. When Mebius returns to the planet's surface, Ultraman and Ultra Seven tell him their hope lies in a half-human Raybrad alien who can control monsters named Rei. Mebius collects Rei and then regroups with Ultraman and Ultra Seven. The quartet travels to the Monster Graveyard where Belial has resurrected an army of monsters. They are unsuccessful in defeating Belial, and at one point, it appears that Seven has been mortally wounded. Before he expires, Seven sends for his son Ultraman Zero, training on a faraway planet with Ultraman Leo. Zero arrives in the nick of time and defeats Belial, who then appears to die and fuse all the monster corpses together into one giant being. With the help of Rei, his pet monster Gomora, and the other Ultramen, Ultraman Zero defeats the giant beast, M78 returns to normal, and peace is restored to the galaxy.

Background & Commentary Encouraged by the success of *Superior Ultraman 8 Brothers* (2008), Tsuburaya Productions set out to make their biggest Ultraman movie yet. Like *Ultraman Mebius and Ultra Brothers* (2006), this film opens with a spectacular off-world battle with Mebius streaking through the stars and hopping off asteroids while battling Bemular. The whole film takes place off-earth, and in an interesting departure, more time is spent with the Ultra beings rather than the human cast. In fact, no humans are even glimpsed until 23 minutes into the movie!

On the negative side, this also makes the film a little harder to connect with. On top of that, the ensemble is so huge it has no central protagonist. At first, it appears to be Ultraman Mebius, who eventually fades into the background. In the middle of the film, it is Rei, a half-human/alien hybrid with the ability to control the monsters (and more importantly, the star of the then-current Ultraman series *Ultra Galaxy: Mega Monster Battle*) who takes over the narrative. And by the picture's third act, the newly-created Ultraman Zero has become the lead.

In spite of its narrative flaws, the film still serves as both a great celebration and exploration of just how rich the Ultra universe is. The score by Mike Verta has a certain *Star Wars* quality to it and is stellar overall, considering most of his film scores are for low-budget rip-offs such as *Independents' Day* (2016). Most importantly for fans, nearly every Ultraman gets a cameo, and just about every fight-match-up imaginable takes place. However, one of the biggest surprises occurs when Dan Moroboshi unleashes his three classic capsule monsters when he is unable to transform on M78. Though gratifying, some of the surprises are a bit too nonsensical, such as Ultraman Dyna popping up out of nowhere. Conspicuously absent from the last two films, Ultraman Leo finally makes his big screen debut training Ultraman Zero.

It's difficult to say just what the highlight battle of the film is, but it's likely when Ultraman Mebius teams up with Gomora (operating as *Ultra Galaxy's* heroic Godzilla-type) to battle the monster army—a strange but delightful sight. The spectacular battle culminates in what appears to be the death of Ultra Seven, and in a very *Star Trek II: Wrath of Khan*-style moment, he "expires" in front of his estranged son, who has only just learned of his parentage. The scene would have been more memorable had Seven stayed dead, but being such a popular character there was no way Tsuburaya Productions would let him stay dead. Consequently, he reappears alive and well during the epilogue.

In the final climactic battle, wherein all the monster corpses fuse together into one devilish beast, it probably looked fantastic on paper—

and it does have its moments—but in the end, it's too reminiscent of the final boss battle in a video game.

Mega Monster Battle aimed for a worldwide release and surprisingly managed to be distributed by Warner Bros, just not in America. Its grosses were healthy at the box office even if they didn't exceed its predecessor, and another sequel—to star Ultraman Zero—was a virtual guarantee.

Final Word Though each and every battle is spectacular, the film is hard to appreciate when watched during its entirety due to battle fatigue by the audience.

DEATH KAPPA

(NIKKATSU)
Release Date: November 27, 2010

Directed by: Tomoo Haraguchi **Special Effects by:** Tomoo Haraguchi **Screenplay by:** Masakazu Migita **Music by:** Uncredited **Cast:** Misato Hirata (Kanako Kawado), Mika (Yuriko), Daniel Aguilar Gutierrez (Professor Tanaka), Matt Alt (Kappa Expert), Hiroko Sakurai (Fujiko Kawado) **Suit Performers:** Kazunori Yokoo (Death Kappa), Toshio Miyake (Hangyolas)

Widescreen, Color, 79 Minutes

Kanako, a failed pop singer, returns to her rural village where her dying grandmother instructs her to care for the Kappa, a Japanese water yokai. A group of Japanese nationalists with ties to the Nazis kidnap Kanako. The group reveals their plan to create an army of kappa-human-fish hybrids. When the Kappa arrives to save Kanako, an atomic bomb goes off mutating him and one of the fish men into giant proportions. The giant fish-man, now more reptilian and named Hangyolas, tramples Japan before it is defeated by the Death Kappa, who, in turn, also tramples Japan before being calmed down by a surviving Kanako.

Background & Commentary 2010 saw the release of yet another kaiju spoof, this time through a recently-resurrected Nikkatsu. Rather than revive Gappa, Nikkatsu crafted the similarly-sounding yet totally new kaiju, Death Kappa, based upon a mythical creature from Japanese folklore. Here, the titular beast shares the same turtle shell and ugly features of a traditional kappa and eventually grows to kaiju size.

Overall, the film is a fairly competent parody of the kaiju genre. The film's first scene is reminiscent of the original 1954 *Godzilla*, set in what looks like Dr. Yamane's study as an unnamed professor talks about the Yeti and Nessie, while in the background the roars of various Toho kaiju can be heard. After this, the title shot is reminiscent of *Varan's* (1958) and has a similar song to boot. The shrine/Nazi bunker that Kanako is taken to is somewhat reminiscent of Asakura's bunker in *Gamera 3: Revenge of Irys* (1999), and the Fishmen are similar to the creatures from

Toei's *Terror Beneath the Sea* (1966). The female villainess, killed halfway through the film, is the story's most interesting character and brings to mind Fatima Blush from the unofficial James Bond film *Never Say Never Again* (1983). Otherwise, the cast generates little interest overall.

Death Kappa doesn't really pick up until the appearance of Hangyolas, the enemy monster. The beast looks like an *Ultraman* foe, coming from the classic Godzilla school of bipedal spiky reptilians. The film's funniest moment, which provides relevant commentary on today's society, occurs when some panicked onlookers stop to take a selfie with the rampaging kaiju in the background. The miniature city set looks like it came straight from the 1970s and the wires are purposely visible on helicopters and jets (the pilots flying those jets are wearing curious, yet still hilarious, eyeliner). The film even spoofs classic 1960s Godzilla volleyball when the monsters pick up the spherical oil tanks at an oil refinery and begin hurling them at one another. In another humorous twist, despite all the destruction he's caused, everything is hunky-dory at the end when Death Kappa leaves Japan, children cheering him on and all. The last shot of the beast swimming out to sea is even a recreation of the final shot of *Gamera, Guardian of the Universe* (1995).

Death Kappa didn't do much in the way of Japanese box office returns, though it quickly made its way to American home video via Tokyo Shock.

Final Word With a better storyline to back up the end's monster action, this film could be much more likable, but instead, it's just a curious dud.

ULTRAMAN ZERO:
THE MOVIE

(TSUBURAYA PRODUCTIONS)
Release Date: December 23, 2010
Japanese Title: *Ultraman Zero - The Movie: Super Battle! Belial's Galactic Empire*

Directed by: Yuichi Abe **Special Effects by:** Masashi Kuwahara **Screenplay by:** Yuichi Abe **Music by:** Kenji Kawai **Cast:** Tomo Koyanagi (Run), Tatsuomi Hamada (Nao), Tao Tsuchiya (Princess Emerana Luludo Esmeralda), Hiroyuki Miyasako (voice of Belial) **Suit Performers:** Hideyoshi Iwata (Ultraman Zero), Daisuke Terai (Glenfire), Tatsunari Fukushima (Jean Bot), Keita Rikimaru (Mirror Knight), Hiroshi Suenaga (Kaiser Belial)

Widescreen, Color, 100 Minutes

When a robot army attacks M78, it signals the return of Ultraman Belial from across an alternate galaxy. Ultraman Zero crosses into the parallel universe to investigate and finds himself on a desert planet where he saves the life of two brothers. When Run is killed, Zero takes on his human form and looks after Run's younger brother, Nao. The duo is joined by Princess Esmeralda and her sentient ship, Star Corvette Jean-Bird, and together the trio searches for the Shield of Barahdi—a mythical object said to have the power to defeat Belial. On their way, they are aided by misfit heroes Glenfire and Mirror Knight and manage to find the shield on the Planet of Mirrors. Belial manages to capture Zero, but the young Ultraman is rescued by his friends. They begin a great battle with the evil Ultraman, who morphs into a new and even bigger reptilian form. Finally, the Shield of Barahdi reveals itself to be Ultraman Noa, who gives Zero a much-needed power boost to finally defeat Belial. With Belial destroyed for good, Zero restores Run's life and sets out for the stars along with his new friends.

Background & Commentary Though it would appear on the posters and advertisements that *Ultraman Zero: The Revenge of Belial* should be even more crowded than its predecessor, *Mega Monster Battle: Ultra Galaxy Legends - The Movie* (2009), it's not. The numerous Ultra Brothers all receive cameos, but this happens at the film's beginning, and they are not seen again very often once Zero transcends universes. It is here that the film finds its footing with brothers Run and Nao, two likable and relatable characters that the film centers on. They are found on a desert planet, which slightly resembles Tatooine from *Star Wars* (their clothes mirror Luke Skywalker's). When Zero takes over Run, it makes for a much more engaging storyline as young Nao is fully aware that this is not his brother. This is just one reason why despite being set in another universe, this film is much more down to earth than its predecessor. Additionally, since the film had a production period of only nine months, this meant the extensive green screen shooting (as done on the previous picture) would have to be scaled back. As a result, the increased on-location shooting for this movie is noticeable. That's not to say the film doesn't have some fantastic CGI locales though; the Planet of Mirrors is especially noteworthy. Another memorable CGI visual is the film's equivalent of the Death Star: a giant, clawed hand the size of an entire planet.

The film is also something of a fantasy quest story and is an exceptionally welcome departure from the usual Ultraman formula. The MacGuffin is the Shield of Barahdi, which turns out to be Ultraman Noa (the hero from *Ultraman: The Next*). Instead of the numerous returning Ultra Brothers of the last story, this film reintroduces heroes from other 1970s-era Tsuburaya TV series heretofore unrelated to the Ultraman franchise. Among them are the heroes Mirror Knight (inspired by 1971's *Mirrorman*), Glenfire (inspired by 1973's *Fire Man*), and Jean Bot (inspired by 1973's *Jumborg Ace*). Naturally, these characters' origins are greatly altered to fit into the parallel world of this movie. For instance, *Jumborg Ace* centered around an airplane that transformed into a robot while in this film, Jean Bot is a transforming spaceship. Though the robot doesn't transform until the climax, its scene battling one of Belial's evil generals amidst some giant, alien skyscrapers is among the film's best moments.

Sadly, the climax falls victim to the usual Ultraman movie bugaboo when Belial inexplicably turns himself into a Space Godzilla-like creature complete with a tail. Zero and his friends somehow overcome him in an overzealous use of CGI ray blasts when their hopes all work to revive Ultraman Noa, who then gifts Zero with a bow and arrow-type weapon to kill Belial.

Shochiku returned as the distributor for the film's release, and it grossed ¥400 million ($3,586,000).

Final Word Despite its flaws and occasional predictability, *Ultraman Zero: The Revenge of Belial* is an enjoyable film that stands head and shoulders above the other Ultraman films due to its well-balanced handling of the humans and monsters.

ULTRAMAN SAGA

(TSUBURAYA PRODUCTIONS)
Release Date: March 24, 2012

Directed by: Hideki Oka **Special Effects by:** Masashi Kuwahara **Screenplay by:** Keiichi Hasegawa **Music by:** Fumio Hara **Cast:** Daigo (Taiga Nozome), Takeshi Tsuruno (Shin Asuka/voice of Ultraman Dyna), Taiyo Sugiura (Haruno Musashi), Sayaka Akimoto (Anna), Ayaka Umeda (Misato), Sae Miyazawa (Sawa), Hideo Higashikokubaru (voice of Alien Bat), Mamoru Miyano (voice of Ultraman Zero) **Suit Performers:** Hideyoshi Iwata (Ultraman Zero/Ultraman Saga), Daisuke Terai (Ultraman Cosmos), Daisuke Fukuda/ Keita Rikimaru (Ultraman Dyna), Tatsunari Fukushima (Alien Bat), Hiroshi Suenaga (Hyper Zetton)

Widescreen, Color, 90 Minutes

On a parallel earth, Alien Bat has abducted nearly all humans and has overrun the world with monsters. A group of female survivors continues the fight by taking over the Earth Defense Force. Coming to their aid from another dimension is Taiga, a human pilot who is joined with Ultraman Zero against his will. Also coming to help is none other than Ultraman Cosmos. And, finally, on this earth is the unconscious form of Ultraman Dyna. As Taiga works through his compatibility issues to finally merge with Zero, he and Cosmos battle the dangerous "space dinosaur" Zetton, the mightiest monster in Alien Bat's arsenal. When the creature morphs into Hyper Zetton, Cosmos, Zero, and Dyna merge together into Ultraman Saga to defeat Hyper Zetton with the aid of the Earth Defense Force.

Background & Commentary After five solid films in a row, *Ultraman Saga* is something of a letdown for the franchise. The film has an undeniably cheaper feel to it than the last five, and it is evident a budget cut of some sort must have been in effect. On top of this, the film's production was delayed by a whole year because of the March 11, 2011 earthquake in Japan.

Like the last film, this story focuses on a heretofore unseen else-world with a fresh history. Ultraman Zero, again the lead Ultraman, jumps universes, and along for the ride are Ultraman Dyna (last seen in 2009's

Mega Monster Battle: Ultra Galaxy Legends - The Movie) and Ultraman Cosmos (the star of the 2001 series of the same name), not seen since the film *Ultraman Cosmos vs. Ultraman Justice: The Final Battle* (2003). Apart from the Ultramen, the film is centered around an all-female team called the Earth Defense Force, an innovative idea for the series. To play the all-female team, Tsuburaya Productions cast girls from the teen idol pop group AKB48 (so named because it initially comprised of 48 members from the Akihabara area of Tokyo).

In another strangely refreshing twist, rather than facing a giant monster that dwarfs them for the final battle, it turns out the alien "dinosaur" (though it looks more like an insect) that Zero, Dyna, and Cosmos initially defeat is just a precursor to the kaiju's final form. Instead, the beast morphs into a smaller, though more deadly, entity called Hyper Zetton. In response, the three Ultra Brothers merge into a new creation called Ultraman Saga—though "Ultraman Groot" might have been a better name as the radical design bears a resemblance to the character from *Guardians of the Galaxy* (2014). In another interesting twist, the lead human character Taiga (not to be confused with *Ultraman Tiga*) refuses to merge with Ultraman Zero despite the fact that he saved his life. Furthermore, Zero and Taiga have frequent conversations/arguments throughout the film via a special bracelet that allows them to communicate. Though for years Ultramen and their human hosts were separate entities, in this way the film explores the concept in an interesting new way. Furthermore, when we think Zero has finally forced Taiga to transform, Zero is only able to grow to a fraction of his normal height until Taiga accepts the transformation fully. Overall, this dynamic ends up being the film's saving grace, and there isn't much to recommend it beyond that.

Ultraman Saga debuted at the #4 spot at the Japanese box office during its first weekend of release and grossed 569 million yen ($5,183,900). To date, the film ended up being the last feature length Ultraman movie as subsequent entries often ran little over an hour in length and were often tied closely to an adjoining TV series.

Final Word Though full of fresh ideas, this Ultraman film has an unfortunate tired and uninspired feel.

PACIFIC RIM

(LEGENDARY PICTURES)
Release Date: July 12, 2013
Alternate Titles: *Pacific Titans* (South America) *Circle of Fire* (Brazil) *Ring of Fire* (Bulgaria) *Pacific Rim: Attack on Earth* (Croatia) *The Ring of Fire* (Greece) *Pacific Fight* (Estonia) *Rudra City* (India)

Directed by: Guillermo del Toro **Screenplay by:** Guillermo del Toro and Travis Beacham **Music by:** Ramin Djawadi **Cast:** Charlie Hunnam (Raleigh Becket), Rinko Kikuchi (Mako Mori), Idris Elba (Stacker Pentecost), Charlie Day (Dr. Newton Geiszler), Burn Gorman (Dr. Herman Gottlieb), Ron Perlman (Hannibal Chau)

Widescreen, Color, 132 Minutes

When aliens send kaiju to earth through a breach along the Pacific Rim, mankind responds by building Jaegers—giant robots operating under a two pilot system. Raleigh, a former Jaeger pilot who lost his brother and partner, is tracked down by his old commanding officer, Stacker Penticost, for one last hurrah before the Jaeger program is shut down in favor of a giant wall. When the wall fails, the Jaegers become more important than ever and a plan is put in place to pilot a Jaeger through the breach and detonate it on the other side. Raliegh finds his new partner in Pentecost's protégé Mako Mori, who lost her parents to kaiju at a young age. On one last drive, Pentecost, Mako, and Raliegh descend to the Pacific Rim where they face off against three kaiju at once. Pentecost and his Jaeger are destroyed, leaving Mako and Raleigh to breach the Pacific Rim and detonate their Jaeger. Both escape in the nick of time back to the other side while their Jaeger detonates, sealing the breach.

Background & Commentary *Pacific Rim* was born in the mind of writer Travis Beacham as he was taking a walk along a beach and imagined a monster battling a giant robot in the distance. His next train of thought was, "What if two people were piloting the robot together and one of them died?" From there, Beacham went home and began writing a treatment based on this idea. The year was 2007, but the film wasn't officially greenlit by Legendary Pictures until 2010. Guillermo Del Toro, whom Beacham was supposed to work with in 2006 on an axed project, took the directorial reigns.

Overall, Del Toro does a great job balancing a Japanese concept for Western sensibilities. The kaiju designs are appropriately weird and seem most comparable to Gamera foes (one even has a knife-shaped head like Guiron). Though all of the battles are great and each has their different merits, the standout of the film is easily the Hong Kong battle with Gipsy Danger and the two kaiju, Otachi and Leatherback. Nothing quite says spectacle like a giant robot carrying a boat through the streets of a city to bash in a kaiju's head. The monster sprouting wings is another surprise which leads to a battle above earth's atmosphere. This sequence isn't just fun for the spectacle, actors Charlie Day and Ron Perlman get to shine during this segment as well. The "bone slums" of Hong Kong are a fascinating locale and the concept of selling kaiju bones (and other parts) as medicine is a fantastic idea.

During this Hong Kong sequence, the film improves and expands upon a concept seen in *Gamera vs. Jiger* (1970); several of Hannibal Chau's men venture inside a dead monster that turns out to be pregnant. The baby monster naturally eats them and makes its way out of the womb and onto the streets where it lunges at Dr. Geiszler before dying. Chau comes up to it cockily and stabs it, stating he knew it wouldn't last more than a minute. The monster then comes back to life, eats him, and then, it seems, dies from eating Chau (who later cuts himself out of the monster in a surprise mid-credits scene).

Though the film was received well, the grosses in America came in under expectations. However, the film proved to be a big enough hit worldwide to warrant a sequel.

Final Word In essence, *Pacific Rim* does everything right that Legendary's *Godzilla* would do wrong next year as the visuals, characters, and monsters are colorful and plentiful.

GODZILLA

(LEGENDARY PICTURES)
Release Date: May 16, 2014

Directed by: Gareth Edwards **Special Effects by:** Jim Rygiel **Screenplay by:** Max Borenstein **Music by:** Alexandre Desplat **Cast:** Aaron Taylor Johnson (Ford Brody), Elizabeth Olson (Ellie Brody), Ken Watanabe (Dr. Ishiro Serizawa), Bryan Cranston (Joe Brody), David Strathairn (Admiral Stenz), Sally Hawkins (Dr. Vivienne Graham), Juliette Binoche (Sandra Brody)

Cinemascope, Color, 123 Minutes

A *horrific accident at the Janjira nuclear power plant in 1999 leaves a devastating effect on Joe Brody, whose wife was killed in the disaster. Fifteen years later, Joe and his son Ford are arrested when they return to the site to investigate. There, they discover the Japanese government monitoring a huge cocoon housing a gigantic insect-like creature that has been feeding on the radiation. When it hatches, Joe is killed in the chaos. The creature, dubbed a "MUTO" (short for Massive Unidentified Terrestrial Organism), comes ashore and wreaks havoc in Hawaii. It is met by another gigantic lifeform—a dinosaur-like monster known as Gojira/Godzilla—an alpha predator whose purpose is to restore balance to the earth. This male MUTO escapes Godzilla's grasp to rendezvous with a female MUTO in San Francisco after stealing a nuclear warhead from the military. Ford, a military bomb specialist, enters San Francisco via HALO jump to disarm the warhead at the same time that Godzilla arrives to battle the MUTOs. On the ground, Ford and the other soldiers manage to destroy the MUTO nest and send the warhead out to sea when they are unable to disarm it. After Godzilla kills the male MUTO, the female MUTO chases down the boat carrying the warhead but Godzilla intercepts and kills her, saving Ford in the process. Exhausted, Godzilla collapses until the next morning, when he reawakens and—dubbed "King of the Monsters" by the watching media—heads back out to sea.*

Background & Commentary In 2010, American Godzilla fans were shocked to learn that Legendary Pictures had acquired the rights to produce an all-new American Godzilla film that would be distributed by

Warner Bros. Fans had always assumed the TriStar debacle (as well as the failure of *Godzilla 2000* in the States) had permanently soured American studios on Godzilla. This surprising move proved this wasn't necessarily the case. Amazingly, concept art was released right away to reassure fans that Godzilla would not suffer another crude redesign and would stay true to his Japanese roots. Slated for release in 2012, Gareth Edwards was chosen as director due to his impressive low-budget feature *Monsters* (2010). Ironically, it would turn out that the very style Edwards impressed studios with in *Monsters* would be the very thing that disappointed many Godzilla fans when the movie was finally released in 2014.

Though Godzilla's redesign is absolutely fantastic, the titular character is rarely glimpsed in his own film! The monster is teased several times before his big reveal in Hawaii, and while the audience is treated to a full-body shot of the monster in all his glory, the scene immediately cuts away to the Brody home where the battle is briefly glimpsed on the news. To many fans' horror (as most were looking forward to a solid first round battle), the POV never actually returns to Godzilla and his battle with the MUTO. Edwards had stated in interviews that he was going for the "less is more" approach in regards to Godzilla just as *Jaws* (1975) had done with its mechanical shark. However, in Spielberg's case, this was a necessary evil since the shark didn't function correctly most of the time. Also, the beautifully-rendered CGI Godzilla had nothing to hide. By the time the monster does finally stay on screen for the final battle, many fans were too embittered to fully enjoy the spectacle.

And what a spectacle the final battle is. Godzilla has never looked so real and the smoldering San Francisco that serves as the battleground is stunningly rendered. The two mutated creatures that Godzilla faces are reminiscent of Godzilla's foes from the Millennium series and surprisingly get far more screen time than Godzilla himself. However, this wasn't anything new to the series and harkens all the way back to the G-films of the 1970s which often emphasized the new monsters over Godzilla himself, who popped up sporadically for the battles. Actually, Godzilla's screen time in this film probably comes close to what it amounted to in 1975's *Terror of Mechagodzilla*.

Oddly, similar to the 1970s Toho films, Godzilla is portrayed as an unabashed hero (though the trailers for the film seemed to imply he would be a serious menace). The final scenes of Godzilla being hailed as "King of the Monsters—Savior of our City?" on the local news as cheering crowds watch him depart is an uplifting and gratifying moment for fans of the heroic Godzilla. As for the humans, Aaron Taylor Johnson makes for a rather blank-faced lead as the audience follows his efforts to reunite with his family. Audiences were also shocked and disappointed to see critically-acclaimed actor Bryan Cranston killed off so early in the film (which the trailers also lied about; they seriously sold the story as a Bryan Cranston vs. Godzilla movie). As for Japanese superstar Ken Watanabe as Dr. Serizawa, G-fans were expecting more from his character due to his name. Instead, he spends most of the film staring dramatically at the camera and giving exposition.

Though not as polarizing as the 1998 *Godzilla*, this film was still incredibly divisive for Godzilla fans angry at Edwards for emphasizing the relatively uninteresting human drama over the monsters. Fan bickering wasn't the only thing this film shared with the TriStar production. Amazingly, the finished storyline bears more than a few similarities to the original rejected 1994 script for *Godzilla*. It would have featured the monster as an earth defender that has very little screen time, and that script also focused around a fractured family unit.

Perhaps more remarkable was the film's performance at the box office. Despite being hailed as a hit, the new *Godzilla* would not outperform the 1998 "flop" if adjusted for inflation, proving that critical reviews count for more than people think. That said though, when one gets down to hard numbers, Legendary's *Godzilla* made $200,676,069 domestically on a $160,000,000 budget. Tristar's *Godzilla* made $136,000,000 domestic on a $130,000,000 budget.

Final Word Whether fans loved the movie or hated it, compared to Sony's 1998 *Godzilla,* this American reboot was wonderfully handled.

ULTRAMAN GINGA S
THE MOVIE: SHOWDOWN! THE TEN ULTRA WARRIORS

(TSUBURAYA PRODUCTIONS)
Release Date: March 14, 2015
Japanese Title: *Ultraman Ginga S: Decisive Battle! 10 Brave Ultra Warriors*

Directed by: Koichi Sakamoto **Special Effects by:** Masaki Nishioka **Screenplay by:** Yuji Kobayashi & Takao Nakano **Music by:** Takao Konishi **Cast:** Takuya Negishi (Hikaru Raido/voice of Ultraman Ginga), Kiyotaka Uji (Sho/voice of Ultraman Victory), Arisa Komiya (Princess Arina), Taiyo Sugiura (Musashi Haruno/voice of Ultraman Cosmos), Yukari Taki (Arisa Sugita), Tatsuhisa Suzuki (voice of Etelgar), Mamoru Miyano (voice of Ultraman Zero) **Suit Performers:** Hideyoshi Iwata (Ultraman Zero), Hiroshizu Iwakami (Belial)

Widescreen, Color, 63 Minutes

On the distant planet Juran, Ultraman Cosmos battles a golden opponent called Etelgar. He uses the magical mirror princess Arina to imprison Cosmos, along with several other Ultramen, within it. Cosmos' human host Musashi shows up on Ultraman Ginga's earth around the same time that Etelgar and Princess Arina arrive with their floating castle intending to capture Ultramen Ginga and Victory. Ultraman Zero appears to help and binds Hikaru and Sho (Ultraman Ginga and Victory's human hosts) together, forcing them to train as one to create a new Ultraman: Ginga Victory. The other Ultramen are freed by Ginga Victory and join forces to fight Etelgar's various monsters. Ultraman Cosmos is able to free Princess Arina, actually a benevolent princess tricked into helping Etelgar by a spell. The Ultramen join their powers into an Ultra Fusion Ray which destroys Etelgar. The Ultramen leave Ginga's earth while Ultraman Cosmos takes Arina back to her home planet.

Background & Commentary For a while, the Ultraman films had been fairly epic—or that is to say worthy of the big screen—with movies like *Mega Monster Battle: Ultra Galaxy Legends - The Movie* (2009) and *Ultraman Zero: The Revenge of Belial* (2010). *Ultraman Saga* (2012) saw a decline in quality that continues here. *Ultraman Ginga S: The Movie* runs only a little over an hour and the cinematography looks more like the TV series than a movie. That said, the past two theatrical Ultraman Ginga "movies" were nothing but a repackaging of TV series episodes. And for those who feel Ultraman is already commercialized enough, the Ginga series took things to the next level with the premise that the Ultramen and monsters were all transformed into Spark Dolls! These Spark Dolls were naturally sold in stores for children—an ingenious idea from a marketing perspective.

Like most Ultraman movies, the joy in this entry is found mainly in amusing character cameos, and, six years since his introduction, Ultraman Zero is still stealing the show. When he arrives on the scene, he spies Ultraman Cosmos' human form and casually says, "Long time no see, Musashi." Later, Musashi makes Sho and Hikaru introduce themselves to the giant Ultraman Zero, who then handcuffs them together for an epic training montage—epically laughable that is. The montage, where Sho and Hikaru somehow manage to take their shirts off while leaving the handcuffs on, is retro 80s at its best, right down to its guitar riffs.

The movie has a decent story concept concerning a revenge-driven mirror princess, which should have had more than enough story to fill a paltry hour storyline—and probably more than that if done right. And yet, every other scene is either the human characters fighting Princess Arina or one of the film's ten Ultramen (Ginga, Victory, Cosmos, Zero, Mebius, Max, Tiga, Dyna, Gaia, and Nexus) fighting Etelgar. Consequently, the movie is more like a video game, and, when the Ultras storm the floating dark castle, the levels are actually listed as "Level 1" and so on. However, having to defeat a new opponent on each level is a neat idea reminiscent of Bruce Lee's original version of *Game of Death* (the film he died while shooting). However, the climax is ruined by one too many power-up moves. Literally every Ultraman gets to show off their finishing move and Ultraman Zero has so many that it strains credibility and falls into parody! The movie premiered at #10 at the box office.

Final Word Though the story concept had potential, the film is too short and bogged down in continuity to be of any merit as a feature film.

ATTACK ON TITAN

(KODANSHA TOHO/NIKKATSU)
Release Date: August 1, 2015 (Part I); September 19, 2015 (Part II)

Directed by: Shinji Higuchi **Special Effects by:** Katsuro Onoue **Screenplay by:** Yūsuke Watanabe & Tomohiro Machiyama **Music by:** Shiro Sagisu **Cast:** Haruma Miura (Eren) Kiko Mizuhara (Mikasa) Kanata Hongo (Armin) Hiroki Hasegawa (Shikishima) Takahiro Miura (Jean) Nanami Sakuraba (Sasha) Jun Kunimura (Kubal)

2.35 : 1, Color, 98 Minutes (Part I); 87 Minutes (Part II)

In the future, humanity has been subjugated into a life of fear due to the emergence of huge, flesh-eating titans. Cities fortified by massive walls protect mankind for many years until one day, suddenly, the walls are breached by an even larger super-titan. Three childhood friends consisting of Eren, Mikasa, and Armin are separated in the ensuing titan attack. They are reunited years later as part of a military unit, lead by a man named Shikishima, to combat the giants. Their mission is to transport explosives to the wall, the hope being that the explosions can seal in the breach at the bottom of the wall by collapsing the top. Terrorists steal the explosives during a battle with the titans. During the fight, Eren gives his life to save Armin from a titan's jaws and gets eaten himself. Moments later, a new titan emerges from that one's body and proceeds to kill all the other titans. The being collapses, begins to dissolve, and Eren emerges from its remains. As it turns out, both Eren and Shikishima have the ability to transform into titans. Furthermore, Shikishima is secretly the leader of the terrorist group, which is really a band of freedom fighters out to overthrow the oppressive government. The only problem is, Shikishima doesn't care how many innocents he kills in the process. In their titan forms, Shikishima and Eren fight, with Eren emerging as the victor. The group then takes the explosives to repair the breach in the wall. They are confronted by one of the heads of state, who transforms into the mysterious super-titan seen years ago. Eren, in human form, is saved from the super titan by Shikishima in titan form, who gives his life to kill the Super Titan and detonate the explosives.

Background & Commentary Based on a manga that began in 2009, an *Attack on Titan* feature film was first announced back in 2011 for a 2103 release. This iteration was to be directed by Tetsuya Nakashima, who eventually left over creative differences. Word has it Nakashima's version would have been closer to the manga. It would have also had a few scenes set in present-day Japan, whereas the final film is all set in the post-apocalyptic future. During the film's development, unlike many authors abhorred by changes to their work, manga creator Hajime Isayama actually suggested many changes as his manga was adapted into a script. The biggest difference was that Isayama pushed for the story to focus on Japan (the manga is international with only one Japanese character).

Eventually, a post-*Japan Sinks*, pre-*Shin Godzilla* Shinji Higuchi was chosen to direct, and an excellent film was born. What makes *Attack on Titan* such a great "monster movie" is that it isn't really about the monsters, it's about the characters. The titans are entertaining when they're on screen, but when they're gone for long stretches, the characters carry the film easily. The film also keeps you guessing, that's for sure. For instance, I was initially thrown for a loop by the beginning. The film had more or less established our three leads, only to have one of them (Mikasa) die around 30 minutes in. However, it turns out that Mikasa didn't really die, we just thought she did, though we don't learn this until another 20 minutes later. The same thing happens with Eren and Armin. We think that Armin is a goner for sure, only he gets saved by Eren. Though it seems as though Armen's imminent doom is a fake-out to surprise us with Eren's death, that takes a turn as well when Eren mutates into a titan himself and bursts out of the very monster that ate him.

Attack on Titan also has some nice subtext on how a government will use a crisis to control and oppress the population. At the same time, the movie does a good job of showing the dark side of the oppressors and their would-be liberators alike. Even though Shikishima plans to liberate the people, he's also going about it in a way that will kill many of them. He even says that he feels no remorse for them because they've allowed themselves to be dominated.

For fans on the fence about non-Godzilla/Gamera kaiju movies like this one, and need some nudging, I would say from a monster perspective that *Attack on Titan* is most similar to *Frankenstein vs. Baragon* (1965) and *The War of the Gargantuas* (1966). Some of the titans look very much like Toho's Frankenstein, especially if he was brought to life with today's effects, whereas the mutant titans inhabited by Eren and Shikishima are comparable to the Gargantuas. It is even said that the battle between Eren and Shikishima's titan forms was inspired by *War of the Gargantuas*. As for more comparisons to the Gargantuas, the titans eat people. Just imagine a hard R-rated movie starring Gaira made today and this is what you'd get. In fact, one Wikipedia editor tried to claim that this was an unofficial sequel set within the same universe! Though they certainly have similarities, this isn't the case.

Attack on Titan was released in two parts within only two months of each other. Though it was a smart decision from a financial perspective (this method, after all, guaranteed a higher profit), from an artistic perspective, it's too bad the film wasn't able to simply be a three hour epic. If one were to remove the opening and ending credits, plus a nearly five-minute-long recap of the first film, Part II really only runs about an hour and twenty minutes.

An American remake has already been announced, though there's really no need for it. *Attack on Titan* was already on par with most American films and did see a limited theatrical release in the U.S. via Funimation.

Final Word If you liked the music and effects of *Shin Godzilla*, and also enjoyed Toho's two Frankenstein movies, this is a must-see. I mean, it should be a must-see anyway because it's so good, but if you *need* a kaiju-related excuse to check it out, there you go.

ULTRAMAN X THE MOVIE: HERE COMES OUR ULTRAMAN!

すぐ

われらのウルトラマン

(TSUBURAYA PRODUCTIONS)
Release Date: March 12, 2016
Japanese Title: *Come On, Ultraman X! Our Ultraman*

Directed by: Kiyotaka Taguchi **Special Effects by:** Tomoaki Miwa **Screenplay by:** Yuji Kobayashi, Hirotoshi Kobayashi, & Takao Nakano **Music by:** Takao Konishi **Cast:** Kensuke Takahashi (Daichi Ozora), Akane Sakanoue (Asuna Yamase), Takami Yoshimoto (Tsukasa Tamaki), Serai Takagi (Yuto Tamaki), Yoshihiko Hosoda (Wataru Kazama), Ukyo Matsumoto (Hayato Kishima), Hayato Harada (Mamoru Mikazuki), Haruka Momokawa (Rui Takada), Michael Tomioka (Carlos Kurosaki), Yuichi Nakamura (voice of Ultraman X), Mamoru Miyano (voice of Ultraman Zero) **Suit Performers:** Hideyoshi Iwata (Ultraman X), Hiroyuki Fukushima (Alien Fanton Guruman), Yoshiki Kuwabara (Zaigorg), Shinnosuke Ishikawa (Ultraman), Aki Okabe (Ultraman Tiga), Kenji Kajikawa (Gorg Antlar), Hiroyuki Arai (Gorg Fire Golza)

Widescreen, Color, 72 Minutes

An ancient temple is discovered by scientist Tsukasa Tamaki and her son Yuto. Another professor/TV personality, Carlos Kurosaki, enters the temple against the warnings of Tamaki and team Xio, unleashing the monster Devil Beast Zaigorg. Daichi Ozora confronts the monster as Ultraman X but is so badly injured that the X Devizer device must be repaired before he can transform again. An orb found in the temple lures Zaigorg to the city where Kurosaki has it in his possession. Tamaki tries to retrieve it but is caught in the monster's rampage, prompting Yuto to try to save her. Using an artifact called the Spark Lens he found in the ruins, Yuto transforms into Ultraman Tiga while Daichi is able to turn into Ultraman X again. The original Ultraman also comes to their aid and all goes well until multiple monsters sprout from Zaigorg's body, prompting help from five other Ultramen. Joining with Ultraman Tiga and Ultraman, Ultraman X is able to finish off Zaigorg with a patented power-up move.

Background & Commentary In 2015, the newest Ultraman series, *Ultraman X*, took the shameless/ingenious marketing ploy that began with Ultraman Ginga's spark dolls and continued to run with it. Rather than a storyline revolving around action figures, it centered on what are more or less trading cards that can give the Xio team the powers of the monsters and Ultraman X the ability to fuse with other Ultramen. As with the previous film, shooting was done parallel with the current series finale.

Unlike previous entries, *Ultraman X The Movie: Here Comes Our Ultraman!* is nice enough to begin with a refresher for those unfamiliar with the series, even though it does give off a very "previously on" TV vibe to the film's opening. The film is set six months after the series finale. Unlike other Ultramen, Ultraman X retains a constant presence in the film through his X Devizer, a communication device via which he talks to the members of Xio. Often it is quite humorous, as the tiny Ultraman X advises his Xio team members on what to eat and even engages in some backseat driving!

Aside from the newest *Ultraman X* series, this story was heavily influenced by the original *Ultraman* (celebrating its 50th Anniversary) and *Ultraman Tiga* (celebrating its 20th). As such, pyramids and ancient ruins again play into the story. Notably, Susumu Kurobe's daughter Takami Yoshimoto, the *Ultraman Tiga* alum who had played Rena, here plays a new character who discovers Tiga's temple along with the usual Apocalypse-bringing monster, Zaigorg. In a fun twist—possibly because actor Hiroshi Nagano wouldn't return—the young boy Yuto transforms into Tiga! Seeing Ultraman Tiga, Ultraman X, and the original Ultraman together is great fun, representing the Showa and Heisei eras of Ultraman perfectly. Each also gets a wonderful battle sequence, and Ultraman Tiga's CGI aerial chase is fast, frenetic, and fun. The other Ultramen are given little more than cameos, and only Zero makes much of an impression as he hams it up as usual.

At the story's end, Ultraman X separates from Daichi. The ending coda is well-executed as the Xio team mopes around sadly after Ultraman X's departure only to get a call from him stating that a new monster is headed for earth. The team rejoices and rushes off for battle.

Final Word Though it suffers from standard Ultraman clichés, this entry is fresher than usual and is an improvement over the last film.

SHIN GODZILLA

(TOHO)
Release Date: July 29, 2016
Alternate Titles: *New Godzilla* (Japan) *Godzilla Resurgence* (brief international title)
Godzilla: Rebirth (Ukraine)

Directed by: Shinji Higuchi & Hideaki Anno **Special Effects by:** Shinji Higuchi & Katsuro Onoe **Screenplay by:** Hideaki Anno **Music by:** Shiro Sagisu **Cast:** Hiroki Hasegawa (Rando Yaguchi), Yutaka Takenouchi (Hideki Akasaka), Satomi Ishihara (Kyoko Anne Patterson), Ren Osugi (Prime Minster Okochi), Akira Emoto (Ryuta Azuma), Mikako Ichikawa (Hiromi Ogashira) **Motion Capture Performers:** Mansai Nomura (Shin Godzilla)

Cinemascope, Color, 120 Minutes

A pleasure yacht adrift in Tokyo Bay is found with a cryptic note stating, "I did as I pleased. You do the same." As the authorities investigate, a huge geyser of water erupts from Tokyo Bay. As the government tries to figure out what it is, they fail to take action quick enough as a giant creature crawls on land and begins destroying Tokyo. As the monster evolves, it is called "Godzilla" by the Americans (though the Japanese decide to use "Gojira" instead) and soon becomes an unstoppable force. Kyoko Anne Patterson, a special envoy for the U.S. President, arrives and teams up with Deputy Chief Cabinet Secretary Rando Yaguchi in exchange for information on the yacht's owner, scientist Goro Maki, who seemed to know something about the mysterious creature's origins. Japan asks for help from the U.S. military but Godzilla shoots their stealth bombers from the sky with his new oral weapon of mass destruction. The prime minister and most of the Japanese government are killed during the assault. Godzilla overheats from exertion and freezes in place. Rando Yaguchi takes over the lead of Godzilla countermeasures in a race against time to find a way to defeat the monster before the U.S. drops a nuclear bomb on Godzilla. In a last-ditch effort, Yaguchi and his team devise a plan to permanently immobilize Godzilla by spraying a coagulating freezing agent into its mouth. The plan works just as Godzilla begins to morph into another stage of development.

Background & Commentary The holiday season of 2014 marked the first anniversary year in Japan since the Godzilla series was launched that a new Japanese film was not in theaters. Instead, during that summer, the new American *Godzilla* from Legendary Pictures was released. Then that December, Toho surprised the world with the announcement that they would be producing a new Godzilla movie. Almost as surprising was the creative team announced to head up the film: Heisei Gamera stalwart Shinji Higuchi and head of the *Evangelion* franchise, Hideaki Anno. Actually, Anno was initially only going to write the film but as he visited the set more and more, he became a co-director.

Rather than try to repeat the original *Godzilla*'s anti-atomic weapons message, Higuchi and Anno wisely took a new disaster as the inspiration for *Shin Godzilla*—the Fukushima Daiichi Nuclear Power Plant disaster of 2011 and the Japanese government's ineffective response to it and the Tohoku earthquake and tsunami that same year. In fact, the Japanese government sometimes seems to be the real threat in *Shin Godzilla*. This is demonstrated over and over again in ways that are shockingly accurate, such as a chain of command so long that it becomes farcical how long policies get back to the prime minister. By the time the prime minister gives the order to fire on Godzilla, so much time has passed that the attack is nearly ineffective. The Minister of Agriculture, who replaces the dead prime minister, is also an interesting character as he faces the possibility of going down in history as the prime minister who willingly let Japan get nuked for a second time. And yet, he seems more upset that his noodles have gotten soggy as he gets bogged down in a meeting on the subject.

The real goal isn't to beat Godzilla so much as to incapacitate him before the U.S. drops a nuclear bomb on him in Tokyo—an angle explored earlier in *The Return of Godzilla* (1984). The most controversial aspect of the new film ended up being Godzilla itself, which went through several Hedorah-like stages of development. In fact, Anno and Higuchi began with the 4th Stage Godzilla and worked backwards from that to create the preceding stages.

Though they should be jarring in their contrast to Shiro Sagisu's new score pieces, the eclectic selection of classic Akira Ifukube tracks integrated into the film work surprisingly well. Tracks from the original *Godzilla* (1954), *Battle in Outer Space* (1959), and *Terror of Mechagodzilla* (1975) are among those used. However, the most stunning pieces of music are easily "Persecution of the Masses" and "Who Will Know?" used to great effect when Godzilla uses his atomic breath for the first time. The scene is truly awe-inspiring and unlike anything ever seen in a Godzilla film before. Godzilla's mouth opens into several pieces and rather than his traditional ray. He appears to exhale a flammable gas that makes the Tokyo streets erupt into an absolute firestorm. Finally, the ray intensifies into a purple beam of light and crazier still, rays also shoot from Godzilla's tail and dorsal spikes!

Shin Godzilla did amazingly well in Japan, where rumor had it the new generation was only vaguely aware of who Godzilla was. The film had a higher attendance than the one for *Godzilla vs. Mothra* (1992) and now sits as the second highest-grossing Japanese-made Godzilla film (after *King Kong vs. Godzilla*, of course). Even more shocking, the film struck such a chord that it won Best Picture and Best Director at the Japanese Academy Awards.

Final Word Though it's talky meeting scenes somewhat lessen the film's re-watch-ability, its win for Best Picture is well-deserved and noteworthy within the history of the Godzilla franchise.

COLOSSAL

(VOLTAGE PICTURES)

Release Date: September 09, 2016

Alternate Titles: *She is a Monster* (Mexico) *My Girlfriend is a Monster* (Russia) *Synchronized Monster* (Japan) *Girl and Monster* (Estonia) *Colossal: An Uncontrollable Monster* (Peru) *Monster* (Poland)

Directed by: Nacho Vigalondo **Screenplay by:** Nacho Vigalondo **Music by:** Bear McCreary **Cast:** Anne Hathaway (Gloria), Jason Sudeikis (Oscar), Austin Stowell (Joel), Tim Blake Nelson (Garth), Dan Stevens (Tim) **Motion Capture Performers:** Uncredited

Cinemascope, Color, 109 Minutes

An alcoholic ne'er-do-well named Gloria gets dumped by her boyfriend and moves back to her small hometown. There, she reconnects with childhood friend Oscar, who runs a local bar. When Gloria witnesses a giant monster attacking Seoul on the news, she soon recognizes that it has some of her ticks and habits. Gloria then realizes that every day she walks through a local park at 8:05 a.m., the mysterious monster treks through Seoul. Gloria uses a live stream of Seoul to prove to Oscar and her friends that she and the monster are connected. When she drunkenly trips in the sand, Oscar steps into the playground to help her up and reveals he too has a giant avatar in the form of a huge robot. While Gloria is cautious not to hurt the people of Seoul, Oscar relishes his newfound power and uses it to blackmail Gloria into doing anything he pleases. When Gloria tries to stop Oscar from destroying Seoul, he beats her badly. Gloria buys a plane ticket and flies to Seoul, and when she stands before Oscar's avatar, her monstrous avatar confronts Oscar in the park. When Oscar won't surrender, Gloria flings him into the air, presumably killing him and saving Seoul.

Background & Commentary When kaiju fans first heard the news of a new monster movie starring Anne Hathaway as a monster it seemed too strange to be true... or to be a good idea in general. The film almost didn't happen due to a lawsuit from Toho. Much like the case of the cancelled *It Ate Cleveland* (which used Godzilla's image and name in a promotional poster), *Colossal* was initially promoted with images from the

Godzilla franchise to generate interest before filming began. To make matters worse, writer/director Nacho Vigalondo was even quoted as stating that he was about to make "the cheapest Godzilla movie ever." Though the final film is set in Korea, it's presumable Vigalondo's initial idea had the film taking place in Japan with a more Godzilla-like monster. Thankfully, Toho and Voltage Pictures settled things peacefully and one of the most unique giant monster films ever was created.

Though the premise is undeniably strange, it works incredibly well and makes for a very unique twist on the giant monster genre. Like *Demeking, the Sea Monster* (2009), this is a film centered more on the human storyline instead of the monsters themselves. While most giant monster movies have an underlying theme relating to nuclear testing, pollution, or bioengineering, *Colossal*'s theme would seem to be the dangers of alcoholism and personal manipulation as expressed through Oscar's controlling of Gloria. As it is, Gloria and Oscar are themselves monsters in real life. However, while Gloria is only self-destructive, Oscar is dangerous, manipulative, and malicious.

It becomes clear by the middle of the film that it is a dark comedy with moments of real drama—there is nothing funny about Oscar beating up Gloria in the middle of the park. This does set up a superbly clever ending though. As the audience watches Gloria board a plane, we assume she is running away from Oscar and back to her ex-boyfriend. Instead, Gloria's plane lands in Seoul. Though Gloria and the audience don't know for certain what will happen, it is presumable that if Gloria stands before Oscar's avatar in Korea, her avatar will appear before Oscar in America. Her plan works, and her avatar defeats Oscar in human form, and by default, his gigantic avatar in the process.

Gloria's avatar probably looked more like Godzilla initially, but the final design, odd though it may be, compliments other Korean monsters (like the 1999 *Yonggary*) rather well. The strange creature can look threatening or sympathetic depending upon the scene and has an interesting range of expressions. Oscar's giant robot, with its singular eye, is naturally rather soulless. However, the monsters' designs really aren't important as they exist solely to service the story (whereas conversely in kaiju eiga, the story usually exists to service the monsters). Also, the effects are excellent and frequent for a $15 million budget.

Final Word Even though it didn't make much of a dent at the box office, *Colossal*—with its positive reviews—is likely on its way to becoming a classic of the genre.

KONG:
SKULL ISLAND

(LEGENDARY PICTURES)
Release Date: March 10, 2017
Alternate Titles: *King Kong: Huge God of Skull Island* (Japan)

Directed by: Jordan Vogt-Roberts **Screenplay by:** Dan Gilroy, Max Borenstein, & Derek Connolly **Music by:** Henry Jackman **Cast:** Tom Hiddleston (James Conrad), Brie Larson (Mason Weaver), Samuel L. Jackson (Colonel Preston Packard), John Goodman (Bill Randa), Corey Hawkins (Houston Brooks), Tian Jing (San), Toby Kebbel (Jack Chapman), John C. Reilly (Hank Marlow) **Motion Capture Performers:** Toby Kebbel (King Kong)

Panavision, Color, 118 Minutes

I n 1973, an expedition headed by the secretive Monarch organization is escorted by an elite military unit to the mysterious Skull Island. Along for the ride are photographer Mason Weaver and tracker James Conrad. When the helicopters begin setting off seismic charges to map Skull Island, the expedition is taken down by a giant ape known as Kong and the few survivors are separated into two groups. The group led by Conrad comes into contact with a native tribe and Hank Marlow, who crashed on the island during WWII. This group begins to view Kong as their key to survival against a group of monsters called Skullcrawlers. The other group led by Colonel Packard believes it is their duty to kill Kong for those killed in his attack. Packard's attempts to kill Kong fail and instead summons a gigantic Skullcrawler to the surface. After a pitched battle, Kong manages to defeat the powerful creature as the survivors escape the island.

Background & Commentary Shortly after acquiring the rights to Godzilla, Legendary Pictures found themselves on the verge of producing a new King Kong film for Universal. However, when the company saw a chance to set up a shared universe à la Marvel Studios, they shifted their Kong film over to Warner Bros, the home of their Godzilla films. As a result, the "Monsterverse" was born with this film and *Godzilla vs. Kong* was announced well before this film's release in March of 2017.

As the second installment of Legendary Pictures' Monsterverse, *Kong: Skull Island* inevitably finds itself compared to the studio's 2014 *Godzilla*. The only major stylistic similarities the films share are their opening credit sequences and the fact that Kong and Godzilla are both presented as benevolent alpha predators that keep nature in check. The similarities end there, however, and in most other ways, the two films are polar opposites. The human characters are all cut from a far less-grounded, more adventurous cloth than those that appeared in *Godzilla*—the standout being comedian John C. Reilly's Hank Marlow, who steals every scene he appears in. John Goodman is intriguing as Bill Randa, an operative of Monarch (a connective continuity thread similar to S.H.I.E.L.D. in the Marvel films), who raises some interesting questions that are never fully answered due to him being unceremoniously eaten by a Skullcrawler (a bit used for shock value more than anything else).

The rest of the cast is solid as well, such as Tom Hiddleston's tracker character, but they soon fade into the background once the stunning visuals on Skull Island take over. There also seems to be a missed opportunity between Brie Larson's female lead and Kong, robbing the film of a more solid emotional connection to the great ape (a given in past Kong films). However, the visuals are still stunning and there are four major battles that Kong engages in, most in broad daylight. The best is undoubtedly Kong's assault on a fleet of helicopters, though the climactic battle is nearly as exciting. In it, Kong uses a boat propeller to gut his enemy and subsequently disembowels it.

The giant Skullcrawler, inspired by a throwaway monster that appears in the original 1933 *King Kong*, has an excellent design and fares much better than the MUTOs from *Godzilla*. Furthermore, due to the relatively recent release of *Jurassic World* (2015), the film contains no traditional dinosaurs and all of Skull Island's monster inhabitants have unnatural traits (though a Triceratops skull indicates dinosaurs once lived on the island, perhaps wiped out by the Skullcrawlers).

Much like *Captain America* (2011) and *Thor* (2011), much of the hype for *Kong: Skull Island* seemed to be based on the fact that it would lead into *Godzilla vs. Kong*. And like Marvel's *Iron Man* (2008), the film ends with a post-credits scene that confirms *Kong: Skull Island* takes place in the same world as *Godzilla*. Though undeniably fun, this tag scene could have been even more joyous had it been a last minute surprise rather than a foregone conclusion.

Final Word Not only does *Kong: Skull Island* stand on its own apart from the Monsterverse, the film also presents an undeniably fun ride that improves upon *Godzilla* (2014) in every respect.

ULTRAMAN ORB THE MOVIE:
LEND ME THE POWER OF YOUR BONDS!

劇場版ウルトラマンオーブ
絆の力、おかりします！

(TSUBURAYA PRODUCTIONS)
Release Date: March 11, 2017
Japanese Title: *Ultraman Orb: I'm Stopping the Power Bond*

Directed by: Kiyotaka Taguchi **Special Effects by:** Tomoaki Miwa **Screenplay by:** Takao Nakano **Music by:** Takao Konishi **Cast:** Hideo Ishiguro (Gai Kurenai/voice of Ultraman Orb), Miyabi Matsura (Naomi Yumeno), Hiroaki Nerio (Shin Matsudo), Kensuke Takahashi (Daichi Ozora), Takaya Aoyagi (Jugglus Juggler/Zeppandon), Oniyakko Tsubaki (Mulnau), Koji Moritsugu (Dan Moroboshi/voice of Ultra Seven) **Suit Performers:** Hideyoshi Iwata/Shinnosuke Ishikawa/Daisuke Terai (Ultraman Orb), Yoshiki Kuwabara (Diabolic), Aki Okabe (Sadeath), Masahiro Omura (Ultraman Victory), Hitomi Adachi (Cicada Woman), Emi Katayama (Garmes Person)

Widescreen, Color, 72 Minutes

While vacationing in Hawaii, Gai battles Galactron as Ultraman Orb with the assistance of Ultraman Zero. After the battle, Zero warns him of impending danger and disappears. Reuniting with the SSP in Japan, Gai comes into possession of the Devizer and Ultraman X beseeches him to find his human host, Daichi Ozora, now trapped in this dimension. Gai finds Ozora in a strange house ruled by Mulnau, a sort of space witch. Gai and the SSP are bailed out with the help of former enemy Jugglus Juggler and Ultraman Orb battles several of Mulnau's monsters in a city. When he is unable to defeat them, Ginga, Victory, and Ultraman X lend him their powers and he forms Orb Trinity. He is further aided by Ultra Seven, who shows up at the last moment, and together the Ultramen defeat Mulnau and her forces.

Background & Commentary Just when you thought keeping up with all the different Ultramen couldn't get any harder, Tsuburaya Productions created Ultraman Orb—an Ultraman who often fuses the forms of past Ultramen into his own. In other words, Ultraman Orb can add design and power elements from different combinations of past Ultras into his being and, therefore the possibilities—but more importantly, the toys—are endless. Naturally, after the series ran its course, a film directed by series director Kiyotaka Taguchi (who also directed the previous Ultraman film) was produced.

The film picks up after the end of the TV series with Ultraman Orb in Hawaii, where the miniature palm trees look a little more toy-like than usual. Nonetheless, the set is still pleasing to the eye and the battle with Galactron is energetic. The city destruction sequences are spectacular, though, and the enemy monster's method of destruction brings to mind Toho's Mechagodzilla. This being an Ultraman Orb movie, he has a new fusion of Ultraman X, Ginga, and Victory to transform into Orb Trinity. Ultraman X is well-integrated into the story with his communication box, which falls into the hands of the SSP. At one point, he nearly spoils Gai's secret identity in front of the SSP in a humorous scene. As for Ginga and Victory, they appear in Ultra form only with their human hosts completely absent. The main Rita Repulsa-like villain, Mulnau, is too silly to be taken seriously, though her flying house has an interesting 1970s Ultra era vibe to it.

Unfortunately, *Ultraman Orb The Movie: Lend Me the Power of Your Bonds* is a film where the parts are much better than the whole, but those parts consist of some truly wonderful character moments. The TV series' main villain, Jugglus Juggler (who has the ability to fuse monsters like Zetton and Pandon), gets many of the film's best moments as he switches sides to become a fun new ally to Gai and the SSP. Ultraman Zero gets two great scenes, one at the beginning of the film and another in what is the series' first Marvel-style post-credits scene.

But the best character moment in the film occurs as a beaten Orb is lying upon the ground and Dan Moroboshi abruptly walks into the frame. Though he comes completely out of nowhere within the context of the story, the scene works as a 50th Anniversary tribute to *Ultra Seven*. As he transforms, each of the Ultramen mutters "Seven?" which humorously recreates *Ultra Seven*'s classic theme song. Ultra Seven (the only Showa era Ultra in the film) then gets some special attention during the end battle, slicing and dicing his way through the enemy monsters with some excellent fight choreography. And, despite comedian Oniyakko Tsubaki's villain Mulnau being weak overall, Mulnau gets a good character moment with Gai, who plays his harmonica after she dies. The film ends atmospherically with Gai walking into the sunset like some Western hero playing his harmonica.

Final Word The parts are certainly better than the whole when it comes to this Ultraman film, but it's worth watching alone for the *Ultra Seven* tribute.

(SABAN)
Release Date: March 22, 2017

Directed by: Dean Israelite **Screenplay by:** John Gatins **Music by:** Brian Tyler
Cast: Dacre Montgomery (Jason Scott), Naomi Scott (Kimberly Hart), R.J. Cyler (Billy Cranston), Ludi Lin (Zack Taylor), Becky G. (Trina Kwan), Bryan Cranston (Zordon), Elizabeth Banks (Rita Repulsa), Bill Hader (voice of Alpha 5)

Cinemascope, Color, 124 Minutes

In the Cenozoic Era, Zordon the Red Ranger hides five Power Coins from the Morphing Grid on Earth to keep them away from the evil Green Ranger, Rita Repulsa. Millions of years later, five troubled teens from Angel Grove consisting of Jason, Kimberly, Billy, Zach, and Trini find the coins. At the same time, Rita Repulsa is fished from the ocean depths and begins to revive—her goal being to resurrect the golden monster Goldar and dig up a Zeo Crystal buried in the earth. As Rita goes about hording gold to revive Goldar, the five teens struggle with the ability to morph under the training of Zordon and his robot Alpha 5. When Rita finally resurrects Goldar, the Power Rangers morph into their armored forms and board their Zords to battle Rita and her monster in Angel Grove. When Goldar proves too difficult to defeat, the five Zords merge into one Megazord and finally manage to defeat Rita and her monster.

Background & Commentary With comic book-based genre movies ruling the box office throughout the 2010s, *Power Rangers* producer Haim Saban thought 2017 would be a good time to do a big-budget reboot of the Power Rangers franchise. Budgeted at only $105 million and produced between Saban and Lionsgate, *Saban's Power Rangers* is a commendable production for several reasons.

In an era of overstuffed, complicated genre movies, *Saban's Power Rangers* is refreshingly simple. Its narrative structure and characters liken to a movie from the 1980s. While concurrently novel, it can also make certain aspects of the characters and their interactions rather cliché. However, the score by Brian Tyler is so good that it elevates the film to another level and the performances of the five leads are satisfactory overall.

Though the original series teen scenes seemed to take inspiration from *Saved by the Bell* (1989), this version was specifically inspired by 1985's *The Breakfast Club*. Several of the characters first meet in detention and all five have the same high school archetype as those in the John Hughes film. Jason is the jock, Kimberly is the cheerleader, Billy is the smart nerd, Zack is the wild rebel, and Trini is the mysterious loner. There is also a brilliant mid-credits scene set in detention that is an homage to a famous scene from *Ferris Bueller's Day Off* (1986) where the detention teacher keeps calling out for an absent Tommy Oliver (the Green Ranger of the original TV series).

As for the rest of the main cast, Elizabeth Banks' Rita Repulsa is a bit too hammy but her new origin story as a Green Ranger gone bad is a fun twist to the mythos. *Godzilla's* Bryan Cranston, who did voice work on the original *Mighty Morphin' Power Rangers* series, now stars as Zordon himself, thanks to his post-*Breaking Bad* stardom and does a stellar job.

Unfortunately, the giant monster scenes are limited to the climax, though this was probably a budgetary necessitation. However, the choreography of the battle is quite rewarding as each individual Zord gets its moment to shine. Somewhat disappointing is the forming of the Megazord. Whereas in the original series, the Zords all coherently formed together, in this reboot, they seem to magically meld together—nor are the Zords distinctly recognizable within the Megazord's body. Goldar's design is something of a disappointment but the redesign was probably necessary as a gold-suited, fanged ape with wings would probably be a bit much for mainstream audiences unfamiliar with the show.

With an impressive opening weekend, *Saban's Power Rangers* seemed destined to become a franchise. However, the global box office revenue was less than anticipated, so sequels seemed unlikely. Since then, Hasbro bought Power Rangers and has stated that future feature films will be reboots. Sadly, this well-done film will never see a sequel.

Final Word Despite its somewhat clichéd nature and "been there, done that" origin story, *Saban's Power Rangers* still manages to somehow be a very well-done, refreshing reboot of the franchise.

BRAVESTORM

ブレイブストーム

(ALBATROSS/BLAST)
Release Date: November 10, 2017

Directed by: Junya Okabe **Screenplay by:** Junya Okabe & Joseph O'Brien
Music by: Takayuki Hattori **Cast:** Shunsuke Daitô (Koji Kasuga/Silver Mask), Shu
Watanabe (Ken Kurenai), Soran Tamoto (Kozo Kasuga), Mitsu Dan (Hitomi
Kasuga), Hisashi Yoshizawa (Kenichiro Kurenai), Chihiro Yamamoto (Haruka
Kasuga), Yuki Matsuzaki (Borg)

1.78 : 1, Color, 84 Minutes

By the year 2050, humanity has been eradicated by aliens called
the Killgis. The aliens arrived in the year 2017 and using their
giant robot Black Baron altered Earth's atmosphere to make it
habitable to the Killgis. Among the survivors are the five Kasuga
siblings. The eldest has constructed a suit of armor for Koji Kasuga,
which transforms him into Silver Mask. Koji and two of his other
siblings travel back to the year 2013, where they enlist the help of
their grandfather, Kenichiro Kurenai, to build a super robot of their
own to counter Black Baron when it arrives. Kenichiro agrees on the
condition that his younger brother, Ken, be the pilot. All goes to plan
except that Black Baron shows up three years ahead of schedule,
forcing an inexperienced Ken to go into battle. While Silver Mask
attacks the Killgis base of operations, Ken manages to defeat Black
Baron via Super Robot Red Baron, and the day is saved.

Background & Commentary In the 1970s, in addition to Tsuburaya
Productions, Toei, and P-Productions, there was yet another production
company that specialized in costumed heroes: Senkosha Production,
which was the television production arm of the Japanese advertising
agency the Senkosha Company. Senkosha debuted heroes like Gekko
Kamen, Iron King, Super Robot Red Baron, and Silver Mask, to name a
few. One could say that *BraveStorm* is a joint remake of *Super Robot Red
Baron* and *Silver Mask* by way of *Terminator* in the style of Adi Shankar's
bootleg *Power/Rangers* short. In other words, it's a lot of fun.

The core concepts from both series are retained aside from a few tweaks. *Silver Mask* focused on a group of siblings, the second oldest of whom transformed into the android Silver Mask, on the run from evil aliens. In *Super Robot Red Baron*, siblings were front and center as well. In this case, older brother Kenichiro Kurenai invented the Super Robot Red Baron that only his younger brother Ken can pilot. Kenichiro is kidnapped and later killed by the bad guys, the Iron Masked Party. Some semblance of those events takes place here but with unique twists. Though the TV series were not connected, in the movie, Silver Mask and the Kasuga siblings hail from the future, and Kenichiro is their grandfather. There are plenty of nods to the *Terminator* franchise when the siblings go back in time to save the Kurenai brothers. One of them even pulls a last-minute parking lot rescue and more or less tells Ken, "Come with me if you want to live." The film also has the grittiness of the controversial *Power/Rangers* bootleg short, and that includes F-bombs, which might be the product of the English dub cast, I'm not sure.

As for other unique updates, Kenichiro has input his consciousness into Red Baron via an A.I. program. This is something that the original series might have done if they knew what A.I. was back then. Kenichiro also gives a practical reason for his brother piloting the robot. Ken is a boxer, and Kenichiro argues that Ken's reflexes can work faster than a computer (that, and when Ken was a child, he asked Kenichiro to one day build him a giant robot). As another nod to the series, Kenichiro is kidnapped by the bad guys and forced to fight on their side.

At the onset of the end battle, Black Baron gets a wicked entrance as he glides through a canal, his shoulder cannons slicing through the water like a shark's fin. Red Baron comes to face Black Baron, and to Ken's horror, he learns that Kenichiro is being forced to pilot Black Baron. This is another fun aspect that takes a concept from the original series and expands on it. Though Kenichiro was forced to do the Iron Alliance's bidding in the original series, he and Ken never had to fight.

The duties between the two heroes are split up well. While giant monster enthusiasts can enjoy a very well-done robot duel in Tokyo, the human-sized Silver Mask is kicking ass on the alien's secret island. While there, he discovers that Kenichiro isn't in the robot. He's still alive and well on the island. The main alien antagonist has holographically taken on Kenichiro's appearance. Silver Mask relays this information to Ken, who quits holding back and finally demolishes Black Baron. It probably would have been more impactful to force Ken to kill his brother for the greater good, but an end teaser establishes that the story isn't over yet (and they probably wanted to keep Kenichiro alive for the prospective sequel).

On the note of said teaser, just when I thought I couldn't love this movie anymore, we return to the future from whence the three siblings came. Oddly, nothing has changed, implying that the heroes didn't actually win yet. Suddenly bursting through the door comes a Japanese cowboy. Could it be? The character does indeed turn out to be a last minute cameo for the character of Gentaro Shizuka, from *Iron King*! As Gentaro and the main characters go outside, a new Iron King can be seen from behind battling an alien menace. Considering that *BraveStorm* saw release three years ago, it's unknown if the sequel will still come to pass, but I certainly hope that it does.

The film was a passion project of Tsuburaya Production's former Vice President Junya Okabe, who secured funding for the project through crowdfunding and other means. Okabe linked up with Albatross, which had acquired the rights to Silver Mask earlier. Okabe's initial vision was to combine *Silver Mask, Super Robot Red Baron,* and *Iron King*, but ultimately that was too complicated, and so Iron King was delegated to an end teaser scene. For what is essentially a giant fan film, there's something about *BraveStorm* that makes it better than it should be (kinda like the *Power/Rangers* bootleg). The score, which has a *Star Wars* vibe to it, also really elevates the proceedings. The effects work (all CGI for the robots) is also stellar for a production of this nature. Ultimately, though I wouldn't say that there's anything wrong with *BraveStorm*, if anything, I only found myself wishing it was longer than its scant less than 90 minute runtime.

Final Word While the uneducated sadly might mistake this for a "*Pacific Rim* rip-off," anyone who has seen either *Super Robot Red Baron, Silver Mask,* or even just *Iron King*, owes it to themselves to check out this gem.

GODZILLA:
PLANET OF THE MONSTERS

(TOHO/POLYGON)
Release Date: November 17, 2017
Japanese Title: *Godzilla: Monster Planet*

Directed by: Hiroyuki Seshita and Kobun Shizuno **Screenplay by:** Gen Urobuchi and Sadayuki Murai **Music by:** Takayuki Hattori **Voice Cast:** Mamoru Miyano (Haruo Sakaki), Takahiro Sakurai (Metphies), Tomokazu Sugita (Martin Lazzari), Kana Hanazawa (Yuko Tani), Kenyu Horiuchi (Unberto Mori), Yuki Kaji (Adam Bindewald), Kenta Miyake (Rilu-Elu Belu-be)

Widescreen, Color, 89 Minutes

In the distant future, mankind has evacuated earth due to a series of monster attacks—the worst of which were caused by a plant-based monster called Godzilla. 20 years have passed for humanity in space when they finally decide to return to earth, where 20,000 years have passed. A landing party discovers a hostile new earth that has changed a great deal. It is ruled over by what appears to be a still-living Godzilla and a group of flying monsters called Servum. When the commanding officer is killed, the revenge-driven Haruo Sakaki takes over and his main goal is to kill Godzilla and reclaim earth at all costs. Sakaki devises a plan to find a weakness in Godzilla's electromagnetic shield located in his dorsal plates. His military forces attack Godzilla with all their might and manage to destroy the monster's leafy dorsal plates. Godzilla is then bombarded and killed but moments later, the original Godzilla from 20,000 years ago, which has now grown to be the size of a mountain, emerges...

Background & Commentary Godzilla's big screen anime debut was a long time in the making. In the late 1960s, Toho toyed with a Godzilla anime series from Filmation that could later be compiled into a theatrical feature. In the late 1980s, Henry G. Saperstein pushed for an animated American Godzilla movie when a live-action one proved too expensive. Apparently, this new film was originally planned exclusively as a Netflix series, but the success of *Shin Godzilla* prompted Toho to release it to theaters instead. Unfortunately, the change from episodic anime to a full-feature film did not suit the narrative very well.

Though *Godzilla: Planet of the Monsters* isn't disjointed by any means, it is evident from its pacing that it wasn't written as a theatrical feature. Overall, the whole thing feels like the first act of a much larger story—which it is. Like the other two 2010 era G-films released up to this point (*Godzilla* and *Shin Godzilla*), this one strangely gives Godzilla very little screen time. While this was somewhat understandable in the two live-action films of the era (due to special effects costs), being an animated film, this wasn't a concern. In this regard, those who watch the film solely for Godzilla may be disappointed, while general anime fans may find more to enjoy. Tonally, one could compare the story to *Space Battleship Yamato* with Godzilla thrown in. As in *Shin Godzilla*, the monster has a new origin and new abilities and finishes the film as the largest Godzilla on record. Other than the finale of *Godzilla vs. Destroyah* (1995), in a series first, there are actually two Godzillas in the film: the smaller Godzilla Filius and the much larger Godzilla Earth, who only surfaces in the last scenes. Along for the ride are several other kaiju that are theorized to be flying offshoots of Godzilla called Servum. Actually, the scenes involving the Servum end up being the film's most exciting sequences overall.

A lack of Godzilla aside, the animation is attractive, and Takayuki Hattori's music score is arguably better than his last score for *Godzilla 2000* (1999) and more or less on par with his work on *Godzilla vs. Space Godzilla* (1994). As is the norm in this current era, there is also some fan service in the film, most of which adds little to the story. In a flashback, it is revealed that monsters Kamacuras, Hedorah, Dogora, Orga, and Dagarah (the villain of *Rebirth of Mothra 2*) attacked earth and then are never seen nor heard from again. Also, aliens from a "third planet" that sunk into a black hole have come to earth and build a Mechagodzilla to counter Godzilla, though they aren't ape-like. Though less obvious, the Exif were also modeled on the Xiians that originated in *Invasion of Astro-Monster*, though that isn't evident until the next entry.

Final Word On its own, or, as an original movie, *Godzilla: Planet of the Monsters* is difficult to judge on its own merits. This is probably why it was ill-received by many fans. If binge watched with the other two as though it's a continuous series rather than a trilogy of movies, it fares better.

ULTRAMAN GEED:
THE MOVIE CONNECT THE WISHES!

(TSUBURAYA PRODUCTIONS)
Release Date: March 10, 2018

Directed by: Koichi Sakamoto **Special Effects by:** Tomoaki Miwa **Screenplay by:** Toshizo Nemoto & Hirotaka Adachi **Music by:** Kenji Jawai **Cast:** Tatsuomi Hamada (Riku Asakura/voice of Ultraman Geed), Chihiro Yamamoto (Laiha Toba), Mayu Hasegawa (Moa Aizaki), Hideyoshi Iwata (Zena), Yûta Ozawa (Leito Igaguri), Hideo Ishiguro (Gai Kurenai/voice of Ultraman Orb), Takaya Aoyagi (Jugglus Juggler), Mamoru Miyano (voice of Ultraman Zero) **Suit Performers:** Hideyoshi Iwata (Ultraman Geed), Aki Okabe (Ultraman Zero)

Widescreen, Color, 72 Minutes

The giant mechanical brain Gillvalis is eradicating planet after planet. An alien princess, Ail, with a device capable of destroying Gillvalis escapes to Feudal era Okinawa in Japan, where she hides away for centuries. She is discovered there by Riku as Gillvalis and the Galactron Army invade earth. Riku, as Ultraman Geed, is aided by Ultraman Zero, Ultraman Orb, and Juglus Juglar to fight the army. Geed only prevails after the death of Ail, who imparts to him the Gika Finalizer/Red Steel, which allows him to destroy Gillvalis once and for all.*

Background & Commentary Continuing the "fusion Ultraman" concept was Ultraman Geed, who, in an interesting twist, is the son of Ultraman Belial. Specifically, Geed is the genetic experiment of Belial and his DNA to create a new type of Ultraman capable of channeling the powers of the other Ultramen. Geed has five different fusions that combines the original Ultraman and Belial, and another that combines Seven and Leo, to name only two.

Connect the Wishes is very much an Okinawan themed movie, revolving around an alien princess who landed there long ago with the MacGuffin, the Red Steel. One of the most fun aspects of the movie is the new kaiju Gukuru Shisa, who being a Shisa, looks like a wild variation of King Seesar. Actually, this colorful quadruped is light years more fun than the King Seesar redesign in *Godzilla: Final Wars*. Another fun, colorful scene has the characters going to an alien bar in Okinawa, allowing for plenty of Ultraman alien cameos along the way. Naturally, a bar fight erupts, which makes a perfect entrance for Gai to walk in playing his harmonica.

The trend of crossing over with the previous series continues here, with both Ultraman Orb and Juglus Juglar having significant screen time in the movie. Of course, Ultraman Zero shows up too, and so does his Ultra Squad comprised of Fireman, Mirror Knight, and the two Jean Bots (all unseen on the big screen since 2010's *Ultraman Zero: The Movie*). The first team-up scene with Geed, Zero, and Orb is fun naturally, but considering that all three have different forms they can transform into the battle gets a little confusing—even for someone like me who basically knows all the different varieties of Geed etc. Essentially, all three change designs willy-nilly throughout the battle which is visually confusing to a degree.

The final battle is your typical Ultraman affair: Geed gains a new form with new powers and blasts the final boss to smithereens saving the day. The epilogue is actually more fun than the end battle due to a clever end joke. As Riku bids farewell to Zero and his squad on the beach, Jean Bot gives Riku a quizzical look and says that he recognizes him. This is a fun nod to the fact that the actor who plays Riku also played young Nao, who piloted Jean Bot in *Ultraman Zero: The Movie* almost ten years ago!

Final Word Like the Marvel Cinematic Universe, if one isn't familiar with the numerous characters, many of the film's best moments will be lost on you. So, if you're up to date on the recent Ultra series, *Connect the Wishes* is sure to delight, but if you don't know who characters like Juglus Juglar and Glenfire are, you're best to wait to see this movie until you're caught up.

PACIFIC RIM: UPRISING

(LEGENDARY PICTURES)
Release Date: March 23, 2018
Alternate Titles: *Pacific Rim: Maelstrom* (working title) *Circle of Fire: The Uprising* (Brazil) *Pacific Titans: Insurrection* (Chile)

Directed by: Steven S. DeKnight **Screenplay by:** Steven S. DeKnight, Emily Carmichael, Kira Snyder & T.S. Nowlin **Music by:** Lorne Balfe **Cast:** John Boyega (Jake Pentecost) Cailee Spaeny (Amara Namani) Scott Eastwood (Nathan Lambert) Charlie Day (Dr. Newton Geiszler) Burn Gorman (Dr. Herman Gottlieb) Rinko Kikuchi (Mako Mori)

Widescreen, Color, 111 Minutes

Jake Pentecost, Stacker Pentecost's son, makes a living in the aftermath of the kaiju war by stealing parts from Jaegers. When he is caught with a young, Jaeger building genius, Amara, both are sent to the Jaeger training facility by Mako Mori. Jake is made into an instructor, and Amara a new recruit. While on a routine assignment in Sydney, Jake, and his partner Nathan are attacked by a rogue Jaeger. When they track the Jaeger to Siberia, they discover that it is piloted by a kaiju brain. The mastermind is Dr. Newt, whose mind has been corrupted by the aliens. Newt uses a new Chinese based Jaeger drone program to open new rifts in the Pacific Rim. Three kaiju emerge and head for Japan, the goal being to use their kaiju blood to ignite the Pacific Ring of Fire and destroy the world. Jake and Nathan pilot Gypsy Avenger while recruits man three other Jaegers to take on the kaiju in Tokyo. Eventually, only Gypsy Avenger is left, and the kaiju morph into one giant kaiju. When Nathan is injured, Amara steps in to be Jake's new partner, and together they finish off the massive kaiju before it enters Mt. Fuji.

Background & Commentary Back in 2012, it was hoped that *Pacific Rim* could launch a whole franchise, and before the film's release, director Guillermo Del Toro mentioned he already had ideas for sequels. But, the first film's box office grosses didn't meet expectations in the U.S., though it did well enough in other territories, particularly in China. As such, there was some doubt as to whether or not the sequel would get made. But then Legendary Pictures was purchased by the Chinese Wanda Group for $3.5 billion. Due to the production company's new backers, the fate of the *Pacific Rim* sequel didn't look so grim after all. Eventually, a sequel was announced, though the previous film's lead, Charlie Hunam, was unable to return due to scheduling conflicts as he was filming *King Arthur: Legend of the Sword* at the time. Likewise, Guillermo del Toro passed on the sequel to direct *The Shape of Water* instead, which won him an Oscar. Television director Steven S. DeKnight (*Smallville*, *Daredevil*) took over for Del Torro and managed to craft a solid sequel overall.

The choreography for every battle is spectacular and makes great use of integrating the buildings and features of the city into the fights. The idea of kaiju possessed Jaegers makes for a great mystery, and the writers should be commended for creating this aspect when they could have been lazy and simply had the aliens make a new rift somehow. This film tips its hat even further to the Japanese giant monster genre in having the climactic battle set in Tokyo, and the goal is to stop the monsters from entering Mt. Fuji.

John Boyega makes for a more interesting lead than Charlie Hunam, whose character's absence is never addressed. As to returning characters, many fans were upset that Mako Mori was not only killed off but was given very little to do. Of the returning cast, it is the comedic duo of Newt and Herman that excel. Newt's new direction from comical actor Charlie Day is particularly interesting. And, just when you think you can see his villainous turn coming, there's a 52 fake-out. Then, after being duped, it was all a red herring as Newt does turn out to be the villain. Ironically, though he played second fiddle to Day in *Pacific Rim*, actor Burn Gorman ends up being the one to shine in comedic terms as Herman. His best scene is easily when he turns out to be proficient at using his cane as a weapon in an elevator scene with Day in what is one of the film's most cheer-able moments.

Though this film was meant to set up a trilogy, it ultimately underperformed worse than the first film did. Some experts even estimated that it didn't even manage to break even, effectively squashing any hope of more sequels.

Final Word If you enjoyed the first *Pacific Rim,* then this one is obviously worth seeing. If you didn't take to the first one, many consider this one to be inferior, and it's probably not worth your time.

GODZILLA:
CITY ON THE EDGE OF BATTLE

(TOHO/POLYGON)
Release Date: May 18, 2018

Directed by: Hiroyuki Seshita & Kobun Shizuno **Screenplay by:** Gen Urobuchi & Sadayuki Murai **Music by:** Takayuki Hattori **Voice Cast:** Mamoru Miyano (Haruo Sakaki), Takahiro Sakurai (Metphies), Tomokazu Sugita (Martin Lazzari), Kana Hanazawa (Yuko Tani), Kenyu Horiuchi (Unberto Mori), Yuki Kaji (Adam Bindewald), Kenta Miyake (Rilu-Elu Belu-be), Reina Ueda (Maina), Ari Ozawa (Miana)

Widescreen, Color, 101 Minutes

Haruo awakens under the care of a strange native woman, Miana, who he chases out into the forest. He finds his fellow comrades in battle with the same woman, or rather, her twin, Maina. The natives, called the Houtua, capture the survivors and take them to their underground city where they keep a huge, unseen egg. There they discover that the Houtua are using a mysterious nano-metal on their arrows. The Bilusaludo recognizes this as the same nano-metal they used to construct Mechagodzilla. The twins agree to lead the crew to the site of Mechagodzilla's remains, but warn that it is dangerous. Haruo and his crew find that not only has Mechagodzilla's AI continued to function, but for thousands of years, it has been building a colossal battle city. The group decides to lure Godzilla to the city with their new mechs, dubbed the Vultures, as the Bilusaludo decide to join with the city as the next step in their evolution. Haruo, Yuko, and Belu-be pilot the Vultures to lead Godzilla into a nanometal trap, but the Bilusaludo tries to force everyone else in the group to join with Mechagodzilla City. Rather than dealing the death blow to the trapped Godzilla, Haruo blows up the city's main control, freeing himself and his team from the city's power.

Background & Commentary After the first entry of Toho's anime Godzilla trilogy left the majority of fans disappointed, many others held out hope for the second installment. After all, perhaps the first entry was just a warmup to introduce the characters, do some world building, etc. before things really hit the ground running. Expectations were also high

186

based upon the fact that this entry would feature Mechagodzilla battling the new Godzilla. Whetting audience appetite further was the concept of a Mechagodzilla City. Unfortunately for most fans, *Godzilla: City on the Edge of Battle* was just as disappointing, if not more so than *Planet of Monsters*. Despite the fact that Mechagodzilla was part of the marketing, and a Bandai figure of the mech-monster was produced, the kaiju doesn't even appear in the movie. Or, at least, not in its traditional form.

It's possible that the concept for this film dates back to both the "Godzilla 2" story contest of the mid-1980s and the development of "Godzilla 7" in the mid-1990s. In 1985 the runner up behind *Godzilla vs. Biollante* was a story entitled *Godzilla vs. the Robot Corps*, about Godzilla battling a massive computer fortress. This idea was sidelined for many years until "Godzilla 7," when it was briefly considered under the new title of *Godzilla vs. the Cyber City*. It's probably a good thing that the story wasn't developed until many years later. For one, in the original concepts, it was never a 'Mechagodzilla City," and two, nanometal was not at that time on the screenwriters' radar. As it is, the nanometal aspect of the story added a lot to the film. Nanometal is used not only metaphorically throughout the movie (the nanometal is what engulfs the Bilusaludo into the city), but it is also used stylistically to good effect. For instance, the title of the movie forms out of nanometal. Hattori's metallic music is also fitting (in fact, this might be the best score of Hattori's career).

When you get right down to it, the core plotline sounds fantastic on paper, that being that the Shobijin must guide planetary explorers to a lost Mechagodzilla City. There is an interesting parallel in that just as Godzilla has grown and evolved to an enormous size over the last several thousand years, so has Mechagodzilla into a literal city. Just the name Mechagodzilla City sounds enticing by itself, which is part of the problem. Fans had visions of a Mechagodzilla-like city coming to life to attack Godzilla, something that doesn't exactly happen. Instead, the sentient city leads Godzilla through a vast metallic corridor until he becomes trapped in a pit. The pit is then filled with liquid nanometal that will hold Godzilla in place while the heroes unleash a vast arsenal of weaponry on him.

If one can get over the fact that this won't be a traditional Godzilla movie and enjoy the twists on the mythos, this can be a rather engaging film—especially if one embraces the characters. Perhaps the most fascinating twist on the typical Godzilla/Mothra/Mechagodzilla mythologies is how all the humanoid species tie into the monsters. The humans who left earth thousands of years ago are tied to Godzilla. The Houtua, a totally new race, have insect traits and are linked to a giant egg housing Mothra (though the big bug's name is never spoken). The update on the Shobijin as human-sized warriors is an interesting one. Their proficiency with a bow and arrow (using arrows made from Mechagodzilla no less) is a fun twist on the mythology, as are their insect traits. The Bilusaludo, which the previous entry established as being from a planet that succumbed to a black hole, is tied to Mechagodzilla in the same way the Houtua are linked to Mothra. The Bilusaludo are the exact opposite of the supernatural-believing Houtua and Exif, though. Their god is science and technology, and as such, they plan to merge themselves into Mechagodzilla City. And finally, there is the Exif, who we learn are tied to King Ghidorah (whose name they refuse to speak it is so ghastly to them, or so we think). That all four species are in some way consumed by their monster, in the Bilusaludo's case literally, is an intriguing idea.

Due to the ill-reception of *Godzilla: The Planet Eater*, the second entry in the Godzilla anime trilogy opened to less fanfare than the original, which wasn't a runaway success itself. It opened in 8th place at the box office and earned ¥100,000,000 in its first week of release. Nor were critics kind to it.

Final Word If you can embrace the characters and accept that this trilogy isn't going to be a typical Godzilla "monster vs. monster" series, there's a lot to enjoy in this rather engrossing story.

GODZILLA:
THE PLANET EATER

(TOHO/POLYGON)
Release Date: November 9, 2018

Directed by: Hiroyuki Seshita & Kobun Shizuno **Screenplay by:** Gen Urobuchi **Music by:** Takayuki Hattori **Voice Cast:** Mamoru Miyano (Haruo Sakaki), Takahiro Sakurai (Metphies), Tomokazu Sugita (Martin Lazzari), Kenyu Horiuchi (Unberto Mori), Reina Ueda (Maina), Ari Ozawa (Miana)

Widescreen, Color, 90 Minutes

After the destruction of Mechagodzilla City, the Bilusaludo want Haruo arrested for what he's done, while the Exif exalt him for his deeds. As the crew of the Aratrum, both on earth and on the ship, fall into despair, the Exif manipulate their hopelessness to their own ends: summoning their god, King Ghidorah. As it turns out, the Exif worship the very creature that destroyed their planet and welcomes the destroyer as an end to humanity's suffering. Metphies needs Haruo, driven by his hatred for Godzilla, to anchor the interdimensional dragon to Earth. Despite Metphies' best efforts to get Haruo to give himself to Ghidorah, currently fighting Godzilla, Maina uses her psychic abilities with the help of Mothra to break the Exif's hold on Haruo. Godzilla defeats Ghidorah, and humankind decides to live with the Houtua. Some time later, Haruo pilots one of the old Vulture mechs into Godzilla in a suicide.

Background & Commentary By the time that this film was released, *City on the Edge of Battle* had more or less solidified for most fans that this would not be a traditional Godzilla series full of monster on monster action. And yet, some still held out hope that the animators were saving the real monster battle for the last entry so that it would have some payoff. While there is something resembling a monster battle, the real payoff only comes for those who are invested in the characters. The biggest twist by far comes in the form of the character of Metphies, who had been odd but still likable for the past two entries as a compassionate figure. For the previous two films, Metphies' race, the Exif, served as the expedition's priests and religious advisors. Though they had often spoken

189

of a god, in this entry, we learn the "god" they worship has been King Ghidorah all along, making them the secret villains of the whole trilogy. With this knowledge in mind, if one goes back and re-watches the first two entries, the Exif's dialogue takes on an entirely new meaning when they speak of religion and their god. As the Godzilla series continues to evolve in later years, it might be interesting if the idea of the Exif/Xiliens worshiping Ghidorah was revisited in another continuity. Say what you will of the lackluster action, but this concept was genuinely thought-provoking, it just needed a better film to go along with it.

If there's one movie this one is comparable to it's probably *Gamera 3: Revenge of Irys* as it is very esoteric. Haruo serves a similar role to Ayana in that his hatred of Godzilla serves as a conduit for the enemy monster. Specifically, the Exif use Haruo's hatred of the beast as part of a ritual to summon King Ghidorah. The end battle is even quasi similar to *Gamera 3*, though certainly less exciting. One will remember that once inside Kyoto Station, Gamera and Irys are limited in what they can do. Here, Ghidorah wraps his necks around Godzilla... and that's about it.

However, Ghidorah makes one heck of an entrance. This entrance also coincides with some rather interesting developments with Miana and Maina. Just as Miana becomes intimate with Haruo for the first time, Maina is caught by Metphies, who forces her to call out Ghidorah's name. Later it is implied that he has murdered Maina as part of a ritual, and it seems he made a broth out of her body! (This turns out to be a 52 fake-out, and the body in the broth was only a hallucination). The surviving members of the *Aratrum* drink the broth, and when the alien leaders call out the monster's name, we see the spectral necks of Ghidorah emerge from a well and begin killing the humans! Physically, Ghidorah then emerges from a portal above the *Aratrum* and wraps one interminably long neck around it, crushing it until it explodes.

Mothra has a cameo, not a full-blown role, but it's quite a scene (to Toho's credit, it was a surprise cameo, nor were any Mothra Bandai figures produced which would have misled fans into thinking she had a big role in the movie as was the case with Mechagodzilla in Part II). As Metphies takes Haruo on a journey through the spiritual plane, Haruo has various flashbacks to his youth, as well as notable moments in Godzilla's history. As they discuss the atomic bomb, there's a scene of the two on the *Enola Gay*, which dropped the bomb on Hiroshima. To free Haruo, Mothra's spirit breaks into the spiritual plane and flies straight at the bomber, enraging Metphies and snapping Haruo out of the trance.

The movie has an extended epilogue that takes place sometime after the defeat of Ghidorah. Things appear to be going well. The crew of the *Aratrum* has integrated with the Houtua, and there seems to be no

190

problems with Godzilla. Haruo even has a baby on the way with Maina. However, Dr. Martin makes the mistake of showing Haruo that he has gotten one of the old Vultures working again. Martin's plan is to rebuild society with its nanometals, despite the fact that everyone seems perfectly happy living with the Houtua. Haruo, unable to let go of the past, takes Yuko's comatose body with him on a suicide mission to face Godzilla. In fact, it is a suicide more than anything else as Haruo knows what he's doing won't kill Godzilla. One could perhaps argue that he's knowingly saving mankind from itself by destroying the technology that would lead to further war with Godzilla.

Ultimately, most Godzilla fans were disappointed with this trilogy. As it was, Toho wanted to try new things and specifically wanted to avoid monster battles, which understandably alienated fans. Apparently, the hope was that if the focus was on the human story, it would appeal to more women, which makes up most of Japan's theater-going audience according to many sources. But it didn't. If anything, it proved that the original course of action (to release it all at once on Netflix to be "binged") would have served the story better. That, and including the traditional monster battles that are a staple of the franchise, of course.

Final Word Now that it has run its course, the Godzilla anime trilogy will likely be more enjoyable for fans who know what to expect upon repeat viewings (it was for me). It may also hold more appeal for first-time viewers who have been warned that it's short on monster battles. Again, if one can watch the trilogy knowing that it's more focused on the human storyline than it is the monsters, it is possible for one to enjoy it.

ULTRAMAN R/B: THE MOVIE
SELECT! THE CRYSTAL OF BOND

(TSUBURAYA PRODUCTIONS)
Release Date: March 8, 2019

Directed by: Masayoshi Takesue **Screenplay by:** Takao Nakano **Music by:** Yasuharu Takanashi **Cast:** Yuya Hirata (Katsumi Minato/voice of Ultraman Rosso), Ryosuke Koike (Isami Minato/voice of Ultraman Blu), Arisa Sonohara (Asahi Minato/voice of Ultrawoman Grigio), Tatsuomi Hamada (Riku Asakura/voice of Ultraman Geed), Yukito Nishii (Yukio Toi), Yuuma Uchida (voice of Ultraman Tregear) **Suit Performers:** Uncredited

Widescreen, Color, 72 Minutes

Katsumi and Isami are brothers who have the power to transform into Ultraman Rosso and Ultraman Blu, respectively. They also have an adopted sister, Asahi, who has special powers. A year after the Reugosite incident, young Katsumi is not sure what path he wants to take with a career, while confident Isami is all set to become a space archeologist. Katsumi goes to visit a friend, Toi, who is even more distraught over his future than Katsumi is. Toi is later contacted by an evil Ultraman called Tregear, who offers to fulfill his wishes, but really just manifests Toi's anger and depression into a giant monster. Tregear also tricks Katsumi into going off-world to rescue a race of Pigmon from a Mecha-Gomora. With Ultraman Rosso off Earth, Tregear unleashes the Toi-possessed monster, Snake Darkness, on Ayaka City. Ultraman Blu and Ultraman Geed, who has jumped universes, teams to battle the kaiju. They are unable to defeat it until Ultraman Rosso comes back to earth. Asahi then transforms into Ultrawoman Grigio. The three siblings then merge into Ultraman Groob, who is able to defeat the monster and expel a repentant Toi from its body, while the mysterious Ultraman Tregear flees to fight another day.

Background & Commentary The *Ultraman R/B* series was unique in that it focused on two Ultramen rather than one in the form of two brothers, each of whom has their own ultra form. In a vague way, the concept dates back to the Showa era. *Ultraman Ace* (1972) began as a fusion of a man and a woman (though, eventually, the female half of Ace

192

left the show, and it was just a single person transformation for the rest of the series). There was also Leo and Astra from *Ultraman Leo* (1974), but Astra was more of a supporting player, nor did he have a human host. Therefore *Ultraman R/B* definitely expands upon the concept by having two main characters, each with their own ultra-form, providing a fresh take on the formula.

Ultraman R/B: The Movie, the last Ultraman feature film released during the Heisei era, might be a little too lighthearted for some. Case in point, the first scene reveals Ultraman Rosso stuck upside down with his head lodged in a building, while his more competent brother Blu battles a pair of monsters with Geed. As Rosso struggles to free himself, Katsumi, Rosso's host, then has a flashback to show us how he got to this point. Since the events of the series finale, Katsumi has been having an identity crisis that is relatable for many youths who are unsure of what they want to do in life. It's even more difficult for Katsumi since his brother and sister have both decided on what they want to do.

Speaking of sister Asahi, who has been away for a while, when the family gets word that she is returning to Ayaka City, they go to spy on her in the town square. It's a goofy scene that should appeal to children— and maybe adults too if they'll let themselves enjoy it. The two brothers and their father hide in plain sight (wearing camouflage) when they spy Asahi with a young man. Suddenly, they see the young man lean in to kiss her. They rush over to stop him, and the young man turns out to be Riku (Ultraman Geed in human form). It should be noted that Geed exists in a parallel universe; therefore, the brothers have never met him before, nor do they know he's an Ultraman too. Soon a pair of monsters attack, and all three rush to transform into their respective Ultramen in the same spot. The brothers and Riku take notice of each other (Geed is also unaware that the two brothers are Ultramen) and sheepishly run off to different spots to transform. When the two ultra-brothers arrive to fight the monster they are then shocked to have Geed pop up next to them. There's a funny moment where they take note of Geed's odd-looking eyes, and one of the brothers chides the other for being rude.

This movie debuts not one, but three brand new Ultras. The first is Asahi's ultra-form called Ultrawoman Grigio. In fact, this is the first and last heroic Ultrawoman to even appear during the Heisei era, as the other two were technically both villains! Ultraman Grood is a combination of Grigio, Rosso, and Blu. Most of the time Grood is brought to life via CGI rather than suitmation. To their credit, Tsuburaya's computer animation has gotten good enough that it's sometimes tough to spot the difference. And then there is the villain of the piece, Ultraman Tregear, who essentially takes the place of Ultraman Belial (possibly vanquished for good in the series finale of *Ultraman Geed).* Though not stated in this feature, Tregear's backstory is that he was a friend of Ultraman Taro's who turned evil for unknown reasons. In some respects, he almost makes for a better "evil Ultraman" than Belial, who became so powerful that he almost ceased to resemble an Ultraman. It's apparent that Tsuburaya Productions has big plans for Tregear since he survives the end battle and also appears in a post-credits scene.

Final Word As with all the Ultraman movies, this one is a richer experience when viewed after watching the entire series. But, even if one hasn't seen *Ultraman R/B* the series, the movie isn't too hard to follow and is still quite entertaining.

ATTACK OF THE GIANT TEACHER

(INDEPENDENT)
Release Date: 2019

Directed by: Yoshikazu Ishii **Special Effects by:** Yoshikazu Ishii **Screenplay by:** Nobuhiko Ishii (from a story by Yoshikazu Ishii) **Music by:** Hiroaki Ito **Cast:** Shogo Aramaki, Takehiko Fujita, Gaichi, Naomi Hase, Michiko Hikosaka, Holly Kaneko, Makoto Kojima, Aoi Kuga

Widescreen, Color, 70 Minutes

Kenzo Miyazawa is an underachieving teacher at a night school. When it is announced that the school will be shut down due to a lack of students, Miyazawa's superior tells him that he must prove himself to get a job at the other school. Miyazawa encourages his students to put on an end of the year musical, but when the students learn that Miyazawa is partly doing this to prove himself worthy of a new teaching position, they become upset. The students decide to go on with the musical anyways. In the middle of the performance, an alien invader descends upon Japan. As it turns out, two of Miyazawa's students were benevolent aliens all along. The evil alien wishes to kill them, and when it does, it will then feed upon all of humanity. Miyazawa's two alien students give him a pill that will increase his size to match that of the giant alien's. Miyazawa takes the pill, allowing his two alien students to escape into space while he battles the alien. Miyazawa defeats the alien menace and redeems himself in the eyes of his students.

Background & Commentary *Attack of the Giant Teacher* is a hard film for a Westerner to judge. It's presumably quite funny if one fully understands Japanese culture, but as it is, many fans—and that includes this author—are more familiar with Japanese tokusatsu films than Japanese culture as a whole. As such, for many of us, *Attack of the Giant Teacher's* main point of interest only comes into play in the film's last ten minutes when Mr. Miyazawa takes a pill that enables him to grow to gigantic proportions.

That's not to say that everything preceding this is of no merit—it's certainly amusing, but it's also hard for a gaijin to fully appreciate at times. The end tokusatsu scenes are very well-staged, and the miniatures are on par with the current Ultraman TV series. Speaking of Ultraman, the alien villain brings to mind the odder, non-dinosaurian alien monsters that appeared in the Ultraman series of the 1970s. Not too many miniatures are destroyed, and the alien is KO'd when Miyazawa swats him into a building.

Attack of the Giant Teacher may be of interest to tokusatsu scholars and enthusiasts due to its pedigree alone, even if the comedy aspects go over one's head. It was made by Yoshikazu Ishii, who is one of the few directors in Japan today to still carry the title of special effects director. He was invited to work on the set of two of the Millennium Godzilla films, *Godzilla 2000* and *Godzilla vs. Megaguirus*, by the films' scripter, Hiroshi Kashiwabara. Ishii eventually served as special effects director on two episodes of *Ultraman Geed*.

Final Word If you like offbeat films like *Monster X Strikes Back* or *Big Man Japan*, you might enjoy *Attack of the Giant Teacher* as well.

DEEP SEA MONSTER RAIGA VS. LAVA BEAST OHGA

(INDEPENDENT)
Release Date: May 7, 2019
Alternate Titles: *God Raiga vs. King Ohga* (U.S.)

Directed by: Shinpei Hayashiya **Special Effects by:** Shinpei Hayashiya **Screenplay by:** Shinpei Hayashiya **Music by:** Keiichiro Kitazono Rengoku & Kozou **Cast:** Makoto Inamiya (Commander Kito), Wasabi Yanagiya (Miyazaki), Anko Hayashiya (Nakagawa), Isamu Ago (First Secretary), Bunzaemon Tachibanaya (Japanese Prime Minister), Mark Jaramillo (CIA agent) **Suit Performers:** Arare Hayashiya/Hiromichi Ebata (Raiga), Yutaka Arai/Naofumi Kanamori (Ohga)

Widescreen, Color, 86 Minutes

It's been several years since Raiga attacked Asakusa, and since then, Commander Kito has been banished to heading up the defense forces branch in Atami. The coastal town is soon assaulted by Raiga and a new, underground monster called Ohga. Rather than stopping the beasts, the Prime Minister of Japan secretly wants the two monsters to destroy Atami so it can be rebuilt into a gambling town. The two monsters do destroy Atami, and in the aftermath, Kito joins the Roppongi branch of the defense force. Raiga and Ohga attack the area, and the military launches a new type of super missile at them. It devastates the area and appears to kill Kito and his team. However, the monsters aren't killed and fuse into a brand new kaiju...

Background & Commentary A wise director once said that art thrives upon restriction, and this is often true. As it is, the third Reigo/Raiga film is not as polished as its two predecessors, but it's still good art. Depending on how you view it, it might be even better than the previous film. Whereas *Raiga* was a quasi-spoof of *Reigo*, *Raiga vs. Ohga* is almost like Hayashiya's bonkers fan film tribute to his previous works.

Hayashiya actually had no plans for a third Reigo/Raiga movie until Mark Jaramillo coerced the director to come to G-Fest in Chicago. Hayashiya was so touched by the fan response to his films in America that it inspired him to do a third film. Raiga even trashes a Crowne Plaza

197

Hotel in Japan, which one can assume was a nod to G-Fest's hotel of choice for many years. Furthermore, quite a few American fans get small roles and cameos in the movie. The best of these is Mark Jaramillo as a CIA agent. His scenes are so well-acted that he easily bests many of the gaijin actors featured in Toho's Heisei Godzilla movies! Jaramillo and his cohort bring to mind the Bio-Major agents from *Godzilla vs. Biollante* as they pop up every now and again during the story.

Actor Yukijiro Hotaru (the lead in the previous two films) doesn't return this time around, and a supporting character from the last film, Commander Kito, takes over as the new lead. The "people parts" are just as funny and amusing as they were in the last movie. For instance, when Jaramillo's CIA agent calls Kito's office and talks to one of his aids, the young Japanese man has only a loose grasp of English. Eventually, he gives up on talking to the agent and says to Kito, "Commander, we've got a foreigner on the phone. I think he's offering us coffee." The aid hangs up, and on the opposite line, the other agent asks Jaramillo's character what happened. He responds, "I don't know, I think he was on a coffee break."

The movie boasts more monsters and mechs than the previous two films did. The mechs include a land-based version of the Gohten called the Gokumei, which fights Ohga underground. Next comes the Auto Tracker Gattling Robot, which looks vaguely like a mecha-Ohga. And then comes an octopus tank, and then some kind of shark car/submarine. Ohga has a good design overall but is often obscured by smoke and other digital effects that make it hard to get a clear look at it. Raiga and Ohga's battles are somewhat limited but still fun to watch. A long shot of the two kaiju fighting in the distance over Atami is a recreation of a similar shot from *King Kong vs. Godzilla* (1962).

The movie's ending is totally bonkers and also a little bleak. All the main characters appear to die in an explosion. The last shot before the credits roll has a soldier (Kyle Yount) revealing that DNA tests proved that Raiga and Ohga had almost identical genetics. The credits roll, and then comes a post-credits scene, which is so long it's almost more of a short film. A new monster, a fusion of Raiga and Ohga, rises from the debris and is dubbed "Kuga, the master of thunder." Though you would think this would be enough to end the movie on, Kuga then flies all the way to Hawaii and begins trashing a city. A new monster rises to challenge him, and then the movie ends.

Final Word Though the first *Reigo* will probably remain the best-regarded entry of the Raiga saga, it's a tough call as to whether *Raiga vs. Ohga* is the second-best entry or the third.

GODZILLA: KING OF THE MONSTERS

(LEGENDARY PICTURES)
Release Date: May 31, 2019
Alternate Titles: *Godzilla II: King of the Monsters* (International)

Directed by: Michael Dougherty **Special Effects by:** Guillaume Rocheron
Screenplay by: Michael Dougherty, Zach Shields & Max Borenstein (Story)
Music by: Bear McCreary **Cast:** Vera Farmiga (Dr. Emma Russel), Millie Bobby
Brown (Madison Russell), Kyle Chandler (Dr. Mark Russell), Ken Watanabe (Dr.
Ishiro Serizawa), Charles Dance (Alan Jonah), O'Shea Jackson Jr. (Jackson
Barnes), Thomas Middleditch (Dr. Sam Coleman), Zhang Ziyi (Dr. Ilene Chen and
Dr. Ling), Bradley Whitford (Dr. Rick Stanton), David Strathairn (Admiral Stenz),
Sally Hawkins (Dr. Vivienne Graham) **Motion Capture Performers:** T.J. Storm
(Godzilla), Richard Dorton (Ghidorah, left head), Jason Liles (Ghidorah, center
head), Alan Maxson (Ghidorah, right head)

Panavision, Color, 132 Minutes

In the aftermath of Godzilla's battle with the MUTOs in San
Francisco, Monarch agents Emma and Mark Russel construct the
Orca, a device that can communicate with the Titans. The couple
divorces, and years later, Emma sides with a terrorist group that has
intentions of awakening various Titans. The group revives a
particularly dangerous extraterrestrial monster called King Ghidorah.
Godzilla and Ghidorah fight off the coast of Mexico where the military
fires their new superweapon, the Oxygen Destroyer, at them. Godzilla
is weakened to the point of death while Ghidorah is unfazed and rallies
the rest of the Titans to his cause: reshaping Earth to his liking. Dr.
Serizawa, a Monarch scientist, gives his life to detonate a nuclear
bomb near Godzilla to help recharge the monster. Emma's daughter,
Madison, steals the Orca and uses it to broadcast from Boston to
soothe the Titans currently destroying the world. King Ghidorah
arrives to stop the signal, and Madison is saved by the recharged
Godzilla. While Godzilla is aided in the battle by Mothra, King Ghidorah
is assisted by Rodan. A fight amongst the four monsters ensues in
Boston as Mark and Emma reunite to search for Madison. They find
their daughter, and in a last act of heroism, Emma uses the Orca to
lure Ghidorah away from Godzilla. Thanks to a power-up from the

dead Mothra, Godzilla enters a supercharged state and kills King Ghidorah. All the other Titans, including Rodan, bow down to Godzilla, acknowledging him as King of the Monsters.

Background & Commentary If Hanna-Barbera had been tasked to make a two-hour movie including Godzilla, Mothra, King Ghidorah, and Rodan, it probably would have turned out something like this. That can be a good thing or a bad thing depending upon your tastes, and therein lies the problem. *Godzilla: King of the Monsters* is not universally loved by any means, ironic considering the fact that it rectifies the main complaint of the 2014 *Godzilla*. Whereas in that film our hero was barely on screen, in this film Godzilla gets a great deal more screen presence. Some might say too much, as in at the expense of the human characters.

The problem seems to be in the pacing. *King of the Monsters* is not a slow film. On the contrary, it's paced too fast. There are no breather scenes to develop the characters enough to truly allow the viewer to connect with them. The exposition scenes seem like cut scenes of a video game, giving you the information you need before moving onto the next mission, or in this case, the film's next action scene. All of the characters have interesting angles to them that the film doesn't seem to have time to explore (though rumor has it, they are explored in scenes cut in order to shorten the film's lengthy runtime... scenes not included in home video releases for some odd reason).

Furthermore, the actors are all excellent choices for the fanbase because each played a rather iconic character on television. Vera Farmiga played Norma Bates on *Bates Motel* and presents a similarly tortured character here. Milly Bobbie Brown played Eleven on *Stranger Things* and manages to be a very likable character as Madison. The problem, again, is not quite getting enough time with the characters. The biggest casualty of *King of the Monster's* runtime is actor Charles Dance, famous for portraying Tywin Lannister on *Game of Thrones*. His character, Alan Jonah, just kind of shows up, and that's that. His motivations are explained once, but it just isn't enough to make him an engaging character, even if Dance is a very engaging actor. Adding insult to injury, Jonah has a post-credits scene even though he will not appear in *Godzilla vs. Kong*. If Jonah's character was intended to be explored in the sequel, then we could have just considered his part in *King of the Monsters* as a teaser for what was to come later. But that is not the case.

We spend most of our time with the Monarch crew of the *Argo*. Kyle Chandler, best remembered as Coach Taylor on *Friday Night Lights*, gives an excellent performance as Mark Russell. To his credit, Chandler manages to spout off lines about Godzilla and Mothra that might sound

200

ludicrous coming from anyone else. Oshea Jackson is also quite likable as G-Team leader Jackson Barnes. Like Burt Gummer's character in the *Tremors* series, Barnes probably has the potential to take over the series one day, if it goes anywhere beyond *Godzilla vs. Kong*, that is. Ken Watanabe gets more screen time as Dr. Serizawa this time around, and also gets a memorable death scene, which is sadly lessened somewhat by the film's overstuffed plot. The same can be said for Vivian Graham's character, who we met in the last film. Actually, none of the film's deaths have the impact that they should, again, due to the rushed overstuffed plot.

The saddest thing about *King of the Monsters* is that the storyline can't prop up the monster scenes well enough, which are spectacular. Monster Zero/Ghidorah's awakening in the Arctic is the stuff that movies are made of. The monster's multiple heads and tails rising out of the icy abyss makes for one of the film's best visuals. Dougherty set out to give all three of Ghidorah's heads distinct traits. Though this might sound like a fool's errand, remarkably, he succeeds via the three motion capture performers. For instance, fandom has nicknamed the left head "Kevin" picking up on the fact that it's the slowest of the three heads.

In a close second for the film's most memorable monster is Rodan. His reveal crawling out of the volcano, the destruction of Isla de Mona via shockwave, and the aerial battle with the jets is pure spectacle. Mothra is probably the most shortchanged of the bunch due to her more complex history. Whereas Rodan is a simple marauding monster, the same can't be said for Mothra. The film has a version of the Shobijin in the form of twin Monarch agents, Dr. Chen and Dr. Ling, but it's not an obvious plot point. In fact, there's so much going on, more than a few people probably didn't even realize that they were twins. The idea of the Shobijin being full-sized, human agents of Monarch could be quite interesting. But once again, it's just another "cool thing" in the background. Mothra probably should have been saved for another movie, but had to be shoehorned in because Legendary had already paid for the monster's pricy rights.

The film is chock full of nods to the Showa and Heisei era. Bear McCreary's score also deserves special mention, as he manages to expertly work in some magnificent Ifukube cues, something not done in the previous two American reboots. Mothra's reviving of Godzilla was presumably inspired by Rodan's sacrifice in *Godzilla vs. Mechagodzilla II* (1993). While Rodan's death powered up Godzilla, Mothra's sacrifice here turns Godzilla into a new version of Burning Godzilla from *Godzilla vs. Destroyah*. Even the film's post-credits scene, where Alan Jonah goes to inspect King Ghidorah's severed head, is staged to resemble the pre-credit scene from *Godzilla vs. Mechagodzilla II* with Mecha-King

Ghidorah's head. Some of the other fan-service doesn't work so well, namely the Oxygen Destroyer. It's shoehorned in so abruptly that the weapon should have been given another name. But, that is the double-edged sword that has become fan-service. While at times it can be amazing (Nick Fury's cameo at the end of *Iron Man*), at other times it can run a little too wild when left unchecked. On the other hand, the film has a unique twist where its monster roster is concerned. When the news hit that the big three were back, many, including myself, assumed the end battle would pay tribute to 1964's *Ghidorah, the Three-Headed Monster*. It did not, and nor did this disappoint many fans. Having Rodan side with King Ghidorah was a rather interesting twist all things considered.

Ultimately, *King of the Monsters* divided the fan base between people who either loved it or hated it. Fans who cared only about the monster scenes loved it (understandable because the monster scenes are gold), while others who also care about the "people parts" were sourly disappointed by that aspect. *King of the Monsters* also underperformed at the box office, and if not for the fact that *Kong: Skull Island* was a hit, not to mention that *Godzilla vs. Kong* was already shooting, a third Legendary Godzilla film may not have even been made.

Final Word As it currently stands, *Godzilla: King of the Monsters* is a hard film to judge due to its runtime, which despite being over two hours long, still seems too brief for all the characters and plot points. I personally believe that a longer director's cut of the film that allowed the characters to breathe would fare better. If by some miracle Dougherty is allowed to do a director's cut, I think *King of the Monsters* has the potential to be one of the better Godzilla movies in the entire franchise.

HOWL FROM BEYOND THE FOG

(INDEPENDENT)
Release Date: November 24, 2019
Alternate Titles: *Land of Fog* (Japan)

Directed by: Daisuke Sato **Special Effects by:** Daisuke Sato & Keizo Murase **Screenplay by:** Daisuke Sato & Yohei Yanase **Music by:** Chouchou **Cast:** Suguru Inoue (Eiji), Akane Kanamori (Takiri), Michiyo Ishimito (Inami), Nana Nagao (Nagisa), Tomohiro Matsumoto (Nebula)

Panavision, Color, 132 Minutes

After the death of his twin brother, Eiji returns to his ancestral village in Kyushu. His only living relatives now are his mother and his blind cousin, Takiri, hidden away because she was born outside of marriage. At night, Takiri ventures to a foggy lake in the mountains to visit with a mysterious creature. A group of land developers wants to purchase the lakefront property, but the family refuses to sell. Learning about the illegitimate girl, the men take her and throw her into the lake. The monster, called Nebula, rises from the depths with Takiri in his mouth, unharmed. Nebula sets Takiri into Eiji's arms and chases the men back into the village. Nebula destroys the village, and the cousins are too late to stop him. The land developers shoot fireworks at Nebula, who, in the end, kills them all.

Background & Commentary This short film takes its inspiration from "The Fog Horn," the story by Ray Bradbury that was adapted into *The Beast from 20,000 Fathoms* (1953). Although set in 1909 Japan, the influences are clear. "The Fog Horn" focused on a remnant dinosaur who mistakes a foghorn he hears for the cry of another dinosaur. Essentially, the dinosaur is lonely and looking for companionship. When he finds that the noise emanated from a strange structure and not another dinosaur as he had hoped, he destroys it. In the case of *Howl from Beyond the Fog*, the monster is lonely, and its roar sounds like a foghorn. Nebula can also suck fog into its lungs, then expel it back out in a decimating power breath.

The movie begins with a very atmospheric pre-title scene reminiscent of a Sergio Leone Spaghetti Western. The sequence has no dialogue and is brought to life with the visuals and sound effects only (namely a howling wind). Like any good monster movie, Nebula is teased but not shown fully when it rears its head from the fog in silhouette. Despite being benevolent throughout the movie unless provoked, here it kills two men crossing a bridge for no discernable reason.

The movie is a miniature enthusiasts dream, as the whole thing is told through puppets and miniatures. That's not to say Nebula looks fake either; the monster could have fit right in with live-action performers in many scenes. Furthermore, Nebula is one of the better designed dinosaurian monsters to emerge in recent years. The beast calls to mind the star of 1977's *The Crater Lake Monster* if it had bits of plant growth attached to it.

When the monsters not on screen, the puppet characters manage to be quite engaging, nor do they wear out their welcome in the short film. The ending, where Nebula trashes the village, is well done. A particularly striking scene shows Nebula backlit by some fireworks, which the villains are using to lure the monster into a trap. The trap doesn't go so well for the villains, and despite scoring one good hit on the monster, Nebula wins in the end. In a surprise move, the monster inhales an immense amount of fog and then blasts it back out, killing the villains who are perched atop a bridge. The film ends on the dawn of a new day. With their home destroyed, the cousins decide they can start anew anywhere they like.

Though directed by Daisuke Sato, one of the major driving forces behind the short film was Keizo Murase, the famous model/monster suit maker. Murase promoted the upcoming film at G-Fest in 2018 and garnered a great deal of excitement from U.S. based fans. The Nebula suit/marionette was the result of a crowdfunding campaign through Kickstarter. The campaign, which began on November 30, 2017, exceeded its goal at 150%. It raised ¥1,269,842 from 140 backers. As a reward for their support, U.S. G-Fans got to see a beta version of the movie at G-Fest in July of 2019, while the finished version premiered at the 2nd Atami Kaiju Film Festival on November 24, 2019.

Final Word As the last Japanese monster movie of 2019, and one of the first of the Reiwa Era, *Howl From Beyond the Fog* is appropriately a beautiful work of art that should appeal to all kaiju fans.

TRIVIA

GUNHED
This film's co-writer Jim Bannon was the future writer of 1991's *Point Break*.

Though this film began life as a potential "Godzilla 2", during *Godzilla vs. Biollante's* lengthy pre-production process, the concept of Godzilla fighting a computer was considered as "Godzilla 3". Eventually it was decided upon to make *Gunhed*, which ironically beat *Godzilla vs. Biollante* to theaters!

GODZILLA VS. BIOLLANTE
Godzilla vs. Biollante was the least-successful film of the Heisei series in Japan.

This is the first movie where Godzilla is actually green onscreen. Even though the same costume would be reused in the following film, it would be repainted his standard charcoal grey color, which he would stay until *Godzilla 2000* (1999).

Toho had big plans for the character of Miki Saegusa from the start as she was also scripted to appear in the solo Mothra film *Mothra vs. Bagan* slated for a 1990 release that never got off the ground due to this film's box office results.

After production ended, the massive second stage Biollante costume became a shelter for stray cats near the studio.

Biollante's voice is derived from the sound effects of the Jupiter Ghost from *Bye-Bye Jupiter* (1984).

Features the first appearance of actor Koichi Ueda in a Godzilla movie, who would appear in every subsequent film until *Shin Godzilla* (2016).

Akira Ifukube was asked if his music could be used for this film. He agreed, "but only if you don't turn them into rock songs." Even though standards like "Godzilla's Theme," "Godzilla Appears," and the "*Monster Zero* March" appear courtesy of Ifukube's recent *Ostinato* album, Godzilla's Theme was transformed into a "rock song" for the opening sequences where a battle for G-cells happens in the ruins of Tokyo.

A 2014 fan poll in Japan asked the current generation what their favorite G-film was. The surprise winner was *Godzilla vs. Biollante*. In 2017, however, it had fallen out of the top five.

Another composer sought for the film was Hiroshi Miyagawa (*Space Battleship Yamato*) who was unable to accept due to scheduling conflicts. Miyagawa had previously written the song "Let's Call Happiness" for *Ghidorah, the Three Headed Monster* (1964).

One design for Biollante had a four-part mouth like a flower, but Tomoyuki Tanaka felt it should look more like a reptile.

When Godzilla first attacks Osaka, much of the footage is stock shots from *Deathquake* (1980). It becomes all-new footage once Godzilla moves into downtown Osaka.

Around 3,000 scripts were turned in to Toho for their script contest.

Shinichiro Kobayashi created the character of Miki in his second draft. In Kazuki Omori's first treatment for the script based off Kobayashi's story, he made Miki the long-lost sister of Erica Shiragami!

Katsuhiko Sasaki has an extended cameo as one of the military men. Kosuke Toyahara is the pilot of the Super X2. Both would go on to bigger parts in the next movie.

Another ending was originally shot in which, after Godzilla is felled by the ANEB, Biollante opens her mouth and, courtesy of anime-style cell animation, sort of devours Godzilla before laying a giant rose onto his body then dissipating into the sky (like in the finished film). The idea was that Biollante took away all of Godzilla's hatred so he would be at peace when he revived. Toho nixed this ending because they didn't want Godzilla to become a Showa-ish superhero again. As a result, the re-edited ending in the finished film seems choppy and random.

The reason this movie took so long to come out is that Dino De Laurentiis' notorious *King Kong Lives* came out in 1986 (as *King Kong 2* in Japan) and just as it did in America and everywhere else in the world, bombed in Japan (where Kong is quite popular). Toho saw this and said "It looks like people aren't interested in monster movies anymore," and put the *Godzilla 2* project on the back-burner. It never once occurred to them that the quality of the movie may have had something to do with it.

ULTRA Q: THE MOVIE
Susumu Kurobe is often listed as Shin Hayata in English sources, but he does not play that character and in fact, only cameos in this film along with another *Ultraman* veteran, Akiji Kobayashi.

This film's director helmed episodes of *Ultraman* and *Ultra Seven*. Ironically, he wrote a script for the original *Ultra Q* TV series but it was rejected!

Nagira's roar is a tweaked version of Biollante's roar.

Amulets like the ones in the Heisei Gamera trilogy figure into the film. Ironically, Shusuke Kaneko was at one point attached to direct.

GODZILLA VS. KING GHIDORAH
The novelization for the movie retained Tomoyuki Tanaka's original idea of King Ghidorah being discovered by the Futurians on Venus and them taking DNA samples to create the Dorats, which they used to create their own version of King Ghidorah. There is no explanation for why Ghidorah is there or how long he's been dormant on Venus.

The Dorats were originally less "cute" and more dragon-like in early designs.

The Godzilla costume is the suit built for *Godzilla vs. Biollante* repainted and refurbished with much larger pectoral muscles and slightly different dorsal plates. Its lower legs can be seen in particularly droopy shape from deterioration since 1989.

Koichi Kawakita was honored with a special technical achievement award at the Japanese Academy Awards in 1992.

Some of King Ghidorah's raid on Fukuoka is stock footage. Citizens fleeing is flipped footage from *Biollante*. A shot of King Ghidorah destroying a factory is actually culled from *Conflagration* (1975) with Ghidorah's gravity beams superimposed in. Additionally, several shots of Godzilla firing his ray in Sapporo are stock footage from *Biollante*.

King Ghidorah was so popular that Tomoyuki Tanaka wanted the next film to be called *The Return of King Ghidorah*. The nixed film would have featured the "real" King Ghidorah arriving on earth from outer space to battle Godzilla.

The Tokyo Metropolitan Government Building, known colloquially by the Japanese as "the Tax Towers," was one of the largest miniatures ever constructed for a Godzilla film at that time. When it was destroyed in the film, Japanese audiences cheered as it was the central tax headquarters of Japan. Additionally, "the Tax Towers" and the battle with Mecha-King Ghidorah takes place in the exact same area of Shinjuku where Godzilla battled the Super X in 1984.

The idea of Emmy piloting Mecha-King Ghidorah to fight Godzilla was inspired by the end battle of *Aliens* (1986). Though pointless being inside a cyborg, Emmy is even caged by something resembling Ripley's power loader.

Akiji Kobayashi, appearing in a Godzilla film for the first time ever, was a veteran of the *Ultraman* and *Kamen Rider* TV franchises. He reprises his role from this film in the sequel, *Godzilla vs. Mothra*.

In Kazuki Omori's original draft, Godzilla was a Tyrannosaurus Rex in 1944. Everyone rightly didn't believe a Tyrannosaurus could change into Godzilla, so the fictional Godzillasaurus was created.

The 1991 Godzilla movie was going to be Toho's 60th anniversary film (in the 90s, for some reason, Toho celebrated anniversaries technically a year early). To mark this occasion, they wanted to do a remake of *King Kong vs. Godzilla*. At the time, Ted Turner owned the rights to Kong and wanted too much money for the character.

The hair from King Ghidorah's three heads was eliminated because it proved too challenging for the effects staff. Specifically, designer Shinji Nishikawa told David Milner during a December 1995 interview that, "The three heads of Ghidorah were modified because it was very difficult for the members of the special effects staff to superimpose all of the individual strands of hair located at the back of Ghidorah's heads onto footage of people fleeing."

208

American actor Robert Scott Field is now a fan favorite, often generously volunteering his services to G-Fest, a Godzilla convention in North America, as a translator and MC.

So Yamamura has a cameo in this film playing—who else?—the Prime Minister of Japan.

Robert Scott Field reprised the role of M-11 for a Japanese-made fan film student project (for a class run by Koichi Kawakita) called *Jet Jaguar: The M-11 Project*.

Kawakita has commented that it was exceedingly difficult to make the animatronic Godzilla head cry during the reunion with Shindo scene. He would do a far better job a few years later in *Godzilla vs. Destroyah* (1995).

During Godzilla's attack on Sapporo, when Godzilla falls into the underground mall, suit actor Kenpachiro Satsuma actually got hurt when his head hit an unbreakable part of the miniature set inside the suit.

When Godzilla surfaces from the ocean with Miki and Professor Masaki looking on, the first "NG suit" built but rejected for *Biollante* was utilized ("NG" is film jargon for "No Good"). The costume was cut in half so Satsuma could more easily move around in the Big Pool with it on.

While King Ghidorah is indeed played by new suit actor, Ryu Hariken, Mecha-King Ghidorah does not have a human actor and is completely held aloft by wires.

Tragically, this film's lead actress, Anna Nakagawa, and the lead actress of *Godzilla vs. Biollante*, Yoshiko Tanaka, would both succumb to cancer in the early 2010s.

GODZILLA VS. MOTHRA
The reason this film is so popular with Japanese audiences is that it builds upon Japanese traditions and Asian mythology that would be completely lost on American audiences. It is perhaps the most "Asian" of all the Godzilla movies; it's literally a case of "you have to be Japanese to get it." It doesn't help matters that American audiences generally watch these films dubbed, and at this point, the international dubs were just making dialogue up and not even bothering translating the original spoken

dialogue. As of 2017, *Godzilla vs. Mothra* was still one of the top five most popular of all Godzilla movies with Japanese fans.

Keiko Imamura and Sayaka Osawa, who portrayed the Cosmos, were both winners of Toho's Cinderella Contest. The duo would cameo as full-sized twin characters in *Godzilla vs. Mechagodzilla II* (1993), and they reprised their roles as the Cosmos for *Godzilla vs. Space Godzilla* (1994). Sayaka Osawa would appear as the new character Meru in *Godzilla vs. Destroyah* (1995).

The main Godzilla costume built for *Godzilla vs. Biollante* (1989) and reused in *Godzilla vs. King Ghidorah* (1991) was meant to be used entirely for this movie. However, before shooting began, someone stole the costume from Toho, which necessitated the construction of a brand new Godzilla suit. However, Godzilla costumes are huge, heavy, bulky, and unwieldy and eventually the 1989 suit was found discarded in a ditch. Apparently, Kawakita's crew (though not Kawakita himself) had some kind of problem with the suit because they were all glad someone had taken it and were dismayed that it was returned. The *Biollante* suit would be used for the battle with Battra on the ocean floor and when Godzilla broke out of Mt. Fuji, but would be retired after this film.

Tim Burton visited the set to watch filming of some of the effects shooting under Koichi Kawakita in July of 1992.

Whereas in *Godzilla vs. King Ghidorah*, Akiji Kobayashi plays his role of Dobashi dead seriously, for this film, Takao Okawara instructed Kobayashi to play Dobashi for laughs. His over-the-top mugging is a scene-stealer throughout the film.

Yoshiko Tanaka reprises her *Godzilla vs. Biollante* role of Asuka Okochi (minus Kirishima, though). She first appears to help Miki locate the missing Cosmos.

Mothra was supposed to land at Haneda Airport for the last scene but a shooting permit could never be obtained.

Battra's introduction, emerging from the arctic ice, utilized stock footage from Toho's 1974 "banned film" *Prophecies of Nostradamus (Catastrophe 1999)*. When Mt. Fuji erupts, there are some brief stock shots from *Submersion of Japan* (1973).

There was an alternate version of Mothra emerging from her cocoon via CGI, but the practical effects looked far more convincing.

Takehiro Murata not only won a Japanese Supporting Actor Academy Award, but also won the same category in the Mainichi Film Awards, Kinema Junpo Awards, and Hochi Film Awards.

In addition to centering this film around Mothra and the Shobijin/Cosmos to appeal to women, Toho also cast Tetsuya Bessho—popular with women as a sex symbol at the time—in the lead male role. Director Okawara has been quoted as saying, "We made *Mothra* for the ladies. The next year, we made *Mechagodzilla* for the guys."

Toshiyuki Honda, composer of numerous films (among them, *Gunhed*), wished to have a cameo in the film. Akira Ifukube arranged with director Okawara to have Honda play one of the self defense force soldiers.

Even though the organization would not be formally introduced until the following movie, G-Force insignias can be found on the maser helicopters that attack Godzilla near Mt. Fuji.

This film's artwork advance poster curiously showcases two normal Mothra larvae hatching from the same egg. Some speculate this poster was based on the script for *Godzilla vs. Gigamoth*.

Frankie Sakai, from the original 1961 *Mothra*, was meant to have a cameo, but a scheduling conflict prevented it from happening.

Koichi Kawakita wanted Mothra to be killed off in this film so he could bring her back as Mecha-Mothra in the next film.

Kawakita staged the whole Godzilla emerging from Mt. Fuji sequence in this film because he felt that he didn't do a good enough job making a big deal of Godzilla emerging from Mt. Mihara in *Godzilla vs. Biollante*. Indeed, he improves upon the sequence, making it a true spectacle to behold and a worthy entrance for the King of the Monsters.

GODZILLA VS. MECHAGODZILLA II
Was officially the 40th anniversary celebratory movie for Godzilla.

First Japanese film to utilize Dolby Digital 5.1 Surround Sound.

The reason that Baby Godzilla's skin is so smooth is because he has not been scarred by the atomic bomb like Godzilla.

Conflicting reports indicate that either Tomoyuki Tanaka or Koichi Kawakita wanted to bring back Minilla but Takao Okawara would have none of it, so Baby Godzilla was the compromise.

Shinji Nishikawa turned in a script for this film that would have utilized Kawakita's beloved idea of the *Fantastic Voyage* (1966) inside of Godzilla, which is launched to stop a nuclear meltdown inside of the monster. After this, Baby Godzilla would absorb his energy and become the new Godzilla.

A deleted scene from Wataru Mimura's early draft would have featured a prehistoric flashback of a Godzillasaurus battling a pteranodon on what would presumably become Adonoa Island.

Garnered a Best Sound nomination at the 1994 Japanese Academy Awards.

In an interview with David Milner, Takao Okawara expressed interest in doing a 160-minute director's cut of the film. Many outtakes (both drama and special effects-related) can be seen in the making of special.

Shelley Sweeney's character is revealed to be an android in a deleted scene, though some say this scene is meant to be a joke being pulled on Aoki, and she isn't really an android.

At a party for the release of *Godzilla vs. Mothra*, suit actor Kenpachiro Satsuma had a little too much to drink and it was he who brashly asked the attending Ishiro Honda to direct the next Godzilla movie. Much to his surprise, Honda said yes.

One of the few times the Japanese version confirms that Godzilla is male. Early in the film, one of the G-Force officers says, in English, that "the time from the radiation of his dorsal fins to discharge of his heat beam is 1.26 second. [sic]". Previous occurrences include the Japanese trailers for *All Monsters Attack* (1969) and *Godzilla vs. Gigan* (1972), which refer to Godzilla as "King of Monsters" (actually "Mr. King of Monsters" in *Gigan*).

The film's prologue explains that G-Force was formed in 1992, likely after the events of *Godzilla vs. King Ghidorah*, but before *Godzilla vs. Mothra,* which would account for the G-Force insignia on the weapons in the latter film.

Strangely and inexplicably, Godzilla's ray once turns into a Showa-style steam ray while he is angry at Baby not coming out when he first tries to collect him.

One ending considered for the film featured Godzilla picking up the baby in his mouth and carrying him out to sea in that fashion.

After filming was complete, the special effects crew merrily destroyed—kaiju-style—what was left of the climactic Chiba set.

Soon-to-be *Gamera* star Shinobu Nakayama has a cameo early on as new scientist assigned to G-Force.

The Godzilla costume built for *Godzilla vs. Mothra* was utilized extensively in this movie, used during many shots of Godzilla on Adonoa Island, when Godzilla surfaces in Yokkaichi, when Godzilla turns to lead Baby into the sea, and when Godzilla and Baby are swimming away from Japan. The water suit constructed for *Godzilla vs. Biollante* was used for early scenes of Godzilla surfacing off the coast of Adonoa Island (as well as the newspaper still of Godzilla heading into Osaka Bay).

KAMEN RIDER J
As was the case with *Kamen Rider ZO*, footage from this movie was used in Saban's *Masked Rider*, an American adaptation of *Kamen Rider*. All of the monsters were used except for Garai.

YAMATO TAKERU
In a *G-Fan* interview 15 years later, Wataru Mimura remained optimistic on sequels commenting, "I am still hoping to complete the story of the trilogy in my lifetime." In a previous December 1994 interview with David Milner, he mentioned that he was writing the script for *Yamato Takeru 2* which would feature "all-new monsters."

Teaser trailers for the film featured a newly-created design for Orochi that more resembled the Showa Ghidorah.

Other cancelled 90s Toho remakes include an updated *Matango* (1963) where the mushrooms hail from outer space and a new version of *The Mysterians* (1957).

The film features a brief stock footage shot of a forest catching fire from 1974's *Prophecies of Nostradamus (Catastrophe 1999)*.

GODZILLA VS. SPACE GODZILLA

Koichi Kawakita told David Milner MOGERA was chosen for the film due to his ability to burrow under the ground and destroy Space Godzilla's energy crystals. However, Kawakita is a huge fan of 1957's *The Mysterians* which likely played a big part in the decision.

Shogo Tomiyama wrote a treatment called *Godzilla: Super Wars* where Space Godzilla has dragonfly-like peons to do his bidding and attack Little Godzilla on Birth Island.

Since Jun Hashizume's character Koji Shinjo doesn't appear in the sequel, in Hashizume has joked in interviews that he and Miki likely broke up because he could not hold a candle to Godzilla.

Rumors that Koichi Kawakita planned a TV spin-off movie called *Little Godzilla's Underground Adventure* are believed to be false.

It's possible Toho president Yoshinobu Hayashi was throwing Kensho Yamashita a bone, so to speak, when he asked him to direct the new Godzilla movie after several of his previous projects at Toho had been cancelled.

Some rumors persist a space version of King Ghidorah was again considered as the villain for "Godzilla 6." (This, according to *Godzilla Dictionary [New Edition]*) Some say this was axed due to the fact that Toho utilized Ghidorah's mythical inspiration, Orochi, in *Yamato Takeru* the same year.

The Godzilla costume built for *Godzilla vs. Mechagodzilla II* was used for scenes of Godzilla entering and exiting the ocean. The water suit in this movie was the suit built for *Godzilla vs. Mothra*. At one point when Godzilla dives underwater, his tail whips into the air and the end of the tail flies apart onscreen from deterioration.

Little Godzilla's design is actually rejected design from *Godzilla vs. Mechagodzilla II*.

Features the debut of Fairy Mothra, who would be much more prominent in 1996's *Rebirth of Mothra*.

214

Contrary to popular belief, the title card for this movie is not stock footage of the title card from *Godzilla vs. Mothra*. It is, however, an alternate take from that film.

According to director Yamashita, after his failure in the previous movie, Commander Aso was supposed to be finished at G-Force (which may account for his much more humble demeanor in this and the following film). However, MOGERA in this film is his attempt at redemption. MOGERA is meant to be even more powerful than Mechagodzilla, but that never once seems the case. Additionally, both Yamashita and Akira Nakao agreed that Aso should no longer be "an angry person."

In the Japanese version, Tomoyuki Tanaka is listed as the sole producer. In the international English version, both Tanaka and Shogo Tomiyama are credited as the producer.

Much like Minilla and Little Man Machan before him, Little Godzilla is played by a dwarf, this time a wrestler, who called himself Little Frankie.

The second Godzilla movie to feature a pop song over the end titles, this time Date of Birth's catchy "Echoes of Love."

Early in the movie, when Miki is at her Psychic Training Facility being recruited for T-Project, there are five psychic-related cards hanging on the wall: a cross, a star, a circle, a square, and... three wavy lines. These are the exact same cards Bill Murray uses during his introduction in *Ghostbusters* (1984). The wavy lines card is partially obscured and can only be made out in HD masters.

Whilst unpopular with American fans, *Godzilla vs. Space Godzilla* was still more successful at the Japanese box office than U.S. fan favorites *Godzilla vs. Biollante* and *Godzilla vs. King Ghidorah*.

GAMERA, GUARDIAN OF THE UNIVERSE
Supposedly film studios toyed with reviving Gamera as early as 1985 in the wake of the 1984 Godzilla revival. Earnest plans to bring Gamera back began in 1991 and one early idea had Noriaki Yuasa returning to direct a short one-hour Gamera film.

Niisan Takahashi, the screenwriter of the Showa Gamera series, turned in a draft for this film, which featured Gamera battling the mythological version of the Japanese Phoenix, the "Guardian of the South."

Takahashi's version was rejected and he turned his script into a novel. Coincidentally, Irys, the villain of the third Heisei Gamera film, is also a version of the Japanese Phoenix.

When this film was first announced to the public, no one in the media took it seriously. Gamera's reputation in Japan was not exactly stellar. Thanks to this and the following two films, that has changed, even for the Showa series.

The original script featured five Gyaos instead of three and also had an aerial battle between Gamera, Gyaos, and the Japanese air forces.

Look carefully on a report and one can see Gyaos' name spelled in English as "Gjaos."

The opening prologue features cameos by Kojiro Hongo and Akira Kubo as the two ship captains.

Yukijiro Hotaru, who plays Osako, is the son of actor Yukitaro Hotaru. Yukitaro had parts in *Gamera vs. Gyaos* (1967) as Hachiko, one of the bumbling road construction workers, and *Gamera vs. Jiger* (1970) in a bit part as a dock worker willing to remove the Devil's Whistle from a ship (he has a towel around his head inside his helmet).

Shusuke Kaneko and screenwriter Kazunori Ito have said that the film's storyline was heavily inspired by *The War of the Gargantuas* (1966).

Kaneko has made the claim that in the universe of the Heisei Gamera, turtles do not exist; an attempt to take the ridiculousness away from the concept of "a flying turtle."

The comma-shaped jewels that connect Gamera with humanity are known in Japan as "magatama" and have a connection with Japan's Jomon and Kofun history periods.

When Yumi Kanayama finished her shooting as Gyaos, the special effects crew gifted her a bouquet of flowers for a job well done. Kanayama also has a cameo in the film as a reporter standing outside the Tokyo Stock Exchange.

Kaneko and Higuchi wanted the new Gamera's arms to transform into a sea turtle's flippers when he flew, but Daiei demanded he resemble the
216

original Gamera. Due to this film's incredible success, the two got their way with the sequels.

GODZILLA VS. DESTROYAH

One of the original storylines had Godzilla battling the ghost of the 1954 Godzilla who had possessed the body of Godzilla Junior. A multitude of ideas were suggested, and there are too many to mention here. See *The Big Book of Japanese Giant Monster Movies: The Lost Films* for a full rundown.

Originally Godzilla was to be luminescent in his meltdown phase and glow with white and red.

The Burning Godzilla suit is the costume made for *Godzilla vs. Space Godzilla* with a new set of spinal plates and hundreds of light bulbs inserted into it to create the glowing effect. The suit made for *Godzilla vs. Mechagodzilla II* was similarly altered for use in water scenes.

In the Japanese end titles, Godzilla suit actor Kenpachiro Satsuma's credit is elevated above the other monster actors.

Screenwriter Kazuki Omori only came back for this "last" Godzilla film because his home had been destroyed in the Kobe earthquake of January 1995 and he needed the money.

Tomoyuki Tanaka disliked the notion of killing Godzilla and insisted people know that one day Godzilla would return. In fact, in one of Omori's later drafts, nearly everybody died. Godzilla died, Destroyah died, Junior stayed dead, and Miki committed suicide out of grief for leading Junior to his death. It was at this point that Tanaka stepped in and told everyone "You can kill Godzilla, but Junior has to live. And don't kill Miki. We may want to bring her back in a future movie."

Stock footage from *The Last War* (1961) is used in a what-if sequence showing what would happen if Godzilla exploded.

On December 03, 1995, a funeral for Godzilla was held in Ariake Colosseum. Koichi Kawakita, Kenpachiro Satsuma, Shogo Tomiyama, Takehiro Murata, the press, and even the public were in attendance. A theater-exclusive glowing Godzilla figure was used as a ceremonial piece. Brief footage of this can be seen in the opening of the Making Of special.

In addition to harkening back to the original *Godzilla*, this movie also reaches back to *The Return of Godzilla* (1984), in which Godzilla, understanding something is wrong with his nuclear energy, appears in the Bungo Channel to raid a nuclear power plant to get new energy to replace it (though he is stymied and placated by the Super X-III's freeze attack).

Though he goes unnamed throughout the movie, Japanese sources site that Saburo Shinoda's character is not the same one he played in *Godzilla vs. Mothra*.

To this day, discussing the death of Godzilla in this movie still affects Satsuma.

When Satsuma was told that Godzilla was going to die, he imagined they would portray it much like when an elephant dies; that Godzilla would win the final battle and then he would go off someplace and we would be told that he had died, reminiscent of the elephant graveyards those animals instinctively go to when they are about to die.

The character of Major Kuroki (previously played by Masanobu Takashima) in *Godzilla vs. Biollante* (1989) returns for this film, now piloting the Super X-III. However, here the character is played by that actor's brother, Masahiro Takashima, who had played Aoki in *Godzilla vs. Mechagodzilla II*.

The Japanese title best translates into English as *Godzilla vs. Destroyer*, which was the English title Toho used for a while until they learned they couldn't copyright the word "Destroyer" as a name and changed it to "Destoroyah."

Two bits that the movie glosses over rather hurriedly are the fact that when Destroyah drags Godzilla into Tokyo Bay, his intention was to dissolve Godzilla with Oxygen Destroyer powers. However, once Godzilla hit the bay, his body boiled the water so much that Destroyah was forced to flee from risk of scalding to death. The other bit is when Destroyah tries to attack Godzilla as a group of Aggregate Destroyahs, they manage to eat away so much of Godzilla's runaway thermonuclear energy that he briefly stops glowing red and his ray turns back to blue in color.

Was nominated for Best Sound and Best Editing at the Japanese Academy Awards.

The final version of Destroyah was designed from parts of the previous Heisei monster enemies. He has Battra's horn, Rodan's wings, Space Godzilla's shoulder spikes, Biollante's mouth, and the mythical Bagan's body.

At one point in the film, Miki remarks to Meru that her psychic powers are declining. In the end, it is Meru who psychically detects the resurrected Junior and not Miki.

In a 2002 *G-Fan* interview, producer Shogo Tomiyama indicated that Toho might at one point create a sequel to *Godzilla vs. Destroyah* starring a fully-grown Godzilla Jr. First drafts of *Godzilla: Final Wars* (2004) used this concept, which is why actors Akira Nakao and Koichi Ueda (originally back as Aso and Hyodo, respectively) pilot the Gohten, but this element was soon dropped.

Akira Ifukube composed a piece entitled "The Birth of the New Godzilla" to be used during the reveal that Junior had resurrected. It is more or less a reprise of Junior's theme used throughout the film with extra harps. It was decided that the reveal worked better with no music at all.

Godzilla Junior's resurrection was initially meant to be a post-credits zinger like today's Marvel Studios movies have. However, Toho feared people would leave the theater before they saw the scene. Junior was to have turned around to face the camera, roared one last time, then blasted the screen with his ray in which a final "Owari" [The End] would have appeared.

According to Ifukube, the bell jingling sound added to the end of Godzilla's Theme at the end of the credits was meant to signify Godzilla's entrance into Heaven.

GAMERA 2: ADVENT OF LEGION
There exists a manga sequel to this film that is essentially a faithful Heisei retelling of *Gamera vs. Barugon* (1966) set shortly after *Gamera 2: Advent of Legion*.

Briefly, there was a rumor that Disney would theatrically distribute the film in America.

American fans erroneously refer to the giant form of Legion as "Queen Legion" and believe it to be female. The Japanese do no such thing; that version is known in Japanese as "Kyodai Region" (Huge Legion) and no gender is assigned that character.

The Gamera suit for this film would be outfitted with a cap the actor could wear on his head that would turn Gamera's head this way and that.

This film begins the overt religious overtones that would come to a head in the third movie. Gamera is dead for three days and then resurrects and a Christian-style cross transforms into the "me" character of Gamera's name on the title card. And of course, Legion itself is name checked from a verse in the Bible.

REBIRTH OF MOTHRA
Won the Silver Excellence Award at the Golden Gross Awards in 1997.

A picture of Ishiro Honda, on set during the shooting of *Ran* (1985), can be seen in the Gotos' house, portraying the Gotos' deceased grandfather. A similar tribute was staged for Tomoyuki Tanaka in Mothra 3.

Mai Hosho was originally cast as Belvera. She dropped out right before filming began and was quickly replaced by Aki Hano.

A scene of Death Ghidorah callously stomping in the face of the Mothra larva was shot, but excised from the final print. Stills do exist of the shot, though. In the movie, the larva's face can be seen squirting green blood for no apparent reason as a result of the cut.

During varying stages of design, Death Ghidorah had no wings and one head, the wings and the other two heads only appearing for its final form.

The story for the film was adapted from an unused draft of *Godzilla vs. Destroyah*, which featured Godzilla dying at the end of the second act and then Junior getting a power up and killing Destroyah (with the aid of Mothra, no less!).

The international dub renames Moll as "Mona" for some reason and Belvera as... "Velveeta."

ULTRAMAN ZEARTH 2

A third Ultraman Zearth film, where he would've learned he was the grandson of Ultraman King, was planned and abandoned in favor of *Ultraman Tiga & Ultraman Dyna* (1998).

REBIRTH OF MOTHRA 2

This film's advance trailer showcased Mothra heading into space to defeat an asteroid, implying Toho may have had ideas to tie this film in with the climax of *Godzilla vs. Mothra* (1992). From this and comments made by Shogo Tomiyama, it is ascertainable that the original story for *Rebirth of Mothra 2* was quite different than what eventually played out on screen.

Masumi Suetani's first idea had this story revolve around a large lake rather than the ocean.

Hikari Mitsushima is a member of the group "Folder" who sings the end title track, "Now and Forever." She does not, however, sing in that particular song.

For filming, *Rebirth of Mothra's* assistant director Kunio Miyoshi was bumped up to the top spot for the sequel though the rest of the team remained the same.

While Dagarah technically engages in some city destruction, it's all accomplished via rear-screen projection without any miniatures whatsoever.

While the international dub still refers to Moll as "Mona," this time it gets Belvera's name correct.

ULTRAMAN TIGA & ULTRAMAN DYNA

Though they missed out on the feature film, Daigo and Jun Yazumi both appear in the series finale of *Ultraman Dyna*.

Originally, there was to be a red, second form Geranda that attacked the island base. The monster was dropped due to the battle already being too crowded.

Shochiku requested the production of this film the success of *Ultraman Zearth 2* (1997).

GODZILLA (1998)

Some people believe a man killed while driving his car when Godzilla first emerges bears an uncanny resemblance to *G-Fan* editor J.D. Lees.

Though many fans hate this iteration of Godzilla, most surprisingly loved the Fox cartoon *Godzilla: The Animated Series*, which premiered in the Fall of 1998 and ran for two successful seasons.

Initially, this Godzilla was nicknamed by fans GINO ("Godzilla in Name Only"). Later, it was rechristened simply "Zilla" by Toho themselves who included the monster in 2004's *Godzilla: Final Wars* where Godzilla easily defeats his American counterpart. Toho's reasoning for the new name was that "Hollywood took the god out of Godzilla."

Roland Emmerich didn't like Godzilla movies and never ever figured out what was appealing to audiences about them.

Dean Devlin and Roland Emmerich wrote the final screenplay for the film over a weekend in Mexico.

This film and its unpopularity actually played a part in driving toy maker Trendmasters to bankruptcy when toys of the new Godzilla failed to sell well. Additionally, Trendmasters was already working on figures for *Godzilla: The Animated Series*, which stores then refused to order. Today, sculpts and prototypes of figures from *Godzilla: The Animated Series* are highly sought after collector's items.

The *Godzilla* Soundtrack featured several hit songs, among them "Heroes" by The Wallflowers and "Come With Me" by Sean "Puffy" Combs, and was quite popular.

The film's aborted sequel focused on the hatchling emerging from the egg in the last scene.

Original Godzilla suit actor Haruo Nakajima allegedly jumped up during a screening, shouted in broken English, "That no Gojira! That iguana!", and left in disgust. Then-current Godzilla suit actor Kenpachiro Satsuma also walked out on a screening, but more succinctly commented "It's not Godzilla. It doesn't have the spirit." Later, he less-diplomatically remarked about the movie that "even *Pulgasari* was better!"

REBIRTH OF MOTHRA 3

This film's design for King Ghidorah is one of the more popular ones amongst the fandom. This incarnation of the monster was meant to appear in 2014's Playstation game *Godzilla (*aka *Godzilla VS.)* but was scrapped due to time constraints.

Many script elements were dropped to the wayside before filming began. Originally, King Ghidorah was to be depicted as the fulfilment of Nostradamus' prophecy that in 1999, "the great king of terror would fall from the sky." Though Nostradamus was removed, the Elias sisters still refer to King Ghidorah as "the king of terror" in the finished film. King Ghidorah was also to be revealed as the father of *Rebirth of Mothra*'s Death Ghidorah, who had come to earth 65 million years ago to finish what his father had started.

Inside the Sonodas' house is a photo of Tomoyuki Tanaka portraying a deceased relative.

Toho considered a solo King Ghidorah film to revolve around the 1999 Nostradamus prophecy as far back as 1995 at the same time they were planning the first *Rebirth of Mothra* film.

Since Lora had to be recast, the story was consciously shifted to focus on Moll and Belvera in an attempt to bring less attention to Misato Tate.

Megumi Kobayashi (the actress who plays Moll) sang the end credits song, "Future."

Popular wrestler Atsushi Onita portrays Shota's manly, though kind, father.

The international dub finally properly refers to Moll as "Moll." It also suddenly refers to Mothra Leo as "she." The film itself also manages to screw up Mothra's gender. The Mothra who was born in *Rebirth of Mothra* has one clasper as an adult, indicating it to be male (the other incarnations of adult Mothra have three claspers, indicating them to be female). While the new Rainbow Mothra prop starts out with one clasper, when he re-emerges from his crystalline cocoon as Armored Mothra, suddenly he has two claspers. And then, when he transforms into Eternal Mothra at the end of the movie, it has three claspers! There is no available answer for this discrepancy.

After Dagarah was conspicuously missing his own toy, the Grand King Ghidorah was released in a highly-detailed, oversized figure.

GAMERA 3: REVENGE OF IRYS
Shusuke Kaneko intended this as the final Gamera film but Daiei was planning on making a fourth Gamera film if the trilogy managed to gross ¥10 billion.

Miki Mizuno was meant to return from *Gamera 2: Advent of Legion*, but a scheduling conflict kept her from appearing.

When asked why his Gamera movies are loaded with women characters as the leads, Kaneko replied, "Because Gamera's a guy!"

The "Nightmare/Trauma Gamera" was created by modifying the suit built for *Gamera 2: Advent of Legion*.

In Japan, the film is generally referred to as *Gamera 3: Irisu Kakusei* ("Gamera 3: Awakening of Irys"). However, the actual onscreen title is given as *Gamera 3: Jishin [Irisu] Kakusei* ("Gamera 3: False God Irys Awakens").

Despite opinions to the contrary, Irys is for certain a male monster, not female.

Some prints of the movie are missing the Toho distribution mark and begin with the Daiei logo.

The first film of the series to have a music video shot for it, Juliana Schano's ethereal "Tell Me Once Again." She stands in a child's pink room singing the song as clips from the movie fade in and out.

Kazunari Ito was intent on delivering a script in which Gamera was the villain. As a result, Shusuke Kaneko had to write his own draft of the script with a character arc for Gamera because Ito wasn't giving him what he wanted.

Many American fans are confused by the motivations of Asakura. According to Japanese sources, she believes herself to be a mediator for the monsters and that if Gamera can be killed, the Gyaos will disappear.

It is speculated that Irys is a good guardian monster like Gamera that goes bad due to Ayana's influence and hatred of Gamera.

Suit actor Akira Ohashi, who played Gamera in the previous movie, switches sides and plays the evil Irys in this one.

A fan-made sequel, *Gamera 4: Truth*, was produced which continues this film's story and even stars Yukijiro Hotaru as Inspector Osako. However, it entirely missed the point that Shusuke Kaneko was trying to get across...

Shinji Higuchi wanted to end the movie with a post-credits sequence that would've revealed Gamera still battling the Gyaos in a future devoid of humanity. However, since this was completely antithetical to the themes Kaneko wished to convey, he rejected the idea outright.

Because of the cost of the movie, Daiei went bankrupt during the two-year-long production of this movie (pre-production started in 1997). While Daiei did keep this secret from the public again, they did not keep it from their filmmakers. Everyone on the crew agreed to finish the movie for no pay in hopes it would save Daiei. Unfortunately (likely due to its overall plot and subject matter), it did not. As a result, this movie has an unusual amount of producing credits: Daiei, Tokuma Shoten, Nippon Televison Network, Hakuhodo, and Japan Publication Sales.

Daiei's official English spelling of the enemy monster's name in 1999 was "Irys." When Kadokawa bought Daiei, they begun spelling the name "Iris." The Japanese agree the proper English spelling should be "Irys" because the Japanese name is transliterated "Irisu" rather than "Airasu."

ULTRAMAN GAIA: THE BATTLE IN HYPERSPACE
The story idea to set the film in a parallel world was that of chief producer Kiyoshi Suzuki and director Kazuya Konaka.

GODZILLA 2000
In the U.S. version, Shinoda was dubbed by Francois Chau, better known as Dr. Piere Chang on the TV series *Lost* (2004).

This film's U.S. version producer Michael Schlesinger wrote a screenplay entitled *Godzilla Reborn* which served as a direct sequel to this film. In it, Godzilla would have battled a giant bat monster in Hawaii. Shiro Sano's character Miyasaka was scripted to return. Joe Dante agreed to direct and genre actors such as Bruce Campbell and Christopher Lee were scripted to have roles.

A subtitled print of the American version received a limited theatrical screening in Japan in November of 2000. Toho has since replaced their original international export version with the U.S. version.

The film cost ¥1.2 billion ($13 million dollars) to produce, and an undisclosed amount to market. The film made ¥1.65 billion ($14,742,420 dollars) at the box office, so Toho seemingly lost money on the production.

The film gives several nods to TriStar's *Godzilla*, notably a scene where a giant footprint is found in the sand. Also in the U.S. version, the TriStar's *Godzilla* roar replaces the Japanese version often on the soundtrack (although U.S. producer Michael Schlesinger swears up and down the sound effects are "all new"). It also mocks the TriStar *Godzilla* with lines like "We know from experience that when Godzilla is attacked, he advances rather than retreats."

A lot of the low U.S. box office returns may be attributed to the general public's belief that this was a sequel to the 1998 *Godzilla*.

In the Japanese version, Orga had Death Ghidorah's voice from *Rebirth of Mothra* (1996). The U.S. version created a whole new roar for the space monster.

The U.S. version renamed Organizer G-1, the newly-discovered part of Godzilla's cells that enhance his invulnerability, to the far-less inspired "Regenerator G-1." This also made Orga's name make no sense whatsoever (even though he is a Millennian alien, his name is taken from "Organizer G-1").

The U.S. version also removed the whole "Millennium" subplot of the Japanese title in which the Millennian aliens were going to awaken at the turn of the Millennium and utilize the information on the internet to conquer the world.

When Godzilla was still Godzilla Junior in early drafts of the screenplay, he wasn't attacking power plants out of maliciousness. He was doing it because he knew the Millennians were about to awaken and use mankind's energy against them and being unable to talk to man, this was the only way he knew to protect them. With this element removed, Shinoda's line in the Japanese version, "Is Godzilla showing his hatred for the energy mankind creates?" no longer has an ironic echo.

According to fan rumors in the U.S., enemy opponents discussed for Godzilla in the concept phase supposedly included Anguirus, King Seesar and Kumonga. However, no Japanese sources can be found to confirm this.

ULTRAMAN TIGA: THE FINAL ODYSSEY
Takeshi Tsuruno (*Ultraman Dyna*) has a cameo as Shin Asuka at the film's ending as he passes Daigo in a hallway and nods to him. Under his breath, Daigo says, "Good luck, junior." The scene almost wasn't shot, as continuity-wise Shin Asuka should be younger than what he appears, but in the end, after talking with Tsuruno, the producers couldn't resist and shot his cameo at the last minute.

Originally the last scene was to be Daigo and Rena's actual wedding, but shooting was canceled for the "real" wedding and as such only the dream scene wedding was shot.

GODZILLA VS. MEGAGUIRUS
The film has supporting and small roles for several of the genre's top stars. Among them are Yuriko Hoshi (*Mothra vs. Godzilla* and *Ghidorah, The Three Headed Monster*), Toshiyuki Nagashima (*Gamera 2: Advent of Legion*). Susumu Kurobe (*Ultraman*) appears in a cameo.

Some sources say this story would have originally fallen in continuity with *Godzilla 2000* until the extensive backstory revolving around Osaka and Green Energy was created. Furthermore, this same elaborate backstory also kept this film from taking place in the same universe as *Godzilla Against Mechagodzilla* (2002).

In Japan, to differentiate itself from the Heisei series, rather than use "vs.", each new film utilized an "X" but they are all still pronounced "tai." It should still be written classically as *Godzilla vs. Megaguirus* in English and transliterated as *Gojira tai Megagirasu* from Japanese.

This is the first Godzilla movie to contain a post-credits scene. In this one, a school has been built on the site where Godzilla disappeared. A young boy staying after school suddenly hears an explosion and then sees Godzilla re-emerge from the ground. The idea is that the Dimension Tide was never really successful at all. All the G-Graspers had created was a giant concussive weapon. Earlier in the movie, the G-Graspers miss Godzilla and it shoves him underground for a few minutes. In the end, they score a direct hit, but it shoves him underground for a few months. How Megaguirus came to be brought into the modern day doesn't actually mix with the explanation; Toho was trying to "have their cake and eat it too."

At the time, this film would end up being the second lowest-grossing Godzilla film at only 1.3 million ticket buyers resulting in a paltry gross of only ¥1.2 billion ($10,746,600). Adjusted for inflation, it just barely did better than *Terror of Mechagodzilla* (1975), which was still the reigning champ of Godzilla box office bombs (though, not for long).

Director Masaaki Tezuka can be seen as a teacher outside the school in the post-credits scene.

ULTRAMAN COSMOS: THE FIRST CONTACT
Initially, Don Ron was going to look like a catfish or a mole instead of the shisa-dog motif it ended up having.

Keiichi Hasegawa likely did not contribute to this Ultraman movie as he did on previous entries because he was working on *Godzilla, Mothra, and King Ghidorah: Giant Monsters All-Out Attack* for Toho.

Hitomi Takahashi, who plays Musashi's mother Michiko, also played the mother in *Rebirth of Mothra* (1996).

GODZILLA, MOTHRA AND KING GHIDORAH: GIANT MONSTERS ALL-OUT ATTACK
Known colloquially as "GMK" on both sides of the Pacific as an abbreviation for "*Gojira, Mosura, Kingu Gidora.*"

Grossed ¥2.7 billion and won a Silver Excellence Award at the Japanese Golden Grosses Awards. While it was the most successful of the Millennium series, it didn't bring in anywhere close to what the Heisei films were doing financially. The success of this movie (and the next one) is somewhat dubious considering it double-billed with an hour-long feature of the incredibly popular cartoon hamster Hamtaro (directed by *Gamera* special effects artist Shinji Higuchi).

The idea of Godzilla as "an avenging supernatural spirit" was actually considered by Toho for a new film as far back as 1998 after the TriStar debacle according to a blurb in the Fall 1998 issue of *G-Fan*.

The first story treatment utilized the Atragon rather than the Satsuma.

A poster for Ishiro Honda's *Farewell Rabaul* (1954) can be glimpsed in the film.

Kaneko was already attached to direct this film during *Godzilla vs. Megaguirus'* (2000) preproduction period. During this time, Kaneko toyed with a swarm of CGI Kamacuras until he learned Tezuka's film would be using a similar insectoid kaiju swarm.

Were the movie to be released in America, it was to have been retitled *Godzilla Must Be Killed* (or GMBK for short, using all four of the monsters' names in its acronym)

Godzilla suit actor Mizuho Yoshida cameos as a panicked fisherman when Godzilla first surfaces in Japan. Moments later, Akira Ohashi (Ghidorah) and Rie Ota (Baragon) can be found inside a building looking on just before Godzilla roars.

The Satsuma submarine is not named for Kenpachiro Satsuma, as is often erroneously believed.

Shinji Higuchi did not direct any of the special effects of this film as is also often erroneously believed. He did, however, storyboard and watch the shooting of the scene where Godzilla battles a squadron of jet fighters (lead by Takehiro Murata) in the Japanese countryside.

Masaaki Tezuka worked as an assistant director on this film to study Kaneko's technique.

The movie takes a jab at the 1998 *Godzilla*. In an early scene, Admiral Tachibana is talking about Godzilla's attack on Tokyo and mentions that a monster attacked New York City at the end of the last century. Two soldiers turn to one another and remark "That was Godzilla?" "They say so in America, but not in Japan." This also implies the 1998 *Godzilla* to be in-universe canon with this film.

ULTRAMAN COSMOS 2: THE BLUE PLANET
Ultraman Justice was a character originally intended to debut on the TV series so screenwriters Hideyuki Kawakami and Hiroyasu Shibuya made sure to include him in the movie.

The Scorpiss, who somewhat resemble Megaguirus, gain a bipedal form in the film. Coincidentally, Toho also considered giving Megaguirus a bipedal form as well (and did have the insect monster assume a bipedal stance for attraction suits).

Some of the members of the Scientific Research Circle Sea division are actors from the GUTS and Super GUTS teams of *Ultraman Tiga* and *Ultraman Dyna*.

Due to the controversy of the arrest of Taiyo Sugiura, a "Boys Edition" of *Ultraman Cosmos 2* was released which entirely excised Sugiura! The film ran 15 minutes shorter, had Kounosuke Tokai reprise the role of the young Musashi from *Ultraman Cosmos: The First Contact* (2001), and was released on September 07th.

GODZILLA AGAINST MECHAGODZILLA
To play together better with Hamtaro, this film's running time was cut by 15 minutes.

Special effects director Yuichi Kikuchi would go on to work on *Ultraman: The Next* (2004).

Suit designer Shinichi Wakasa wanted to put tiger stripes on Godzilla for this film. Masaaki Tezuka was rightfully having none of it.

Tokyo Tower was supposed to be destroyed in this film, but due to shooting difficulties, it didn't get destroyed until the next film.

Godzilla vs. Megaguirus' lead Misato Tanaka cameos as a nurse saved by Kiryu with Toshiyuki Nagashima, who played her commanding officer in that film's pre-title scene.

One version of the script featured Anguirus and a fight with Kiryu, but the idea was abandoned.

Many staff members, former Toho stars, and celebrities have cameos in the film. Among them are writer Mimura, director Tezuka, and baseball player Hideki "Godzilla" Matsui, who expressed interest in appearing in the next Godzilla movie after the success of *Godzilla, Mothra, and King Ghidorah: Giant Monsters All-Out Attack* (2001). Makoto Kamiya, Shinji Nishikawa, Tsutomu Kitagawa, Hirofumi Ishigaki, and Kenji Suzuki also appear in cameos. Takehiro Murata makes yet another cameo in the typhoon sequence as the self defense forces truck out to face Godzilla.

Footage from *Rodan* (1956) and *Varan* (1958) were also meant to be shown but was scrapped. In fact, the universe this movie (and its sequel) inhabits includes the films *Godzilla, Rodan, The Mysterians* (1957), *Varan, Frankenstein vs. Baragon* (1965, though set in 1960), *Mothra, Atragon* (1963), *Space Monster Dogora* (1964), *The War of the Gargantuas, King Kong Escapes* (1967), *Space Amoeba* (1970), and *Gorath* (1962, though set in 1979/80).

When Godzilla lands in Tateyama City in the prologue, it is November 3rd, the same day of release of the original *Godzilla*.

Prime Minister Tsuge was male in the screenplay, but became female when it was decided to cast Kumi Mizuno.

The opening shot of the Prime Minister's residence is stock footage from *Godzilla vs. King Ghidorah* (1991) and a shot of Kiryu destroying a factory is doctored footage from *Conflagration* (1975).

Contrary to many fans who believe it to be CGI, a new half-suit of the original Godzilla was built for the scene re-depicting his death by the Oxygen Destroyer.

ULTRAMAN COSMOS VS. ULTRAMAN JUSTICE: THE FINAL BATTLE
A submarine model used in this film is supposedly the leftover sub prop from *Godzilla vs. King Ghidorah* (1991).

Actor Taiyo Sugiura would return as Musashi several more times, first on the TV series *Mega Monster Battle: Ultra Galaxy* (2009), the movies *Ultraman Saga* (2012), *Ultraman Ginga S: The Movie* (2015), and on TV again in *Ultraman Orb: The Origin Saga* (2016-2017).

GODZILLA: TOKYO S.O.S.
The new Shobijin were the winners of Toho's Cinderella Contest.

The identity of the monster corpse that washes up on the beach went through several stages. First, it was to be a Liopleurodon (a short-necked plesiosaur that looked more like a Mosasaurus), then Anguirus until Shogo Tomiyama intervened saying Anguirus was too popular for a throwaway cameo like that, so Kameba from *Space Amoeba* (1970) was chosen.

In the post-credits scene with Godzilla's DNA, there are several other visible chambers containing other monsters' DNA samples. The only name plate other than Godzilla's visible in the shot is one for Kameba. However, name plates for Varan, Sanda, Gaira, Ganime, and fictional monsters "Tezuka" and "Futami" were created but are not onscreen.

Masaaki Tezuka (in the last scene) and Shogo Tomiyama (as a refugee) have cameos in the film. Norman England, a popular writer for *G-Fan* and *Fangoria*, also has a cameo in the pre-title sequence with Mothra.

In much the same way that Toho produced *Zone Fighter* in the 1970s, during the same time as this film, they were producing another tokusatsu series called *Chouseishin Gransazer* and one episode featured Hiroshi Koizumi reprising his role as Dr. Chujo. However, the series is not meant to be in continuity with the Tezuka Godzilla films.

Kiryu's "Sayonara Yoshito" message to Yoshito Chujo was not in the shooting script, but had been in preceding scripts. It was added back in during shooting.

This film is loaded with stock footage, at least for modern day standards. Shots from *Godzilla Against Mechagodzilla* (2002), *Godzilla vs. Destroyah* (1995), and even *The Return of Godzilla* are trotted out to pad the film.

GODZILLA: FINAL WARS
A scene was shot where the locals in Okinawa react in shock at their protector King Seesar attacking them (one of them asking "What did we do, Mr. Seesar?!").

In addition to playing Godzilla, Tsutomu Kitamura also served as the suit actors' fight choreographer. While he is credited as such in the Japanese version, he is only credited as Godzilla in the international version.

After Godzilla defeats Rodan, Anguirus, and King Seesar, he was scripted to roast them with his flame breath but the scene wasn't shot. Shogo Tomiyama wisely felt a scene where Godzilla kills his old allies would be ill-received by fans. Also, he wanted to keep the suits in good condition for publicity purposes.

In May 2004, the Chinese sent out a fraudulent press release that in this film, Godzilla would lose to a "fire dragon" and die near the Oriental Pearl TV Tower in Shanghai. They go on to claim that the plot of the movie entailed Godzilla's child being killed by humans, which sends Godzilla on a world-wide rampage of destruction. The purpose of this remains unknown, other than the fact Godzilla isn't particularly popular in China. The Oriental Pearl TV Tower does appear in the movie... briefly in the background of a shot as Anguirus howls in the foreground.

The giant octopus, the Mothra larva, Mechagodzilla, Gorosaurus, and King Ghidorah (rather than the new Keizer Ghidorah) were initially slated to appear as well.

This was the last Toho film to utilize the "Big Pool," and it was demolished soon after the final shots of Godzilla and Minilla swimming away were filmed.

Some sources postulate that at one point in development, this film was a sequel to *Godzilla vs. Destroyah* (1995), taking place many years in the future after Godzilla Jr. has been frozen in the Antarctic. Supposedly, when Kitamura came in with his writer, they removed all the references to the Heisei series.

Kyle Cooper's opening credits montage utilized footage from *Godzilla* (1954), *Godzilla Raids Again* (1955), *Rodan* (1956), *Mothra* (1961), *King Kong vs. Godzilla* (1962), *Mothra vs. Godzilla* (1964), *Ghidorah, the Three Headed Monster* (1964), *Invasion of Astro-Monster* (1965), *Destroy All Monsters* (1968), *Submersion of Japan* (1973), *Godzilla vs. Mechagodzilla, Prophecies of Nostradamus (Catastrophe 1999)* [1974], *The Return of Godzilla* (1984), *Godzilla vs. Biollante* (1989), *Godzilla vs. King Ghidorah* (1991), *Godzilla vs. Mothra* (1992), *Godzilla vs. Mechagodzilla II* (1993), *Godzilla vs. Space Godzilla* (1994), *Godzilla vs. Destroyah, Godzilla 2000, Godzilla vs. Megaguirus, Godzilla, Mothra, and King Ghidorah: Giant Monsters All-Out Attack* (2001), *Godzilla Against Mechagodzilla,* and *Godzilla: Tokyo S.O.S.*

The opening prologue features stock footage clips from *Varan* (1958), *Frankenstein vs. Baragon* (1965), *The War of the Gargantuas* (1966), *Space Amoeba* (1970), *Terror of Mechagodzilla,* and *Godzilla vs.*

Megaguirus. Additionally, the same footage from *Conflagration* (1975) of a factory exploding is superimposed over that monster footage and shown *again* when Ebirah appears in Tokai.

The Mothra marionette was leftover from *Godzilla: Tokyo S.O.S.*

Yoshio Tsuchiya begged to be allowed to play an Xilien in the film (and possibly Masato Ibu's part). He was denied.

Tomoe Shinohara, who was the woman callously killed in a hospital by Godzilla's tail in *Godzilla, Mothra, and King Ghidorah: Giant Monsters All-Out Attack*, plays herself in this film during a TV talk show scene.

Yoshimitsu Banno said he had lunch with Ryuhei Kitamura and the director told him Hedorah was his favorite Godzilla monster. When Banno saw the film, he said he was perplexed as to why Hedorah was in the film so little. Elsewhere in the press, Kitamura had said King Seesar was his favorite Godzilla monster.

Toho's working titles for the film included *The Godzilla* and *50dzilla*.

Allegedly, when Shogo Tomiyama saw the movie for the first time, he let everyone leave the room, then turned to his assistant and said "We're in trouble."

ULTRAMAN: THE NEXT
This film wasn't originally called *Ultraman*, but *Yellow Eyes* (in reference to the fact that all Ultramen had large yellow eyes).

Later, this iteration of Ultraman was named Ultraman Noa.

GREAT YOKAI WAR
Yokai expert Shigeru Mizuki consulted on the film and also has a cameo as the Great Elder Yokai in the film.

Won the Silver Excellence Award at the 23rd Japanese Golden Grosses.

SAZER X: THE MOVIE
Though one might assume this film used the leftover model from *Godzilla: Final Wars*, in a *G-Fan* interview, Kawakita implies this is a new model, more faithful to the original 1963 Atragon.

To fill the void left by the Godzilla series, this was released as Toho's New Year's Blockbuster for 2005 but it only grossed ¥640 million ($5,741,696).

GAMERA THE BRAVE
In the novelization, it is revealed Zedus was once a lizard who ate pieces of a Gyaos carcass and became mutated.

Kaho, who played Mai, was the lead in a popular Japanese TV series called *Cellphone Detectives*. She was also (and still is) a popular singer in Japan.

A humorous reference to Guiron is made when the juvenile Toto crawls through a kitchen and encounters a giant butcher knife. Toto then hisses at the knife and blasts at it with his flame-breath. Toru's father amusingly picks up the knife and can't understand how it became charred.

Photos of the full-scale Toto prop hauled on the back of a truck were passed off as a real giant turtle on the internet.

Miyuki, Toru's deceased mother, is played by Megumi Kobayashi, Moll of the *Rebirth of Mothra* trilogy.

Initially Daiei wanted to do *Godzilla vs. Gamera*. When Toho rebuked this idea, Daiei decided to make Gamera's opponent a Millennium-ized version of Jirass (the monster created from a Godzilla suit on the original *Ultraman* series). In Japanese, they almost have the same name. "Jirasu" and "Jidasu."

THE SINKING OF JAPAN
Shinji Higuchi has said he changed the ending from the book so that the film could come to a more definite conclusion.

Tetsuro Tamba, who played Prime Minister Yamamoto in *Submersion of Japan*, has a cameo as Reiko's grandfather.

Originally, the explosives were going to be nuclear but TBS objected to this and they were changed to the N2 explosives.

ULTRAMAN MEBIUS AND ULTRA BROTHERS
Originally the *Ultraman Mebius* TV series was to have centered around the children of the original Ultramen growing up on earth.

Early scripts had Ultraman Taro's former host, Kotaro Azuma, working as the curator at the aquarium in this film. The reason Taro's human host never appears is partly for continuity's sake, as Taro was the only Ultraman to ever permanently separate from his host during *Ultraman Taro's* series finale in 1974.

DRAGON WARS
The original cut ran 110 minutes before it was edited down to only 90 minutes.

Robert Forster played the voice of Jack Chapman in the "Wedding Bells Blew" episode of *Godzilla: The Series* (2000).

The music that plays over the end titles is a Korean folk song entitled "Arirang." In *Yongary, Monster from the Deep* (1967), when Yongary wakes up and dances around, the soundtrack plays a surf rock version of this same piece.

MONSTER X STRIKES BACK
This was not the first live-action appearance of Guilala since *The X From Outer Space* (1967). Guilala actually has a stock-footage cameo in *Tora-san's Forbidden Love* (1984).

Shunya Wazaki, who played Sano in the original film, has a cameo in this film as Dr. Sano. Susumu Kurobe (star of the original *Ultraman*) and Satoshi Furuya (Ultraman himself!) cameo as generals as well.

Yosuke Natsuki (*Ghidorah, the Three-Headed Monster; The Return of Godzilla*) turned down the director's request to appear in the film several times but finally relented.

So much stock footage from *The X From Outer Space* was used, that the actor who played Guilala in the original film, Yuichi Okada, was given credit here.

Guilala is brought to Earth by the Chinese Mars probe "AAC-Gamma," and when shown, it is an exact replica of the AAB-Gamma from *The X From Outer Space*.

The real-life Marusan Guilala figure is used here to represent the monster's position on a military strategy map.

The Guilala costume constructed for this film was utilized in an extensive TheLadders.com job-finding ad campaign in America.

SUPERIOR ULTRAMAN 8 BROTHERS
Kenji Sahara has a cameo as an advisor on the news.

A black and white photo of Shin Kishida, one of the stars of *The Return of Ultraman* (1971), can be seen in the background of Hideki Go's office.

The first Japanese science fiction film released on Blu-ray format in Japan.

DEMEKING THE SEA MONSTER
The squid on the Mamahama Marine Park promotional button looks just like Gezora from *Space Amoeba* (1970).

Lead actor Takeshi Nadagi (Nakajima) eventually went on to star in the *Kamen Rider* franchise.

Toy company Medicom made a figurine of Demeking.

MEGA MONSTER BATTLE: ULTRA GALAXY LEGENDS
Former Prime Minister Junichiro Koizumi was offered the chance to voice the Ultra King and declined the first time but accepted the second time and voices him in this film.

Originally, Ultraman Hikari was to lead the Ultramen to the Monster Graveyard but instead, he is among those frozen on M78.

DEATH KAPPA
Features future *Shin Godzilla* (2016) directors Hideaki Anno and Shinji Higuchi in cameo roles.

ULTRAMAN ZERO: THE REVENGE OF BELIAL
Like the first *Ultraman* series, when Zero separates from his host, Run can't remember the events of the last several days.

Director Yuichi Abe told Fabien Mauro in *G-Fan* #110 that one of the on-location filming sites was Mt. Aso, heavily prominent in *Rodan* (1956). However, filming there was difficult due to heavy rains. The film finished shooting only one month before its release.

The film's main stipulation from Tsuburaya Productions was that it had to focus on Ultraman Zero. The inclusion of characters from *Mirrorman*, *Jumborg Ace*, and *Fire Man* came later.

ULTRAMAN SAGA
Was the first Ultraman movie presented in 3-D.

Five of the classic Ultramen receive a very brief cameo in a scene set in the Land of Light, with Susumu Kurobe, Koji Moritsugu, Jiro Dan, and Keiji Takamine finally being joined on the big screen by *Ultraman Leo* star Ryu Manatsu.

Originally, Ultraman Legend and Justice were supposed to appear alongside Cosmos. However, since Justice and Cosmos had to jointly transform into Legend, perhaps this was deemed too confusing.

PACIFIC RIM
In an early draft, Mako and Raleigh were to have a language barrier before they connect in the drift.

Nearly a hundred different kaiju and Jaegers were designed, even though only a handful appear in the film.

GODZILLA (2014)
For the Japanese version, Katsuhiko Sasaki (*Godzilla vs. Megalon*) dubbed David Strathairn into Japanese. Shiro Sano (*Godzilla 2000*) dubbed Taylor Nichols. Ken Watanabe, meanwhile, dubbed his own voice.

Immediately after playing husband and wife in this film, Aaron Taylor Johnson and Elizabeth Olsen were cast as twin superhero siblings in *Avengers: Age of Ultron* (2015). In one of the early drafts for *Godzilla*, the duo were actually siblings, not husband and wife.

Godzilla was originally to be unearthed in an ice cap, the same introduction the monster received in the aborted Terry Rossio and Ted Elliot script from the original TriStar *Godzilla*. Legendary Pictures claims this scene was changed because of a similar icy scene in *Man of Steel* (2013).

The reboot had its origins in an aborted IMAX film by Yoshimitsu Banno entitled *Godzilla 3-D to the Max*, a quasi-sequel to *Godzilla vs. Hedorah* (1971).

238

Ken Watanabe's costume in his first scene is meant to evoke Eiji Tsuburaya's style of dress.

Supposedly, King Ghidorah was the villain in one draft of the script but Gareth Edwards felt an extraterrestrial monster didn't suit the "balance of nature theme" he was striving for.

Akira Takarada filmed a cameo as an immigration officer that was later cut.

According to Japanese wikipedia, Ishiro Serizawa's father's name was, of course, Eiji Serizawa.

ULTRAMAN GINGA S: THE MOVIE
Ultraman Max was included in the film because it was released on his tenth anniversary.

This movie and *Ultraman X The Movie: Here Comes Our Ultraman!* (2016) were dubbed into English and released for a limited theatrical run in the U.S.

Originally Leo and Astra were to train Hikaru and Sho, but the producers decided only Heisei Ultramen should appear prominently, so it was changed to Ultraman Zero. Leo, Astra, and Ultraman King do get cameos, though, and are the only Showa era Ultramen to do so.

Etelgar's name comes from the word eternal and the character was originally immortal.

Originally, Arina was to come from a sand planet in a parallel dimension.

Takuya Negishi was overjoyed to be working with Taiyo Sugiura who was his Ultraman as a child.

Ultraman Saga was supposed to appear but didn't make the cut—likely because he was a fusion Ultraman of Zero, Cosmos, and Dyna.

ULTRAMAN X: THE MOVIE
Takami Yoshimoto's character was meant to use the Spark Lens to transform into Ultraman Tiga until it was decided her character's son would instead. This idea came from director Kiyotaka Taguchi.

In one story draft, Evil Tiga was to appear until director Kiyotaka Taguchi said it was too similar to *Ultraman Tiga: The Final Odyssey* (2000).

The spikes on Zaigorg's back were reportedly influenced by Varan.

Kiyotaka Taguchi was a huge fan of the Heisei Godzilla series and tried to include as much miniature work in the movie as he could.

SHIN GODZILLA
Hideaki Anno and Shinji Higuchi had plans for a fifth form of Godzilla that Toho refused to approve. Apparently, they aren't even allowed to show off concept art for the fifth Godzilla form drawn by M. Maeda Mahiro!

Motion capture performer Mansai Nomura requested that he have a stage mask to play Godzilla as is traditional in the Japanese art of kyogen. Higuchi had a special wooden Godzilla mask made for him to wear along with a lightweight tail and dorsal plates.

Akira Takarada and other Godzilla alumni tried to get a cameo part in *Shin Godzilla*, but were turned down because Anno didn't want any actors from the past Godzilla movies in his film. Apparently, no one told him Akira Emoto was Yuki in *Godzilla vs. Space Godzilla* (1994) or that Jun Kunimura was Komura in *Godzilla: Final Wars* (2004).

Heisei Godzilla star Megumi Odaka has mentioned that she was trying drive down a street one day to find it had been blocked off for shooting *Shin Godzilla*. The policemen on duty told her she couldn't drive down the street because they were shooting a new Godzilla film. Odaka's immediate thought was "What? Miki can't see Godzilla???"

Godzilla's ray was changed from blue to purple in honor of the musician Prince who died during production.

New sound effects and music based on the Showa era were tried but the directors felt they didn't surpass the originals and stuck with them.

In 2017, a poll with Japanese Godzilla fans asked them what their top five G-films were and *Shin Godzilla* emerged as number one. The remaining four titles of the top five were, in order, *Mothra vs. Godzilla* (1964), *Godzilla* (1954), *Godzilla vs. Mothra*, and *Ghidorah, the Three Headed Monster* (1964).

KONG SKULL ISLAND

John C. Reilley's character was originally to be played by Michael Keaton and Samuel L. Jackson's character was originally meant for J. K. Simmons. Both actors had to bow out due to scheduling conflicts.

The title credits scene was designed by Kyle Cooper, who also did the title credits for *Godzilla: Final Wars* (2004).

The makers consciously removed dinosaurs from Skull Island because they didn't want to be in competition with the *Jurassic Park* movies.

The post-credits scene originally had Brooks, Conrad, and Weaver observing Godzilla surface in the arctic before it was decided it could create a continuity problem between this film and *Godzilla*. Therefore, the cave paintings of Godzilla, Mothra, Rodan, and King Ghidorah were shown instead.

Legally, Legendary is not allowed to refer to Kong as "King Kong" as Universal owns that trademark, though the name and character of Kong itself are allowed.

ULTRAMAN ORB: THE MOVIE

Koichi Yamadera (Japanese dubbing voice of Lloyd Wilder in *Ultraman: Towards the Future*) has a role as one of the alien villains.

The tears in the last scene were supposed to be fake but Oniyakko Tsubaki managed to cry real tears on camera.

In the scene where Daichi is held captive in a chair, actor Kensuke Takahashi fell asleep due to the early morning filming hours.

SABAN'S POWER RANGERS

Despite the mid-credits scene mentioning Tommy Oliver, some fans have petitioned for the new Green Ranger to be a woman.

Early rumors seemed to suggest that this film would somehow be in-continuity with all of the preceding series rather than a reboot but that was quickly proven not to be the case.

Haim Saban has already stated that future sequels, if they materialize, will focus on the Green Ranger saga as well as other iterations of the Power Rangers.

BRAVESTORM
Ryuhei Kitamura helped with ideas during the script writing phase.

Albatross had already decided on titling a movie *BraveStorm* when he approached them with the *Silver Mask/Red Baron/Iron King* combo movie. He does not know how or why the name came to be, but accepted it nonetheless.

GODZILLA: PLANET OF MONSTERS
Toho commissioned a prequel novel, *Godzilla: Monster Apocalypse*, which explains much of this film's history. The novel explains that Godzilla killed many of the monsters seen in the flashbacks. There is a great deal of fan service in the novel, such as making a team out of Anguirus, Baragon, and Varan in a nod to Shusuke Kaneko's original version of *Godzilla, Mothra, and King Ghidorah: Giant Monsters All-Out Attack* (2001).

GODZILLA: CITY ON THE EDGE OF BATTLE
Though this news will certainly pour salt in the wounds of people who wanted to see more fights in the anime trilogy (including this author!), the original plan for Mechagodzilla City was for it to come alive at the film's climax—possibly morphing into a 1km tall robot. Another idea was for it to transforms some components of the city into Mechagodzilla's head to battle Godzilla. This was rejected for two reasons. First, Toho had stipulated that they didn't want "silly looking monster battles" in the movie, and second, co-director Kôbun Shizuno was also not a fan of "silly monster battles." What could have been...

GODZILLA: THE PLANET EATER
The Exif at one point were designed to have the eye visors of the Xiliens, hence the name Exif.

ULTRAMAN R/B THE MOVIE
Ultrawoman Grigio's initial designs depicted her as having long strands of hair and pink eyes.

GODZILLA: KING OF THE MONSTERS
Anguirus gets an unofficial cameo as a skeleton scene in the background of the sunken city.

The 2014 Godzilla had ties to the Avengers: Age of Ultron (2015) due to its featuring Aaron Taylor Johnson and Elizabeth Olson playing husband and wife. The duo played siblings in the Avengers film. Here, actress Lexi

Rabe portrays the younger version of Madison. Rabe portrayed Tony Stark's daughter in Avengers: Endgame. Stark's cabin in Endgame is also Mark Russel's cabin in King of the Monsters.

The articles seen during the end credits are full of Easter Eggs, including an article written by Steve Martin.

All the Monarch outposts names correlate to dates of monster movies. Mothra is located at Outpost 61 as her debut film came out in 1961. Rodan is located in Outpost 56, Kong/Skull Island are at Outpost 33, and so on.

Of the cast O'Shea Jackson was the biggest fan of the series, listing Gigan as his favorite monster apart from Godzilla.

REFERENCE MATERIALS

The Illustrated Encyclopedia of Godzilla by Ed Godziszewski (By the author, 1998) Originally, Godziszewski was commissioned to do this book to coincide with the release of Tri-Star's *Godzilla*. When the publisher backed out, he published it anyway. It remains the single most authoritative volume on the G-series detailing its every aspect up to 1994.

Japan's Favorite Mon-Star: The Unauthorized Biography of the "Big G" by Steve Ryfle (ECW Press, 1998) The best critical filmography of the G-series with tons of interesting background information and trivia on the production of the series.

An Unauthorized Guide to Godzilla Collectibles by Sean Linkenbach (Schiffer Publishing Ltd., 1998) An all-color photographic guide to Godzilla posters and collectibles from around the world.

A Critical History and Filmography of Toho's Godzilla Series by David Kalat (McFarland, 1997) An excellent review of the series by critic David Kalat which closely analyzes its many themes.

Eiji Tsuburaya: Master of Monsters by August Ragone (Chronicle Books, 2007) The most authoritative English language book on Tsuburaya. It is also the best illustrated book on Toho/Godzilla/Ultraman as it was officially licensed by Toho and Tsuburaya Productions.

Japanese Science Fiction, Fantasy and Horror Films by Stuart Galbraith IV (McFarland, 1994) Features a synopsis and brief analyses of every film under the heading of the title genre up to 1992's *Godzilla vs. Mothra*. Its most useful aspect is the many quotations it contains from critics when the films were actually released in America.

The Official Godzilla Compendium by J.D. Lees and Marc Cerasini (Random House, 1998) A wonderful, though unfortunately out of print, officially endorsed volume on the G-series illustrated with color/b&w

photos and illustrations. Written by novelist Marc Cerasini and *G-Fan*'s editor himself J.D. Lees.

Kaiju For Hipsters: 101 "Alternative" Giant Monster Movies by Kevin Derendorf (Maser Press, 2018) If you liked reading about the more offbeat entries from this book, then you'll love Kaiju For Hipsters, as it covers 101 rare films!

Essential reading for all fans also includes several notable fanzines (fan-produced magazines) either dedicated to kaiju eiga or strongly focused on them which began with Greg Shoemaker's The Japanese Fantasy Film Journal in the 1970s among others. Below is a list of fanzines still running today.

G-Fan Magazine
Currently the world's longest running fan-made magazine at over 100 issues over the course of twenty plus years published by J.D. Lees. In addition to reviews, retrospectives and other features, it contains interviews with stars like Kumi Mizuno and Akira Takarada to bit part American actors to behind the scenes players like Haruo Nakajima, Teruyoshi Nakano, and Shusuke Kaneko to name a few.
www.g-fan.com

Xenorama: The Journal of Heroes and Monsters
Featuring an eclectic group of pop culture topics from Kung Fu, Swords and Sandals Epics, Superheroes, and more often than not Dai Kaiju Eiga and Sentai series by David McRobie. Xenorama.blogspot.com

Mad Scientist
Covers sci-fi and horror films from the 1950s, 60s, and 70s usually with a high emphasis on Godzilla and other Japanese giants. Published by Martin Arlt. www.madscientistzine.com

SPECIAL PREVIEW
A Chapter from the upcoming book
EDITING JAPANESE MONSTERS
A comprehensive reference book that covers the differences between the original Japanese versions vs. overseas versions such as *Godzilla Raids Again* vs. *Gigantis, the Fire Monster*, *Varan* vs. *Varan, the Unbelievable*, *Gamera* vs. *Gammera the Invincible*, *Great Monster War* vs. *Monster Zero*, *Submersion of Japan* vs. *Tidal Wave*, *Conflagration* vs. *High Seas Hijack*, *Legend of Dinosaurs and Monster Birds* vs. *The "Legend of Dinosaurs,"* and many more!!!
Available in 2021

JURASSIC CITY

GODZILLA V/S MECHAGODZILLA

Toho/Japan	Unknown/India
Godzilla vs. Mechagodzilla	*Jurassic City: Godzilla v/s mechagodzilla*
Release Date: December 11, 1993	unknown
Running Time: 108 minutes	102 minutes (PAL)
Cut Scenes: None	Added Scenes: None

It's unknown whether or not this Hindi-dubbed version of *Godzilla vs. Mechagodzilla* is endorsed by Toho or not, or if it's a pirated re-edit. Whatever it is, "Jurassic City" has been altered quite a bit compared to other Heisei era Godzilla films, which were relatively unchanged when exported to other countries. While it cuts no footage (the difference in run times is due to a faster frame rate in *Jurassic City*), the Hindi dub changes nearly all of the character names as well as a few minor story details. **Aoki** is now **Mr. Robert George**, **Azusa Gojo** is **Saluja**, **Miki** is **Misha**, **Professor Omae** is **Professor Humai**, **Lieutenant Jun Sonezaki** is **Tony**, and **Mechagodzilla** is called **Mahabali**. Godzilla's name is the same, but throughout most of the dub **Godzilla is referred to as being female and "Baby's mother."**

The Toho Logo is removed, which suggests that this is an illegal cut, and we fade in on the severed head of Mecha-King Ghidorah. On the first C.U. on Mecha-King Ghidorah's head, **some new music is laid over the original score**. As such, **we can't hear General Aso's line about "finally being able to kill Godzilla."** Ifukube's score eventually overpowers the new composition which fades out upon the CGI scenes of Mechagodzilla being formed. When we get to the live action footage of Mechagodzilla in its docking bay, **we fade out before the Japanese title can be superimposed over Mechagodzilla. We fade to a black title card with white lettering reading "JURASSIC CITY Godzilla v/s mechagodzilla"** (yes, the 'm' is not capitalized).

A different version of the international English credits from Tri-Star's *Godzilla vs. Mechagodzilla II* print are used which credits Tomoyuki Tanaka, Wataru Mimura, and Akira Ifukube before the actors, while in Tri-Star's version the actors come first.

That this version takes some interesting liberties with the dialogue is apparent upon Aoki/Robert's first meeting with Captain Sasaki. It's all rather funny, with **Sasaki telling Robert that he better not be putting up dinosaur posters in his room! He also lets Robert know that he doesn't think he is the right man for the job.**

During the training montage, **Ifukube's score becomes drowned out at the point that the commander gives a training briefing on Godzilla**, where we can see footage from *Godzilla vs. Mothra* on the monitor. **A new, more ominous score replaces Ifukube's music.** The original score resumes upon Aoki's sparring session with Catherine. Apparently the new editors wanted to give Godzilla a more threatening tone in this cut, because again, **when we cut to the simulation within Mechagodzilla the music changes again to fit a darker tone.**

Despite there being English slates earlier, the slates for Adonoa Island are in Japanese. When the team is shown the pteranodon bones, **ominous music plays replacing the original score. The rescoring occurs all the way up until Baby's egg is loaded into the chopper.** When Rodan arrives, and Baby's egg begins to glow, **a new score is briefly inserted before Ifukube's track resumes. Another new track rears its head in the scene where the group takes cover and Professor Humai explains what Rodan is.** For a brief moment, when Godzilla emerges, **Ifukube's score is briefly replaced by the ominous tracks that played over the Godzilla related scenes at G-Force earlier.**

Aoki/Robert's dialogue as he leaves Gojo/Saluja's office is cringe worthy. **"I'm going to haunt you in your dreams tonight," Robert tells her as he leaves rather than, "This was meant to happen," as he says in the Sony dub.** Following soon after is the scene where "Misha" meets Robert in the G-Force cafeteria and suggests that they take Robert's plant sample he stole to the Center for Psychic Development. While there, **Misha calls Hosono (Tadao Takashima's cameo character) "Brother" in this dub.**

After Baby hatches, and Omae is explaining the parasitic egg theory, **some new music is dubbed in with a lighter tone.** When Mechagodzilla/Mahabali launches **a few strange random bits of new music are thrown in.** After Godzilla defeats Mahabali and walks away from the battlefield, **scenes thereafter are scored with Ifukube's music where there was none before.**

Then, as radar predicts Godzilla's course, one of the officials says that the monster is **"headed for Jurassic City near Kyoto!"** Also, though no footage is reshuffled, **when cutting back and forth between the military parade and the control room the Ifukube scores are completely different!** One is the zippy military march, while the other is Mechagodzilla's slower launch theme.

248

During the final battle, when Aoki holds off Godzilla, there's a scene where he tells the Mechagodzilla crew to hurry up. **In this dub he jokes with his boss that he never wants to work in the parking department again.** During the scene where Godzilla's secondary brain fuses back together, **it sounds as though a new music score is input**, but the sound quality is so poor that it's difficult to know for sure.

The biggest alteration to this cut comes in the final scenes. **Saluja tells Misha that Godzilla is baby's mother and he must go with her.** Now, in all other cuts, Miki simply projects the song to Baby, but here she speaks the following to him: **"Baby, you're not safe amongst humans. Me or Saluja, whom you think as your mother cannot protect you. Our world is based on hatred. You've your mother, who's a epitome of motherhood. You will have to go with your mother. Because we humans are not worthy of raising you. Your life, your world is with your mother. .where there's no war, weapons or hatred. There's only love. Only love."**

Even Captain Sasaki feels the love, as this dub changes his line to be, **"This is an image of love and care." When Godzilla and Baby enter the water, Joe asks what they should do and Catherine, rather than talking about "life vs. artificial life," says, "What we should do to live on."**

"It's been proven that 'Live and Let Live' is the best motto," Sasaki says.

Robert speculates that one day mankind will annihilate itself and the age of dinosaurs will return, not exactly what Aoki says, but tangent at least. **Saluja responds, "[The dinosaurs will] awaken the feeling of love and caring amongst humans."**

JOHN LEMAY

WITH TED JOHNSON

THE BIG BOOK OF JAPANESE GIANT MONSTER MOVIES

THE LOST FILMS

MUTATED EDITION

FROM THE FILES OF THE BIG BOOK OF JAPANESE GIANT MONSTER MOVIES

WRITING JAPANESE MONSTERS

JOHN LEMAY

FOR MORE LOST FILMS CHECK OUT
THE LOST FILMS FANZINE (PUBLISHED QUARTERLY)

JOHN LEMAY

KONG UNMADE
THE LOST FILMS OF SKULL ISLAND

For Brown Scale, adaptive evolution is a curse.
The Flock Matriarchs want to kill him because he is different.
Mankind wants to kill him because he is better than The Flock.
This baby kaiju's only hope is to become an adult. The race for survival is
on—I Shall Not Mate.
Pick up your copy on Amazon.com

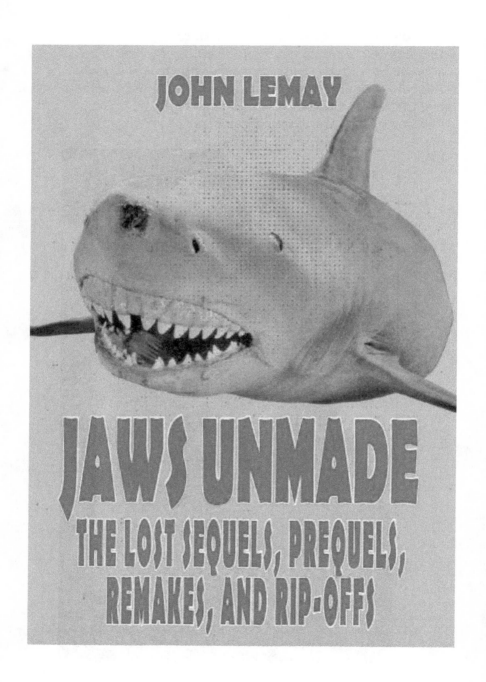

JOHN LEMAY

JAWS UNMADE
THE LOST SEQUELS, PREQUELS, REMAKES, AND RIP-OFFS

BE SURE TO LISTEN TO

Join hosts Byrd and Matt as they discuss all things giant monsters, tokusatsu, and Japanese fantasy films. We'll also cover comics, cartoons, toys, books, and more! Come here for a regular dose of everything from Godzilla and Gamera to King Kong and Ray Harryhausen to Ultraman, and everything in between!

ABOUT THE AUTHOR

John LeMay is the author of several lost film histories such as *Kong Unmade: The Lost Films of Skull Island*; *Jaws Unmade: The Lost Sequels, Prequels, Remakes, and Rip-Offs*; *The Big Book of Japanese Giant Monster Movies: The Lost Films;* and *Terror of the Lost Tokusatsu Films*. He is also the editor and publisher of *The Lost Films Fanzine*, published quarterly. LeMay also writes on the history of the Old West, with a focus on folklore. Some of these titles include *The Real Cowboys and Aliens* series with Noe Torres, *Tall Tales and Half Truths of Billy the Kid*, and *Cowboys & Saurians: Dinosaurs and Prehistoric Beasts as Seen by the Pioneers*. He is a frequent contributor to magazines such as *G-Fan, Mad Scientist, Xenorama, True West,* and *Cinema Retro*.